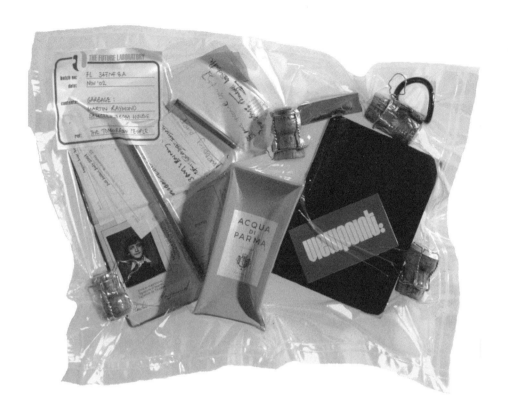

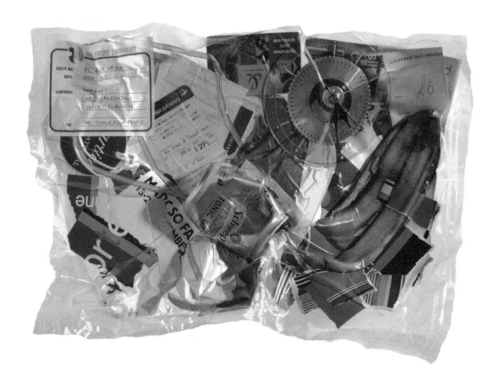

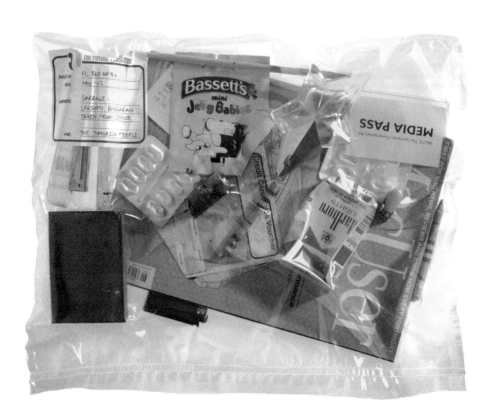

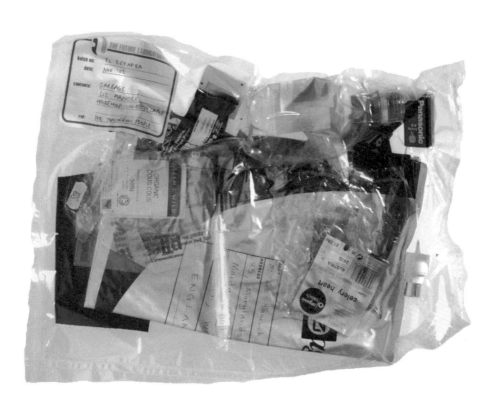

# The Tomorrow People

# The Tomorrow People

## Future consumers and how to read them

MARTIN RAYMOND

FINANCIAL TIMES

*An imprint of* **Pearson Education**

London • New York • Toronto • Sydney • Tokyo • Singapore
Hong Kong • Cape Town • Madrid • Paris • Amsterdam • Munich • Milan

PEARSON EDUCATION LIMITED

Head Office:
Edinburgh Gate
Harlow CM20 2JE
Tel: +44 (0)1279 623623
Fax: +44 (0)1279 431059

London Office:
128 Long Acre
London WC2E 9AN
Tel: +44 (0)20 7447 2000
Fax: +44 (0)20 7447 2170
Website: www.business-minds.com

First published in Great Britain in 2003

© Martin Raymond 2003

The right of Martin Raymond to be identified as Author of this Work has been asserted
by him in accordance with the Copyright, Designs and Patents Act 1988.

ISBN 0 273 65957 X

*British Library Cataloguing in Publication Data*
A CIP catalogue record for this book can be obtained from the British Library.

10 9 8 7 6 5 4 3 2 1

Typeset by Northern Phototypesetting Co Ltd, Bolton
Printed and bound in the UK by Biddles Ltd, Guildford & King's Lynn

*The Publishers' policy is to use paper manufactured from sustainable forests.*

# About the author

**Martin Raymond** is Editor of *Viewpoint* magazine (a biannual trends and consumer lifestyles journal for the design, fashion, brands and marketing sectors) and is cofounder of the Future Laboratory, a leading futures consultancy for brands and market leaders in Europe and the US.

When not working with the Future Lab or editing *Viewpoint*, Raymond lectures at the London College of Fashion, Nottingham Trent University and Central St Martin's College. With his forecasting team, he regularly briefs advertising agencies on the next big cultural trends set to impact on consumer consciousness.

A frequent conference speaker, he contributes regularly to Radio 3's *Nightwaves* and *Front Row*, Radio 4's flagship arts programme.

# Contents

# Introduction

The future has already happened, it just isn't very well distributed. And this is what good forecasting and trend analysis are about – reading or 'brailling' those bits of the culture that are already living and making tomorrow happen.

But it is also about using the tools, technologies and techniques that make forecasting a science rather than an intuition – the future something you can depend on rather than something you are forced to gamble with.

These are the things we do at the Future Laboratory, and these are the things this book will teach you to understand – how to 'mine' the future and how to take the ideas, innovations and trends you find there and plug them back into your business or brand in ways that make it future-faced and consumer-centred.

The process is a simple one – in Parts 1 to 4 we show you what the future is, and how it is set to shape up according to our own Lifesigns Network. Then we look at how you can use the latest developments in network science, emergence and complexity theory – growth laws, weak and strong tie links, superhubs, distributive systems, deviant nodes – to establish your own brailling, or deep listening and learning stations that inform and grow your brand on a 24Seven basis.

These stations or 'hides' will plug you into the future by connecting you into a group of thinkers, doers, dreamers and antenna group 'prosumers' that we've dubbed the power curve 20. 'Power curve' because they contain within them the 'trend arc' or narrative bridge along which most trends move or enter the mainstream, and '20' because they are the vital 20 per cent that drives the dreams, desires and future choices of 80 per cent of the population.

This is why we talk of the 'average many' and the 'vital few'. Why we teach you to abandon quantitative measuring techniques, focus groups, telephone polls and clipboard questionnaires in favour of a new set of insight tools and observational methods that allow you to plug into tomorrow's consumers in ways that win their approval but also allow them to suggest and create the next generation of consumer-faced products for themselves.

These networks – consilient networks – and these techniques – designed to measure 'brand poetics' and the 'customer narratives' – are at the heart of a handful of very successful creative brands and companies. We shall profile these, and borrow from them their best practices in ways that make them universally useful and relevant.

We haven't, however, lingered on big business or familiar brands for the simple reason that many are still unable to grasp the future as it should and must be grasped – with emotion, with poetry, with irrationality, with innovation and by listening rather than telling.

This then is not a book of glib case studies on names like IBM, KPMG, Accenture, Ernst & Young, Hewlett Packard, Dell, or GE (the usual case study suspects) but a book of ideas, structures, and knowledge and insight nodes located on the farther shores of corporate experience – ideas from biology, the social sciences, from emergence, ethnography, behavioural research, even evolutionary theory and practice – but ideas that are set to drive business and brand insights into a new and fascinating era – the age of consilience, to quote the biologist and social philosopher E. O. Wilson. An age of integrated knowledge streams, and federated and federal consumer and business hubs that connect, overlap and flow into each other in ways we are just beginning to understand and mine.

Tomorrow as you will see is about collaborative brands, 'tactile' products and intuitive technologies – and this is what you will learn to create and develop in the following pages. Brands that are live, brands that are tactile, brands that are immersive, and brands that use their insights on Big Picture trends and key societal, social and lifestage shifts to arrive in the market on trend and in context.

And now more than ever, brands need context, relevance and an aura of multiplexity that allow them to be all things to all men and women – for the consumer of tomorrow is self-actualized, self-learning and self-aware and wants the future to address the vital few – them – rather than the mainstream many.

This book is about plugging into the few to connect with the many. It is also about something else – about getting a life, or rather living life and using that living of the customer's experience – your experience – to make brands live for them. And of course for you!

# Acknowledgements

This book has many authors. They are the editors, journalists, creative directors and networkers of *Viewpoint* magazine and the Future Laboratory – Chris Sanderson, David Shah, Liz Hancock, Lakshmi Baskaran, Hester Lacey, Max Natham, Sean Pillot de Chenecey, Leon Kreitzman, Tom Savigar, Jeremy Brown of SenseWorldwide and Gwyneth Holland. There is an even larger number of thinkers, academics and 'contrarians' from our worldwide network, impossible to credit individually, who contributed in one way or another to the ideas, narratives and possible future scenarios outlined.

Grand scenario ideas however came from the works, words and 'on the fly' conversations with a large number of writers, theorists, academics, designers, economists, scientists and sociobiologists who should be thanked individually for insights offered and advice given.

High on our list is Malcolm Gladwell, author of *The Tipping Point*, who introduced us to the writings of Zeth Godin, who wrote *Permission Marketing*, and Jane Jacobs, an architectural critic and urbanist, whose seminal work, *The Death and Life of Great American Cities,* laid the foundation stones for much of our thinking on how communities, social systems and creative networks gel together to generate the kinds of opportunities and serendipitous encounters needed to make good networks great and insightful.

All this led us to Richard Florida's Bohemian and Gay Indexes, and to his book, *The Rise of The Creative Class*, which articulated much of what our networkers had been arguing all along, especially when briefing 'big business' about network etiquette – that deviancy pays, matters, and is probably one of the few things guaranteed to return real dividends – in terms of creativity, ideas and ultimately, profits.

Gladwell and Godin also made us aware of Edward O. Wilson, whose works *The Ants, Consilience* and *The Future of Life* informed much of our thinking on how consilient networks should be created and cultivated.

Wilson's writings in turn opened our sensitivities to those expressed by Richard Dawkins in his book *The Selfish Gene*, which in turn connected us to Howard Bloom's *Global Brain* and his theories on the evolution of hive minds from the Big Bang to 21st century connectivity.

Much discussion was had (and still continues) by our network discussion groups on the evolutionary nature of networks, ideas and trends spreads in the population. These subsequently led to thoughts and ideas on evolutionary thinking processes, higher skill sets and limbic systems and how they operate. Thus to *Driven* by Paul R. Lawrence and Nitin Nohria – an incisive and revealing work on what makes us human and the four innate drives that make us live life and think the thoughts we do on a daily basis. These are the drive to acquire, the drive to bond, the drive to defend and, the one we were most interested in, the drive to learn.

*Driven* connected us to Steve Johnson's *Emergence: The Connected Lives of Ants, Brains, Cities and Software*. This is one of the first books that did in its text what Wilson was doing in  life – making connections, drawing together apparently disparate facts, fictions, scientific, social and economic theories and using their distilled knowledge pools to create new and core insights about the world we live in, and how we live in it.

This taught us about network theory and introduced us to *Linked: The New Science of Networks* by Albert-László Barabási, much of which informed our chapters on network development and network architecture. It also allowed us to create structures and frameworks within which to design, build and deploy our own Lifesigns Network using models created originally by Paul Baran around 1964 – specifically those that he referred to as centralized networks, decentralized networks and distributed networks.

Networks, or rather underlying theories about chaos, fractals, complexity and emergence, led us to *Harnessing Complexity* by Robert Axelrod and Michael D. Cohen, a book that laid out complexity and complex adaptive systems in a way that even our magpie-like minds could understand and appreciate.

Here, as with Barabási, we learned about Mark Granovetter's theories on weak ties and strong ties and how the former, rather than the latter, are of greater benefit when assembling networks or harnessing knowledge. We also learned about the economist W. Brian Arthur, whose writings and asides, in turn, introduced us to the Sante Fe Institute and its work on complex adaptive systems and how these impact on everything from wind systems to organizations, to economic and social modes and models of behaviour.

Enter then Thomas Homer-Dixon, the director of the Peace and Conflict Studies Program at the University of Toronto, whose book *The Ingenuity Gap* encouraged us to investigate the way that knowledge streams emerge within certain complex systems, and how we can divert and harness these streams to encourage and cause insight and sublime moments of creativity and ingenuity.

Homer-Dixon also directed our attentions to the work of 'irrational' economists such as Robert Shiller and Paul Ormerod. *Butterfly Economics*, Ormerod's book, lays out in a simple, compelling and poetic way the eddies, sweeps and hidden currents that make economics the fascinating story of human endeavour and behaviour it really is – why we call it humanomics rather than the dry area of study economics has become, linearly divorced from the dreams, tides and affairs of man.

Ormerod and Shiller made us better aware of the writings and theories of David Doyle of the New Economics Foundation. His *Tyranny of Numbers* is proof, if proof is needed, that measuring and metrics tell you everything except what is useful and beneficial in terms of reading or understanding the future. Their work also led us on to the work being carried out at the Ernst & Young Centre of Business Innovation and to *Blur* – the book, the theory, and the subject of an entire issue of *Viewpoint* magazine inspired by a still compelling and relevant book of the same name by Stan Davis and Chris Meyer.

Here, while researching the background to Issue 11 of *Viewpoint*, we spoke to the design teams at IDEO, Philips, Ford and Apple, who in turn mentioned names like Paco Underhill, Bill Abrams of Housecalls, Peter Schwartz of the Global Business Network, Max Natham and his colleagues at the Work Foundation, Michael Willmott of the Future Foundation, the Sputnik collective and network, and Jeremy Myerson of the Helen Hamlyn Centre at the Royal College of Art, London. All these helped us to develop the systems and methodologies now used by many of the brands, design houses, advertising and marketing agencies we work with.

Myerson's book *IDEO: Masters of Innovation* looks at IDEO and its work methods and is of particular relevance to designers and brand strategists who are still wary of applying method to the creative process. Abrams' *The Observational Research Handbook* says all there is to say about how and why focus groups are dead, and why the new age of the engaged, tactile and tenacious market and brand strategist is upon us.

Schwartz and his *The Art of The Long View – Planning for the Future in an Uncertain World* is also required reading for all planners, trend forecasters, futurologists and new networkers – it remains a key book in all the academic programmes we run or are involved in. In it Schwartz has outlined how we can harness our imagination and our ability to look and dream ahead to generate viable and incisive snapshots of things and trends to come and for this we are truly grateful. From it we derived new levels of insight and understanding with which to inform our own narrative and scenario planning theories and practices.

And those 'bin dives' we do? A technique and discipline learned from William Rathje's and Cullen Murphy's *Rubbish! The Archaeology of Garbage* and the University of Arizona's ongoing Garbage Project.

The sources above established our connective threads but many other books were used by the Future Laboratory team and our networkers to flesh out key chapters and sectional headings. These are detailed in the bibliography to this book but we would like to mention by name Michael Lewis, Naomi Klein, Noreena Hertz, George Monbiot, Alan Burton-Jones, John Grant, Francis Fukuyama, Thomas Frank, David M. Fetterman, John Micklethwait and Adrian Wooldridge, E. F. Schumacher, Francis Cairncross, Pico Iyer, Patrick Dixon, Leon Kreitzman, Matt Ridley, Mike Hammer, Linda L. Price, Eric J. Arnould and George M. Zinkhan, Jeremy Rifkin, Michael G. Zey, and Richard Koch.

For these, and all the other works read but not credited, we are truly grateful and recommend them to your own networkers.

*The Future Laboratory team, London, 2003*

# Brands in the dock:
## survival of the most flexible

# What's new?
## The only question worth asking

The big truth: a brand loses its way when it loses touch with its customers' needs. Marks & Spencer was one such brand. At its zenith, the company posted profits above £1.2bn and its then chairman and chief executive Richard Greenbury could do no wrong. In Baker Street, home of the brand's head office, the boardroom was awash with management awards and every UK family, so the myth went, wore something with the St. Michael label on it.

Or, if they didn't, they would. It was only a matter of time. Customers needed Marks & Spencer more than Marks & Spencer needed its customers. They didn't say that, but that was the impression you got when you spoke to the Marks & Spencer press office. That they knew and had a direct line to what was hot and what was not – as the hackneyed pens of the UK fashion press were so fond of writing at the time. And what was hot from 1994 to 1997 was anything and everything Marks & Spencer. Bodies? They had them. Boxer briefs? Which size? Classics with a contemporary twist? Only say the words . . . they knew and you couldn't tell them otherwise.

That's when and why we had our first polite communiqué from them. A number of Future Laboratory founders were editing and working on *Fashion Weekly* at the time, a trade magazine that had been languishing behind the then market leader *Draper's Record* – or 'Drab Person's Record' as it was known in the rag trade for its unique ability to make one of the world's most glamourous industries seem like a month in New Jersey, no remission offered.

> **The big truth: a brand loses its way when it loses touch with its customers' needs.**

We decided to make *Fashion Weekly* everything its rival publication wasn't – international, glamorous, upmarket and, above all, a business journal that industry players turned to for the latest trends, tastes and consumer shifts which, then as now, were all about brands, lifestyle, market segments and retail as experience, theatre, therapy and relationship selling. Especially the latter, for at the top end of the market, as brands in the lifestyle sector became all too similar in price, strategy and position, relationship selling and 360 degree customer service were two of the few things beginning to distinguish one overpriced designer brand from the other.

Against this backdrop, the letter from Marks & Spencer seemed doubly odd, written we suspected at the time by a company crank, or one of our many mates on the inside looking for a well earned respite from all those pleated skirts and bottle green jackets with breeze block shoulder pads.

No such luck. The letter was real and suggested politely, as only a company with a supreme and unshakeable belief in its own ego can suggest politely, that we should desist from calling Marks & Spencer a fashion retailer, or St. Michael, for that matter, a lifestyle brand.

They were a clothing retailer, or a *clothier* – a word our student help had to look up in the dictionary – and not to be confused with that fast, racy rather impetuous and shallow end of the business determined to sell a thing called 'fashion'. This was something the British consumer wasn't keen on, or at least the Marks & Spencer customer – theirs was a world of genteel styles and classics with a contemporary twist.

Note that there was no mention of service, or brand, or the idea that fifty-something middle England had moved on from its ration card, post-war roots – the one time heartland of the Marks & Spencer customer – just this focus on the company being a clothing company, a clothier, and this of course was meant to say it all.

And it did say it all – about Marks & Spencer, about *Fashion Weekly*, about the world we were living in and writing about at the time. A world of incredible contrast and, when you look at it now, one on the edge of great temporal, spiritual and commercial flux.

This was the world BD (before dotcom) in the nascent stages of a thing called flexecutive work patterns, on the western cusp of latte culture, 'No Logo', the celebrity moment, Big Brother, Middle Youth, yes even Grunge, Britpop and the Teletubbies. So in many ways you can forgive Marks & Spencer for getting it so wrong, or having their collective heads embedded so deep in the ground that seeing really was a case of disbelieving.

And why should they believe? Their profits rose from £165.5m in 1991 to £924.3m in 1995, and above £1.2bn in 1997. And everything else seemed trivial, or at least not 'them'. We're thinking here of a conversation we had with one of their trend forecasters at the time. One of those rambling, hipper-than-thou affairs that take place when trend scouts or 'cool hunters' meet and try to impress each other with their respective grasps of the latest buzzwords or cultural shifts.

Naturally then, this being 1994, the talk was of ecstasy and Thai beaches, of Britpop and Britart, or Irvine Welsh and Heroin Chic. Of designers and architects and interiors that were all about things going minimal, spiritual, or back to deconstructed basics. Of organizational change and a way of working that would see the rise of serial careerism, open plan offices with astroturf receptions and live-in sushi chefs.

It should have been, but it wasn't. Like the letter, the person in question (happily gone now) demonstrated a stupendous lack of insight when it came to consumer trends – lack of because they weren't interested, or rather that their core customer base wasn't interested, so why should they be?

And e-commerce, social and ethical trading, the global label, the global soul, the shift to third way politics, dress-down culture, that other thing we kept banging on about then, values instead of value?

## ▓ If it isn't broke, all the more reason to ask why

All these things, all these changes, but inside Marks & Spencer a world like the 'shopping and fucking' 90s wasn't happening. Consumers entering stores were still confronted with rails of slacks, blouses and 'horrible little suits in cheap fabrics', as the editor of *Harper's and Queen* wrote at the time.

Worse, once you were in it was difficult to find your way out, or find a product or clothing category that might or might not fit. Signs telling you where things were located were hard enough to come by, and made less noticeable by the fact that staff were even harder to locate. There were rumours too of changing rooms, but few ever saw them, and if you were unfortunate enough to find the shoe department and wanted to try something on, it was necessary to clutch at tubular steel fittings, or at the arm of a passing customer, to maintain your balance since chairs, like fashionable items of clothing, were dim and distant memories. This had been the policy of Simon Marks and, give or take a few chairs, remained the policy of the present incumbent, Richard Greenbury.

Likewise the stores' refusal to accept credit cards, stock brands other than their own, or to take on board lessons and messages from a flurry of consumer surveys (by groups like Verdict, Mintel and Datamonitor) which pointed to the rise of a new brand-conscious, label-driven, designer-aware generation of ethically and socially-aware consumers who wanted more from the high street than their 'quality at a price' parents.

As Marks & Spencer spoke of middle England, middle England in turn was speaking of Middle Youth and Third Agers, of lads and ladettes, slappers and celebrity culture being embraced in ways that were redefining our notions of market, class, youth and teenagers, who, rather than finding their parents a bore for being too old, found them borrowing their clothes and down-aging to become a tribe called Kidults.

Not to be outdone, and perhaps seeing less and less point in childhood, kids themselves shopped at the kinds of shops and bought the kind of looks that turned them into betweenagers, a marketer's dream and hard-pressed parent's nightmare.

Instead of fearing debt, we became what has been dubbed DFLs (deficit finance livers) and embraced a 'live rich, die broke' approach to enjoying ourselves that has seen the rise of celebrity culture, the Limelight Syndrome (the desire to be treated as a VIP) and shopping as buzz rather than shopping as purchase. It was the age of the superclub and slapper holidays, of designer drugs and the Union Jack as a rising icon of cool – in fashion, on the football pitch, in abattoir style East End galleries. Yet we weren't getting any of this in Marks & Spencer – or indeed from many other British retailers of brands for that matter – where the only designer label on sale was St. Michael's, and in conditions that reminded one critic of department stores in Moscow.

## ▓ Listen, look, ask, then act

Worse – and this is where our story really begins – the consumers of this period wanted to buy items that reflected THEIR lifestyle, made THEM feel better about who THEY were and where THEY were going. And Marks & Spencer, like many brands before and many to follow, had forgotten about doing this – about asking a question which, during better times, one of its founders (Simon Marks) would always ask himself and his managers when visiting the brand's flagship store at Marble Arch – what's new?

If nobody knew, or he saw a garment that didn't reflect what he thought was new – a mood, an ambience, a subtle shift in the desires of his customers – he would take the garment in question and hurl it to the floor declaring, 'You are ruining my business.'

Towards the end of his tenure, Richard Greenbury – who had walked the floor with his mentor many times, and many times had heard him ask that telling question – had stopped asking it himself.

Worse, he had stopped listening, looking, brailling – as in reaching out and touching the very people, things and cultural shifts that would tell him why a brand which 89 per cent of customers trusted 'very highly' in 1995, would become one which only 61 per cent trusted to deliver on quality and value with style by 1999. It happened because he had stopped looking at the future, stopped listening to his customers – facts very clear to us when we read that letter, recalled that conversation with the store's alleged trend forecaster. Now, happily, Marks & Spencer has moved on, has started listening to the market, runs its own insight unit, has a sharp and very focused trend department, and above all now works with designers and merchandisers who understand fashion, sell lifestyle, promote and deliver customer-centric service policies.

> **❝ It happened because he had stopped looking at the future, stopped listening to his customers. ❞**

However, this is not the story of Marks & Spencer. A brilliant and telling version of the brand's decline and phoenix-like recovery can be found in Judi Bevan's award winning book *The Rise and Fall of Marks & Spencer*. It is about why Richard Greenbury forgot to ask that question, along with countless CEOs and marketing departments before and since – at Enron, at Microsoft, at McDonald's, at Arthur Andersen, at WorldCom, at many of the brands we've been working with since (yes, Marks & Spencer included). It is becoming the only question worth asking – what's new?

It is also the question most of the companies entering the top ranks of the fabled Fortune 500 forget to ask – one of the key reasons we believe that 91 per cent of the names that achieve such dizzy and dizzying heights slow down so much that the only way they can grow is via acquisitions rather than new ideas.

But to succeed, this question must be asked 24Seven – and not just in fashion, for this is a small, ever elusive and shifting area of popular culture we all dip into, whether we admit to it or not – but what's new in the culture itself. The mood abroad, the changes in the wind. The key cultural, social and consumer shifts that impact on the bottom line – your bottom line. We continue assuming that the brand is king, that brand matters, that customers care. They used to. David Lubers, a senior advertising executive in the Omnicom group, once famously compared consumers to cockroaches, 'You spray them and spray them and they get immune after a while.'

They do, but they are also doing something else as we shall see – they are getting even.

# S**t happens –
## so you'd better be prepared

Getting even is exactly what customers did at Marks & Spencer because the retailer failed to ask what one of its founders asked every day – what's new? And getting even is what anti-global protesters are doing when they blockade the streets of Davos, Seattle or Genoa; when food protesters like Jose Bové trash a McDonald's outlet in his hometown of Millau or anti-fuel activists in the UK blockade garage forecourts.

It is also what anti-GM activists are doing when they uproot genetically modified crops in the heart of Wiltshire; what South African civil rights protesters are doing when they take pharmaceutical giants like GlaxoSmithKline and Pfizer to court and challenge their right to charge high prices for badly needed Aids and anti-HIV drugs.

It is also what more and more consumers and stakeholders are doing daily, not just speaking out, but acting up – occupying Easyjet planes; taking tobacco giants like R.J. Reynolds to court where they were fined £15m for advertising in teen-friendly magazines like *Spin*, *People* and *Sports Illustrated*; targeting AGMs or investors and the banks and financial institutions of companies and brands like Gucci, Corus and Vivendi who they feel have wronged them in some way or other.

It can be a small, quiet victory – like the residents of Hampstead, one of London's more affluent areas, campaigning successfully against plans to open a Starbucks along their street. Or a major moral victory like that achieved by child labour activist Marc Kasky in the Californian Supreme Court against Nike when judges ruled 4–3 in his favour that a PR campaign run by the brand to 'inform' the media about its work practices was in fact first and foremost a commercial speech – in short a thinly disguised form of advertising designed to sell products rather than to dispense truth.

## ■ Brandlash on the increase

Activists aside, even ordinary Americans are falling out of love with brands. Once upon a time poll after poll reported that people were satisfied or very satisfied with how American businesses worked, but not anymore. According to a *BusinessWeek* poll, consumers believe that having profits is more important to big business than developing safe, reliable, quality products for consumers. They also believe that brands are squeezing out local business and reducing local variety and culture.

Very worrying when you consider that these were the very consumers who, only a few years ago, were all too happy to repeat the mantra that 'what is good for business is good for most Americans!'

When asked to comment on this very statement in a *BusinessWeek* poll in 1981, only 47 per cent said it was still true, compared to the 71 per cent who believed it in 1996. This poll was carried out before the Enron, WorldCom, Tyco and Arthur Andersen accounting scandals hit the headlines, so you can imagine what they are thinking now! In case you can't, here's something to think about. A Burson–Marsteller poll found that the proportion of senior executives answering 'No' to the question, 'Would you want to be a CEO today?' had more than doubled in just one year from 26 to 54 per cent due to the personal antipathy they had felt from colleagues and the public. Add to that, a new and highly popular network series in the US called *Just Cause* in which a hard kicking, book touting, morally superior paralegal goes about whip-assing Ken Lay types (tag line: 'Cleaning up America one crooked CEO at at time . . .') and you can see just how low American business, and the brands that made America great, are now rated.

In Europe, things are no better. According to the Future Foundation's nVision consumer monitoring service, shoppers who believe that brands and companies are fair to them is down from 58 to 36 per cent. Half of those spoken to also agreed with the statement, 'You can't trust large multinationals nowadays', while a whopping three-quarters believed that such companies 'have too much power and should be stopped now' or that they 'need to be policed and controlled more than they are at present'.

However, things are never so bad that they can't get worse, as more and more brands are discovering. And they have only themselves to blame as we shall see – not for not asking that question, what's new? – but worse – for asking it and not paying attention to the answers. Why? Because it didn't suit their target objectives or didn't suit their sense of brand. But also because they believed, like Marks & Spencer, that success made them invincible, or that their coolness made them untouchable. Which of course is one of the greatest problems of being cool – you risk going off the boil pretty quickly.

# Prey now –
## and you'll pay later

In a survey carried out by the Work Foundation, even brands hailed for their coolness and street credibility have been outed and condemned for practices that seem acceptable to them but less than acceptable to the consumers they deal with.

Asked to rate names like Nike, Coca-Cola and Marlboro against a list of 30 negative and positive adjectives, Nike was seen to be ambitious, aggressive, greedy, exclusive and cynical, and Coca-Cola the same, but with the terms secretive and ruthless replacing exclusive and cynical.

Ruthless and deceitful were the words most commonly associated with Marlboro – once regarded as hip and edgy – which is understandable when you consider how tobacco companies have attempted to suppress research on the links between cancer and smoking, but puzzling when you consider that these were the kinds of adjectives also used to describe a brand that makes soft drinks and another that makes trainers and sportswear!

Puzzling but hardly surprising – brands, retailers and corporations are now so far away from where consumers want them to be, one wonders if the former and the latter are living in parallel universes, especially when you look at how business continues to address consumers and sell to them in ways that are woefully out of step with their long term needs and new century desires. And it is this process, this constant need to make a brand a 'happening' one that is causing much of the negativity consumers are feeling towards brands at the moment.

> **❝ Retailers and corporations are now so far away from where consumers want them to be. ❞**

As Susan Fournier, associate professor of Business Administration at Harvard Business School, sees it, brands and marketers are under tremendous pressure to do a one up. This means constantly raising the bar, using more tools – guerilla marketing, disruption marketing, viral marketing – and entering more domains. But what actually happens is that the discipline spirals downwards and validity is reduced.

Fournier continues, 'Take that whole buzz or "under the radar thing", advertising in non-traditional spaces and places, everybody's doing it now . . . There are too many brands, too much product development and too many boundaries being crossed at once. This credo just produces a "you've got to be kidding" reaction.'

Consumers then are suffering from brand fatigue, or brand blur as we've dubbed it – we are now subjected to more than 3000 brand messages or statements on a daily basis and many of us, rather than succumbing, are just saying no. Which, to borrow a term from the world of complexity theory, has brought us to that point in culture where things become ever more complicated and complex, before, yes you've guessed it, they fall apart or implode into something far simpler and more in tune with the market's needs.

## ▧ Brand basics and simplified customer solutions

There are three stages to this process, according to W. Brian Arthur who has pioneered complexity theory studies out of the Sante Fe Institute, New Mexico. The explosive or creative stage when ideas are new, fresh and so impregnated with energy that these in turn spin off ever better and far more ingenious and creative ways of doing something – in this case creating brands or redefining new or emerging consumer markets, which happened between 1985 and 1990 when 'lifestyle' became the mania we all bought into, brands the way of doing it, 'designer' the way of making those brands more appealing and exclusive. Here there is growth, diversity, a sense that things created are the things needed. Remember those days? When you created something consumers actually wanted!

Then comes stage two – 'structural deepening' when the brand horizon becomes more complicated, more convoluted and complex, with add ons, extras, bells and whistles. Arthur reports, 'The steady pressure of competition causes complexity to increase as functions and modifications are added to the system to break through limitations, to handle exceptional circumstances, or to adapt to an environment itself more complex.'

This is where advertising and brands are at now in a market of total complexity, of mindless similarities where more and more add ons or even greater or sneakier ways are needed to sell what is in essence the same product, in many cases products or brands that few consumers want – only 60 per cent of TV viewers actually pay any attention to on-air commercials according to the latest research, and it now takes 300 spots to reach the same number of viewers, whereas five TV spots would have succeeded 25 years ago.

Hence 'guerilla marketing', 'viral branding', 'immersive advertising', 'emotional selling', the creation of so-called brand spaces like Shiseido's brand garden in Tokyo, or Nike's all ages Presto music venue in Toronto, or reality TV brand shows like *Murder in a Small Town X* in which real contestants attempt to solve a semi-scripted mystery in a purpose-built Taco Bell, billed not as a product placement but as a pivotal plot device in its own right. Oh yeah.

We've also witnessed the rise of 'community branding', 'e-banners', 'memetics', 'SMS advertising', 'permission marketing', 'brand gaming' (Nokia runs a Europe-wide brand game via mobiles, e-mails, phones, TV and print advertising which involves up to 600 000 players at a time) and, as Frederic Beigbeder suggests in his slash-and-burn skit on the French and UK advertising scenes, £9.99, free telephone calls paid for by 'informotionals' from advertisers allowed to interrupt your conversation with regular words of wisdom on their latest offers.

'Just imagine,' writes Beigbeder in his novel, 'the telephone rings, a policeman tells you that your child has just died in a car crash, you dissolve into tears and the voice on the other end of the line says, "Mouts Ulther? Bon Jela!"'

When this point is reached, the system itself begins to bite back or at least takes on a personality and flavour that work independently of, and in many cases contrary to, those originally designed by its creators.

This is Arthur's third stage – the one in which the system, because it has become so complex and so unmanageable, takes on a personality of its own and bites back. This is why, when you dip into chatrooms, scan bulletin boards, read rant sites, peruse Blogg diaries, or look to the editorial pages of niche or boutique reads like *ID, Dazed, Surface, Vice, Tank, Adbusters* (even biannual consumer trends and marketing publications like *Viewpoint, TNB* or *Antenna*), views on brands are not only negative, but expressed in a very political, aggressive and none too pleasant tone.

Is that bad? You bet. Especially when you consider that one group of online consumers identified as e-fluentials because of their collective click power, say that if a brand or service appeals they will tell, on average, 11 people about it, but if the brand fails them in any way, they will e-mail 17 or more about their experience! And with 11 million e-fluentials currently connecting online, each reaching up to

155 million other adults with their messages and comments, you can see just how damaging word of mouse can be.

## ■ Consumanism is politics the people's way

But e-fluentials are part of a much broader and more pan-political shift in affirmative consumers using Zapatista style tactics – mobiles, the internet, chatrooms and cell-like organizational hubs to 'net them up' – to get their messages heard.

> ❝ **Using their buying power to punish errant brands or those who fall short.** ❞

And this is just the beginning. Consumers are only now gearing up for the many fights they see ahead of them. So look out for more of the kind of actions carried out by anti-vivisection protesters on Huntingdon Life Sciences and their shareholders; or the protests that led to Benetton's U-turn on using death row prisoners to sell their products in America.

Also, as politicians engage less and less with community-based issues, watch out for an increase in the number of people voting with their credit cards rather than their polling cards, using their buying power to punish errant brands or those who fall short of the social, ethical, environmental, and – bad for some – moral agendas consumers are now setting for them. These are what we call 'consumanists', a generation of proactive shoppers with humanist principles firmly at the heart of all their shopping decisions. And it's set to become a very powerful movement indeed as we shall see.

For this is a consumer 'values' system that can be, and usually is, an issue-based one rather than one based on shared social backgrounds.

## ■ Single issue protests

The reason why beleaguered and puzzled brands, pharmaceutical companies or biotech researchers are just as likely to find gays, anti-abortion groups, Christian fundamentalists, non-governmental organizations (NGOs), organic farmers, Women's Institute members and militant animal rights activists all standing shoulder to shoulder outside their doors is that protest is no longer about politics but about policies.

And what works across seemingly disparate social groups, also works across continents, as Huntingdon Life Sciences found when anti-vivisection protests in the UK forced them to cancel their London Stock Exchange listing and move to the US with a name change to boot. Here they were targeted once more by US protesters working with those in the UK, and found investors there to be equally nervous and worried about the damage the residual publicity could do if they were seen to be supporting the company in its researches.

Although some investment groups stuck with them, Charles Schwab told his investors in the company that they had a month to transfer stock elsewhere because of the possible damage such investments would do, not just to their stock but to that of other investors Schwab was handling.

The point being made here is a simple one – brands, or corporations, may have the law on their side but the consumanist will break it if it is believed there is a greater moral argument at stake.

And in the future even more so – as 'acting up' becomes become the new way of making brands and organizations pay up.

# Tactile futures –
## tomorrow's brands are about human values systems

You get the message – consumers really are revolting. And this is why the future isn't about using ever more sophisticated or 'beneath the radar methods' of selling or brand building – consumanists see this as intrusive, invasive and a very good reason for taking you to court! It is about going back to fundamentals – building brands, designing products and creating corporations that people want and are happy to endorse because from the beginning they are part and parcel of the creation process. But to do this properly, you have to create and inhabit a very particular kind of company or brand – one we call tactile.

The tactile brand isn't about touching or feeling things in the traditional sense. It is about tactility in the way that we understand reaching out, as in connecting, digging down into a culture. It's about brailling – feeling, touching and seeing the world around us as it shifts and moves in an engaging, measured, emotional and poetic way.

As Interbrand CEO Rita Clifton puts it, 'A brand has to be about a lot more than a mere logo'. If it works, she insists, if it has meaning, emotion, tactility, you should be able to block out the logo or name with your thumb and still understand 'what the brand is, what it means' – not just its intangible assets, but its emotional and poetic ones as well.

### ■ Brand poetics and the death of rational expectation

Yes, poetic! Future trends cannot and should not be measured rationally, or quantitatively, as we shall see, but emotionally, intuitively, empathetically and with a battery of technologies, techniques and observational and field study processes that are more familiar to the artist, the sociologist, the ethnographer or the anthropologist than they are to the traditional manager, marketer, planner or brand manager.

This is marketing by engagement – living the consumer life rather than asking about it, or indeed attempting to direct it. This is a way of seeing and anticipating change that puts the consumer at the heart of all decisions and strategies. A way of reading the future by rewriting the rules of brand inclusiveness (or brand relevance), fit and what we call brand poetics – the emotional and tactile, but invisible, constructs that make your brand ultimately appealing because it connects with, and plugs into, the mood or trend that people are subscribing to at that point in time.

This fusing of brand to moment, of product to trend is known as brand harmonics and this, if we read the future correctly, can be achieved seamlessly and smoothly because the brand, when grown properly, will be a brand grown from the same needs and spiritual yearnings as those of the consumer – in other words you won't decide what your brand characteristics are to be, they will. And in this world of live research, of tactile engagement, the consumer will become your brand doctor, brand regulator, builder and deployer.

And while they are creating their own lifestyle and lifeprism platforms to operate from, the Limelight Generation (who want to be treated like VIPs), Lone Wolves (single males who want to be treated as ME-brands), the New Essentialist Shoppers (who want to be dealt with preferentially) and SINDIES (or single income now divorced, who want to be dealt with fairly) will, if you work with them honestly and inclusively, allow you to participate in this process.

This is why future-faced brands are not brands that are omnipotent, or consistent in the traditional sense that brands are consistent or standardized across all territories, but rather that they accommodate the personal, the individual – as brand analyst Robert Jones explains (of Wolff Olins, the brand consultancy that gave us Orange, one of the first and most enduring tactile brands), 'People don't want totally defined, totally replicable experiences.'

They want difference and diversity, but inside those they still want to know that there is a consistency in terms of promise, of delivery, of values and service, not just at the point of purchase or engagement with the consumer, but five years down the line.

Brands then need to do to us what familiar places, people and things do to us – reassure, protect, calm, offer emotional security, physical warmth, honesty, trust, a sense that all is well; that we are here to be stimulated, assuaged, wooed, revitalized or romanced.

'It is precisely what is not easily mass producible that adds most value now to a product or service,' believes economist and analyst Diane Coyle – what she calls weightless economics. Brands have to get real, get involved, believes Clifton. 'Real in the sense of who you are, what you are here for, and how is that going to make the world a better and happier place.'

And making the world a happier place might, as we shall see, mean doing less rather than more of what you are doing at the moment – of distributing profits in different ways, of measuring your worth not in terms of what you can get out of your customers, but what you can give them back, and also how you give it back to them.

What Coyle refers to as serendipity – 'by far the most fruitful source of genuine innovation and fresh thinking' – is one way the future-faced company or tactile brand can dance more effectively with its customers. 'But if your customers don't enjoy the dance,' as Michael Wolff, one of Europe's few tactile brand developers sees it, 'they won't continue it'.

> **This is why old marketing techniques must be abandoned.**

And in a brand-rich and brand-wary culture where choice isn't just everything but also everywhere, consumers have so many brands to dance with that those which don't do it their way are going to be left on the shelf.

Like all good dance partners however, those that anticipate the moves are far better placed to please partners and collect plaudits than those whose only desire it is to follow and come in an adequate but unremarkable second.

This is why old marketing techniques must be abandoned and why we recommend the following to all our clients – if you see your marketing department at their desks on a regular basis, you should sack them. They can't be doing their jobs! Why? Because marketing is no longer about gathering – it is about doing, engaging, being.

# 5

# Brailling the culture –
## to read change, you have to live it

True forecasting or brailling isn't just about anticipation or passive observation, but about interaction. It's about living customers' lives or 'lifestyle narratives' in a way that keeps you connected to them online. In the field, in their homes, offices and heads, in their spiritual and emotional lives, in their dreams, desires, and daily needs. And with their full consent. We didn't say this – it was said to us at a number of meetings with top creatives and brand strategists such as Ogilvy & Mather's Mark Earls, and John Grant, cofounder of St. Lukes, one of the UK's most successful and creative advertising agencies – but we sincerely believe it.

And to do this, you have to understand, accept and open up to new ideas about the market and how it works – not rationally, as traditional economists and marketers tell us, but irrationally, emotionally, chaotically and idiosyncratically.

More than ever, markets are driven not by Mr and Mrs Average (as if these categories really exist!) but by a small, radically connected set of doers, thinkers, activists and deviants who are driving markets in new and increasingly complex ways.

And these power curve consumers or hub group members (risk takers and cultural anarchists whose very genes and jeans demand that they say yes to everything twice) are not the kind of passive consumers your marketing department has become used to selling to, or your design department all too used to creating products for.

They are the kind of people that have already designed the products you will be selling tomorrow (think Dean Kamen here and the Segway human transporter; think Lexus cars who visualized the autodrive cars for Steven Spielberg's *Minority Report*; or GE's AUTOnomy, a fuel cell concept car already setting standards for others to follow). These are now creating the brands you will be offering, are already giving birth to the services you will be providing them with.

Few of us however see or even believe this. In our hearts, we still regard consumers as passive – as takers, colluders – still see brands as ways of getting us off the hook, as Mark Earls puts it. We hide behind the promise, we tinker with the small print, make one too many exceptions in the terms and conditions and then hope that nobody will notice, or that these exceptions make those unhappy with the rules as we've laid them down, less likely to complain because, after all, we did say there 'might' be problems.

## ◼ Solutions shouldn't be compromises

The British Airways flat bed for first class business flyers is a good example of this attitude, believes Michael Wolff. 'Yes, you can lie down flat but it's so uncomfortable, and you're sleeping right next to people that it is clearly not right.'

In other words, it is in breach of its potential, its promise. Worse still, it is not truly the product of a company or brand that is listening, merely the compromise of one that is attempting to save money – and consumers see through this (especially our power curve ones) whether your brand manager or advertising agency likes it or not.

Did BA's research with its business class passengers, for example, really come up with the following? That they wanted a bed that wasn't quite a bed, but a bit of a seat that opens out like one, and thus looks like a bed and gives you a nice image for your ad, saves you some space and keeps things within budget, but gives its users an uncomfortable night and bad back problems to boot.

Or did those travellers say simply – we're assuming here that they were asked, and that these things were designed with passengers making input and suggestions at all stages of the design process – that 'we want a bed we can sleep in with blankets, a nice pillow and a comfy mattress.'

Probably.

But ah, we hear you say, what about cost, space, ergonomics? What about them? These are your concerns, not the consumers' – they simply want a bed, and a proper bed at that. And if you don't comply, don't complain when somebody like Boeing comes along with its Airbus 380 series which comes with cabins, beds, a gym, cocktail bars, even designer boutiques as standard – for standard class passengers to boot.

## ■ Tactile means versatile

That's what characterizes a brand or company that is tactile, or as we say, one that can dance – it refuses to entertain compromise as far as consumers are concerned. Refuses to place constraints on its solutions, refuses to set parameters on its brief. Rather, it takes its customers as they are, and works with them accordingly – not just in terms of using them to look at new and innovative products and ways of taking them to market, but for reading trends correctly and seeing why some technologies and products work, while others fail to get off the starting block. Why, for example, products like the Sinclair C5, Apple's Newton, Betamax, or eight-track stereos have become the stuff of kitsch TV specials along with K-Tel compilation albums and DIY haircut combs, while other products like IDEO's Palm V, the microscooter and the Tate Modern have become fast spreading consumer trends.

But tomorrow's consumers don't just want solutions and simplifications – they want to be seen as people, not numbers or statistical groupings to be audited or broken down. They want a clarity and a cohesion of transaction that treats them as individuals, not segmented bundles.

Customers have lives – that's the reason why economists are being forced to consider new ways of reading them – but worse still, they now see themselves as 'prosumers' or proactive consumers with billing capabilities just as businesses and services have billing capabilities, and more than ever they are ready and waiting to use them.

A mother's time isn't her own – it's part of a community network she runs called the family. A single person's time likewise is part of an increasingly radicalized concept called the cat's cradle network. Likewise, the dual income lone kid household, or the full or part time student – they are all brands or connected webs with rate per minute billings, and just as you charge them when they fail to show up for a dental appointment, a restaurant booking or a flight, so too will they start billing you for having to wait indoors, hang on a telephone, queue, write interminable letters because nobody in your company really understands how customers are changing and just how little it takes to anger them!

Tomorrow's consumers want things their way and if their way changes, as real people change on a daily basis, they want the service, brand or company they are dealing with to change with them – this is why the old ways of reading and defining brands no longer work; why the old ways of profiling consumers, or measuring market shifts are redundant.

We are living in blurred times on a connected, ever shrinking, ever netted-up planet where, as forecasters Stan Davis and Christopher Meyer very succinctly put it, 'Products and services are merging, where buyers sell and sellers buy, where neat value chains are messy economic webs, homes, offices, process difficult to separate from structure.'

It is a world of knowledge companies, knowledge brands and knowledge needs. A world of ideas and intangibles, and companies that see these things. One where the consumer wants products when they want them, without having to wait.

This is the connected world gone mad. But one – as people become more vocal and more determined to stress the I, the ME, the individual, and the personal – that you have to read in very much the same way. But what will this future look like, how will it feel, what kind of brands and organizations live there?

part

## Future imperfect:
the shape of trends to come?

# 6

# Through the looking glass –
## a world turned inside out

This future, the one we are looking into is at once familiar, but also different and disturbing. It is a looking glass world of changes that bother because they seem not to be changes at all – a place where familiar voices are heard from unfamiliar mouths,where things done one way are now executed as their polar opposites.

In this future natural borders still exist – in China, Russia and India they will be stronger than ever, nationalistically, but also notionally in terms of embracing change, brands and a staggered or staged market economy – patent, copyright and intellectual properties are now flaunted and ignored in favour of 'copyleft' agreements (where everybody has the right to copy what they want when they want to under law) as bamboo curtains and caste divides are torn down or swept away in a race designed to make the First World come in second.

The world atlas rolling out before you contains many areas marked in blue – regions or super-regions that have been designated specialized zones of knowledge and connectivity, hubs that connect to each other across borders and cultures, countries and political ideologies.

**ff These transborder zones contain a new type of consumer. JJ**

These transborder zones contain a new type of consumer, or 'transumer' – plugged-in, wapped-up merchant princes that travel along, serviced by an interconnecting grid of songlines and social pathways that settle over these blue areas like ever thickening gossamer.

They refer to themselves as the hypermobile – men and women connected to each other and to the places they shuttle to and from, not by culture, class, or tradition but by ideology, by technology and a single language that dominates all business and social discourse.

They are serviced in their constant criss-crossing of cities and zones by free floating, nationless groups of migrant workers – medieval serfs in all but name – that work the roads, airports, technoparks, hotels, ideas and Ballard-like industrial zones this new world order is conjuring up. They don't even speak like the rest of us, or indeed follow traditional work routes, patterns or business diaries.

Like swallows, they are ever on the move, carrying with them everything they need to work, rest or play – this then is a future of perpetual mobility, virtual nomading; of intranets and extranets; of handhelds, wi-fi, 3G, laptops, BlackBerrys, Palm Vs, video conferencing; departure gates, arrival halls, transit lounges; three-way calls, four-way conversations; wheel-on and wheel-off cabin luggage cases; and lives that contains a thing called the 96-hour wardrobe, a 26-piece flat pack capsule collection of clothes, shoes and night shirts in cosmocratic colours of grey, black and charcoal. Four nights, five days – the time a cosmocrat stays away from home, base or, more unusually, office. Only no longer an office in the recognisable sense of the word – in the future we're looking at, hierarchies have been banished, demarcation lines between departments removed, departments themselves made up of flexecutives who sit next to strategists, who sit next to planners, who sit next to CEOs who work alongside R&D, marketing and customer services, who even have customers working with and against them on an ongoing basis.

## ▉ Insight over marketing

There is even a thing called an 'insight' unit. Indeed the term insight now describes ALL activities the company or brand involves itself in – all associates carry that word built into their round the clock activities. Insight, interconnecting, interplay, interfocus.

Another thing you'll notice is the company structure, or configuration – no longer like a pyramid but a federal splash of smaller cell-like minihubs of 50 or fewer people, each connected 24Seven to the other but each, depending on its own micromarkets or the localized requirements of its partners, allowed to make its own policy and strategy decisions independent of the other hubs scattered about the super-regions or territories that make up our map.

Some even change the brand logo or corporation letterhead as personal or professional etiquette requires; others create microbrands or 'flat pack' brands that are assembled or broken down in a week, a day, an hour, a nanosecond.

## ▉ The 'Hollywood' corporation

Brands that are rolled out, or released Hollywood movie style – for a day, a week or a month as the audience or prosumer requires it. And when they are no longer required, they will be taken off the shelf or the brand circuit (think of your supermarket in terms of a theatre or cinema) and mothballed. No need for brand stretch, brand building, brand segmentation, all that brand nonsense and multi-layering that has made branding such a despised activity – in this world the transumer is king, and in this world they are promiscuous to a fault.

And this brand promiscuity is the one thing you openly encourage. Every time a customer spurns you or moves on they are giving you the best kind of feedback and encouragement a customer can – a cry for the new, the different, something more original and outré than the last!

That's why brand or production teams are contracted and disbanded on a regular and ongoing basis – the most creative demanding royalties instead of wages, or accepting buyout rights or territorial royalties in greater recognition for the fruits of their efforts, or the risks attached to their efforts if the consumer doesn't like what they see.

Some brands live and die by this process. Others, if the insight and market intelligence is right, become a thing called a classic and have a shelf life longer than its owners could have hoped for. Nothing to do with advertising, or repackaging, or free giveaways, but all to do with the consumer, their whims, their needs, their desires.

## ■ Knowledge and innovation – the new profit centres

In this future our way of developing brands and retail concepts is nothing like it used to be, but more like the old Hollywood studio system where creatives, ideas, knowledge and innovation are the only assets worth measuring. Management, administration, human resources, secretarial support, PR, advertising and marketing – if you still have such an antiquated department – are all farmed out or contracted in.

Imagine an economy where profits from ideas and creativity outstrip those made from the sale of clothes, chemicals, cars, household goods and planes – not singularly, but combined. One where you really are as good as your last idea, where creativity rules, ideas sell – and the intangibles have become more important than the physical or measurable.

Likewise, if the top few names in the FTSE 100 now trade in ideas, all of them will in this future that we are glimpsing. Tomorrow is a brandscape with few physical boundaries – brands are immersive rather than confrontational; sonic rather than visual; quiet rather than loud; implanted, embedded and interactive as opposed to items that occupy shelves or can be packed into bags and taken home.

It is a world of 'edutainment' where knowledge, fun and brands collude to create games, zones, headscapes or interactive learning areas that teach and sell as they go.

It is a world of experience marketing – of content culture and content brands; of knowledge and ideas corporations. A world where knowledge is profit and interconnectivity is power – where enabling and personal empowerment is key to all B2C transactions.

It is also a world where brands have become social workers, healers, enablers, sources for moral and spiritual guidance.

# Terms of engagement –
## plugging into the shopped out

In this future then, the Fortune 500 is dominated by brands and corporations that offer socially, ethically and environmentally audited products as standard. They will also offer ever demanding customers services that were provided by governments once upon a time – and free with no obligation of purchase required.

Some call these concepts 'Citizen Brands', others 'Halo' or 'governance' marques but all do essentially the same thing – use something called a 'brand tariff' to raise money for hospitals, universities, knowledge shops (they used to be called libraries), sports centres, rehab programmes, leisure parks, environmental programmes, childcare facilities, pensions and Rainbow Youth retirement ships.

**❝ Brands with customer values systems at their heart, brands that are about governance. ❞**

These are brands with customer values systems at their heart, brands that are about governance, and open source monitoring procedures – allowing their books to be monitored by independent trust boards or consumer appointed organizations 24Seven.

## ▧ Citizen brands

Initially these things were done for mixed reasons – as a way of wooing prosumers (air miles regarded as silly were replaced by life miles or health miles regarded as useful); of winning over their loyalty; then as a way of not falling foul to prosumer rights groups who regulate and monitor a thing called the Prosumer 500. This is an index that is fast outstripping the FTSE and the Dow Jones because it measures brands not in terms of what they take out of the community, but what they put back into it. It is an index now used by investors and public alike to determine which companies or brands best deserve their support.

All this has come about because of something called connectivity – the way the net, mobiles, laptops, and interactive TV allow people to hook up and talk politics and enable social involvement of a different and far more radical sort.

Things work differently in the future – brands need 'trust marks' to trade. These are issued not by governments but according to your brand league position, as determined by viewers giving your 30-second pleas for their attention an approval rating on their TiVo handhelds.

Now the people regulate and rate your company and how it issues its shares or trust marks. Yes, you now have to go to market with your offer and see what people think of it – no more lavish advertising roll outs, no more cooking the collective books (popular in the naughty noughts) or faking the test results (a favourite with cosmetics, pharmaceutical and fragrance houses), no more doing business as it used to be done, which is why most brands or product categories are now created in the field, live or on things called extranets where customers, creatives, marketers, R&D, sales, CEOs, planners and project managers can all log on, or live out there in the field, live, ongoing and yes, interacting with – God forbid – a thing called the prosumer.

Data jockeying – what marketers once did – has been replaced by ethnographics, brand and retail anthropology, behavioural scientists, social profilers, story tellers, researchers and field operatives who live consumer behaviour, attitude, insight and a thing we'll call poetics and harmonics of place on a daily basis.

# NEW CONSUMING WORLD ORDERS

BRANDTOCRACIES → BRA
political &
social animal

CITIZEN BRAND
MENTOR BRAND
STATUS BRAND
BENEFIT BRAND
VALUE BRAND

It's all about fulfilling
a promise — creating a
pathway — simplifying
clarifying a need
SATISFYING A DESIRE

"NEVER FA
EVEN IF REALITY
OF EXPECTATI

A notebook produced by our Lifesigns Network in association with anti-global protestors and concerned shoppers. The notebooks were designed to reflect the needs and obsessions of their creators, but also to act as visual narratives designed to explain concepts such as 'consumanism' and 'citizen brandship'.

NO AS personal,
ethical +
statement

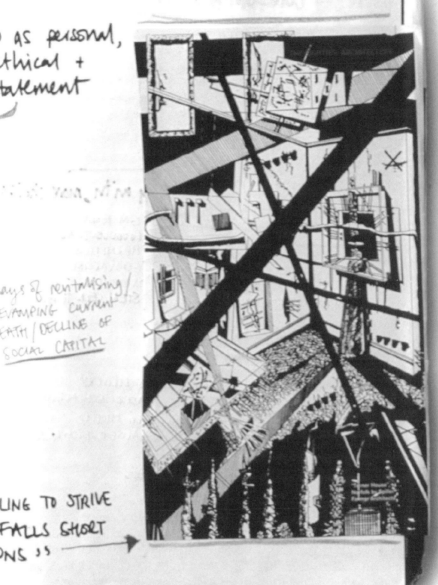

ways of revitalising/
REVAMPING current
DEATH / DECLINE OF
SOCIAL CAPITAL

ILING TO STRIVE
FALLS SHORT
ONS ,, ⟶

But it is also a future riven by food fundamentalism, social contradictions and single issue causes relating to health and well-being. Foods once permitted – fatty ones, calorific ones – and even the right to bear shopping bags from the supermarket will all be subject to health tariffs, warnings and environment taxes.

We have become sequential puritans remaining abstemious during the week, cutting down on alcohol, using dermal medicines to regulate our cravings for everything from tobacco, to fat, to sugar, to alcohol, to sex – only to indulge in a trend called 'compression hedonism', a weekend of 24Seven party excess where anything goes until Detox Monday where cosmeceuticals – breakfast cereals or foods with enhancement cosmetics, or so-called brightening or psychotropic ingredients – are consumed to bring your over-partied system back into line.

## ■ Food fundamentalism

Food fundamentalism, and the contradictions that come with it, are reflective of the much bigger fundamentalist ideas and contradictions found abroad in the general culture where philosophers, ethicists, and mainstream religions, especially Islam, are enjoying a renaissance as all things biotech divide not just the world, but zones of the planet where biotechnology is accepted and used – in China, India, Russia and the megacity states of South East Asia; where GM crops, transgenic livestocks, genocaste children and skin, organ and body part pharms or stem cell factories, are revolutionizing the markets and the fortunes of these countries and continents – the so-called genotocracies. This has led to the growth of body banks, organ farms, biolakes or centres where cells are stored and bodies grown *in vitro*, so that donors can avail themselves of spare parts when they need them without fear of organ rejection.

There are debates of course, and this is why philosophers and ethicists have once more come into their own – do clones have souls? Do transgenic species – those containing the genes of many animals, including humans – have rights? And if so, are they equal to those enjoyed by mankind?

And what of the plants that now contain human genes, or animal cells? Are they higher up the evolutionary ladder because of our tinkering, or has all this tinkering made everything more inhuman, more bestial?

These debates rage and so too does the one about longevity and the growing divide, not between rich and poor, the haves and have nots, online and offline people, but concerning those in their seventies still supporting sectors of the economy unable to work or fend for themselves – those in their childhood and teen years deemed to be unproductive in a society increasingly marginalized by twenty-somethings who are in decline, and sixty- and seventy-somethings who are in the ascendant.

## ■ Rainbow Youth exacts its revenge

In the past, the old were seen as a burden and a liability, but they are now increasingly politicized, wealthy, affluent and, thanks to advances in genomedicine, transplants, and psychotropic technologies, able to live into their nineties and beyond. More actively and mentally alert than ever, they have become a powerful lobby against the so-called tax burden of youth, of family and teenagers living off an increasingly overburdened social welfare system.

To compensate for declining birth rates, an ageing population and escalating health costs, immigrants and migrant workers have ceased being a problem and are now a highly sought after asset. So much so that recruitment fairs are held in key super-regions where countries like Japan, Korea, Britain, Italy, Spain, Russia, Brazil and China – dogged by falling birth rates – offer increasingly attractive settlement packages to the growing number of guilds, collectives and trade-craft federations that have been formed by immigrants in association with an increasingly powerful lobby of NGOs and cross-border citizen and civil rights organizations.

## ▧ Copycat culture

Social divides still exist, class divides are more endemic than ever, the divide between the so-called digerati or 'netocrats' and those denied access to even basic technological advances ever more pronounced. But a moral imperative to catch up has brought forth a Robin Hood class of brands, businesses, product cloners and concerns in high and low places determined to use all in their power to make technology, drugs, and all that passes for entertainment hardware or software more available to all.

This is a world where open source, open plan and open door approach to copyright have come into their own – along with the idea that copyright patents and protects intellectual property agreements, far from protecting creativity and advances in knowledge, actually restricts it to the privileged few. So now people are encouraged to do what was hitherto banned – to copy and be profitable.

Likewise, cloning and fusing, or collaborative technologies, brands, softwares or companies are the rule rather than the exception. Things connect, link up, become organic and fluid in ways that are creative and beneficial, but not always to the liking of the brands involved. Once you monitored and cruised consumer databases, once you eavesdropped on their bank accounts, their e-mails, their phone calls. Now they do this to you – and with the law's approval. And oddly enough for your own good, as well as theirs.

# The future happened yesterday –
## you just missed it!

A familiar and shocking world? We assume so, because the world we've just described has already happened. From babies bred for their cells to gene kits sold over the counter at Boots or Brooklyn chemists to test for hereditary diseases.

If you didn't spot this or weren't familiar with most of the scenarios or terms outlined in the previous chapters, you are not doing what you need to do to survive in this new world slowly settling on us – you are not reading it, or engaging with it in the way it needs to be read or engaged.

> **A familiar and shocking world? We assume so, because the world we've just described has already happened.**

What we have outlined is the world as it is, but distilled, and this is what good forecasters and brand builders must do – create the Big Picture before they can break it down, and see how it impacts on the little one, or on the life of the prosumer. But let us stay with this view of the world for a moment and break it down so that you can see it a little better.

Our hypermobile elite – or cosmocrats as we've named them – are very much a part of that cross-global grid of companies, brands and corporations that are already transforming the shape and geography of our planet. A glance at A.J. Scott's atlas *Global City Regions* proves this. In it we are confronted with a very different world from the one once dominated by the colour pink, or showing regions, countries and borders framed by dizzying mountain ranges, or sharp, straight lines that indicated signed treaties and negotiated borders. Technologies have removed borders; brands and economic charters have merged whole countries; population shifts from green to brown sites have created 300 or so megacities, most with favelas, banlieus and barrios carrying millions more people and problems in their wake.

Immigration certainly is a big issue – the US now takes more than a million immigrants a year – while declining birth rates and a growing grey market in Europe will see immigration rocket, and no bad thing. In Europe alone, the number of children under 15 has shrunk by 23 per cent since 1970 and, according to the UN Population division, the number of working age people to support every European over the age of 65 will fall from four to two. If Europe is to counter this, it must boost its productivity by two-thirds by 2020, which means opening up its borders to immigrants on a scale hitherto unimagined. If Europe is to remain a buoyant, profitable zone, immigration will become the norm.

## ▧ Knowledge capitals and elsewherevilles

We are are witnessing the rise of so-called IQvilles – cities that exist only because technology allows them to – edge cities like those that grew up around Atlanta in the 80s and 90s; aero or conference centres like Kuwait and Dubai, which have become hub centres because they are easy to get to; cities or regions like Singapore, Jakarta, Seoul, Tokyo, Lagos, Taipei, KL, Sydney, Manila and the Pearl River Delta in China that have used technology, hyperarchitecture culture, low labour costs and position to broker city states and super-regional enclaves in everything but name – regions and states that have more in common with each other and with the 20 million or so hypermobile elite commuting between them, than they have with the populations living in the shanty towns and slums growing around them.

These are cities and regions welded together by hotel chains offering an elite, deluxe, but consistent service across cultures (the Hyatt, le Meridien, the Hilton, the Oberoi, the Radisson); by brands like Gucci, Prada, Louis Vuitton and Versace that allow you to buy a shirt in Taipei and exchange it, no questions asked, in the marble malls of the Hong Kong Peninsula; by architects like Pelli, Foster, Rogers, Yeang, Tange, Piano and Gehry who create towers and palaces and shimmering skyward slivers (the Petronas towers, the Bilboa Guggenheim, the Reichstag, the World Financial Centre in Shanghai, Norman Foster's City of London Gherkin). These knit all these cities together into futuristic, fast forward myths where London and New York have become one – a megacity called NyLon – a conceptual, connected, multicultural zone of commerce and cross-cultural consequence.

Here you can already buy that 96-hour wardrobe we've mentioned – by Puma. Here too you'll find the kind of federal structures for the future companies and corporations we've been talking about. Companies like Shell, IBM, HP, Philips and Ford have already gone some way down this route, slicing out tier after useless tier of C-class management, replacing them with more autonomous, cell-like systems and hubs connected with ICT, intranets, even virtual jamborees, where brands like IBM convene 8100 managers from 50 countries online to share ideas, swap working methods and bond across geographic, cultural and digital divides – the 'ultimate watercooler experience', as John Rooney, its head of development, describes it.

But you'll also find concept design consultancies like IDEO who have made the federated system a power to be reckoned with, a design company that offers autonomy to its federated cells in ways few of its more moribund contemporaries would dare to risk – to alter personal logos and letterheads at will. Companies – like Orange, Allied Irish Banks, Happy Dog, BMW, Nissan, WCRS – who use ethnography and the kind of future-faced, customer-centred techniques we believe offer the kind of spiritual, design and intellectual insights needed to drive business in a world dominated by ideas, knowledge and consumer desire.

Some companies are playing with notions of flat pack labels, of 'keyboard brands' – like Oki-ni in London, where one-off products are created and ordered online, the shop becoming a virtual outpost but also a canny interactive tool for brands to use customers to design and customize products; or Hong Kong's Cyber Express, a virtual shopping mall that exists within a real one to allow brands to come and go when consumers demand; or even Rem Koolhaas' Prada store in New York with its public spaces, virtual changing rooms and theatre areas that make shopping a cultural activity and knowledge bringer in its own right.

Even the paradigm shifts in consumer behaviour patterns described previously are already up and running. As well as shopping with our feet, we are increasingly shopping with our consciences, with our ombudsmen and, when all these fail, with the law, with lawyers and the knowledge that even time will not prevent the truth about a company or a country's immorality from coming out, as IBM and Swiss banking organizations found when attempting to deny their part in the Holocaust. Brands are now being judged by a values index whether they like it or not.

## ■ Tomorrow's tribes today

In tandem with groups motivated by historic and political reasons for punishing wayward corporations, there are those like our e-fluentials – the new middle classes, our Rainbow Youth, Lone Nesters, Late Nesters, Lone Wolves and New Essentialist Shoppers – who are all demanding that brands take on a more socially responsible role. Become citizen brands, as Michael Willmott, the writer and cofounder of the future forecasting consultancy, the Future Foundation, calls them – brands that broker and engender change. Brands that embody the old value systems of the great philanthropic families of the past – the Cadburys, the Guinnesses, the Carnegies. Or people ownership movements like the Chartists that put useful, beneficial and badly needed things back, without demanding that their logo be everywhere or that their products be sold prime position.

Citizenry and brand governance in the way we know consumers want it, is about an approach to brand management and profit deployment that few companies are yet equipped to tackle, tied in as they are to outmoded ideas of cause-related marketing, sponsorship and advertising activities.

But as brands fall under more and more scrutiny – socially, ethically, environmentally and morally – more and more consumers take class action suits against them for false claims or damage to their health. Following civil suits against tobacco companies, we are seeing similar ones being pursued against fast food corporations. And brands, to overcome this, or to nail their colours to the supermarket aisles, will have to do more for less – to give as much in altruistic endeavours as they take in profits – or suffer the legislative consequences.

And if customers don't get these things or feel they are being duped they will sue – as consumers are now suing burger giants for failing to inform them of the true dangers of fast foods, mechanically recovered meats, or the low levels of chicken in such items as chicken nuggets – usually less than 7 per cent!

Fast food suppliers, supermarkets who fail to inform, and clothing or product manufacturers who fail to disclose how goods are produced are all liable to experience the same kinds of lawsuits currently being experienced by the tobacco industry, as consumers, believing governments to be in cahoots with big business (see George Monbiot's excellent *Captive State*) use the law more and more to defend their rights.

We are likely to see similar class action suits against mobile phone companies (because of fears over cancer, leukaemia); alcohol producers (alcoholism, cirrhosis of the liver); brands or retailers that sell GM food, or foodstuffs contaminated with genetically modified genes. Ignorance will not give protection from this new generation of highly articulate and litigious consumers waiting in the wings.

But anticipating their needs or going some way towards their desires and points of view might. Shell has done this to some extent, reversing a poor public image and low value rating as a brand concerned about ethical and environmental images – Brent Spar, its atrocious record against ethnic minorities in Nigeria – and recast itself as ecowarrior and champion of ethnically marginal groups and local tribes.

## ■ The future is about being proactive

But you can do this only if you know and feel what consumers want, how the future is shaping up. In one area in particular – biotech and GM – brands and governments (in the UK especially) still fail to understand the true depth of consumers' concerns.

It is important that you don't fall into this trap – even if biotech is the future (and it is), you can't go there without the customer's approval. We haven't yet reached the world of biotech babies and transgenic brands we wrote about earlier, but we're closer to it than even the most optimistic of us think. Already in Brazil, the US, India and parts of northern Africa, GM crops have become an everyday reality. In India, Bt cotton (which contains a gene that kills bollworm) is a necessity, while in US supermarkets 75 per cent of all soya-based products are GM.

> ❝ Amid these changes then, you need to be prepared, to be able to see and envision these futures long before they happen. ❞

Transgenic cows, sheep, mice and pigs are alive and kicking in US, UK and French laboratories, while Israeli scientists, aware of Middle Eastern tastes for chicken à la everything, have cloned a plump, extra succulent but featherless chicken to cut down on plucking time.

In the UK alone, six companies are already offering genetic screening to couples who wish to create the best conditions for conceiving the 'perfect' child. Another, Sciona, also sells over-the-counter screening kits for £120 which allow users to identify up to nine potentially life-threatening illnesses that may or may not be lurking in their genes. Even the creators of Dolly the Sheep are now turning their attentions to cloning humans, fearing perhaps that less scrupulous organizations and religious cults have already beaten them to it.

Amid these changes then, you need to be prepared, to be able to see and envision these futures long before they happen – you need to have strategies in place, a game plan already deployed. Know how to read the future, yes – and this is what we will teach you to do – but you might just also know how you can influence it and make the future your future, rather than that of your competitors.

# Blinding by numbers:
## or how data jockeys murdered the marketing stars

# Data jockeys –
## their part in your downfall

The future really is another country then – and a strange one at that. And to understand it, and the kinds of companies or brands best suited to inhabit it, requires the application of a particular kind of brain, and a particular kind of reasoning and logic – emotional reasoning, irrational logic – only then will the questions you ask and the answers you receive make sense, or become the kind of a thing that adds value, usefulness, imagination and insight to such details that have been gathered.

But to do this, it is important that you understand the difference between 'data' and 'information', 'information' and 'knowledge', 'knowledge' and 'insight' and the part each plays in helping us mine the future and create the kinds of products, services and brands best suited to living there.

This is important. For years marketers, analysts and advertising agency planning departments have confused one with the other – we are forever being introduced to departments or department heads and shown reports with the words 'knowledge' and 'insight' figuring prominently only to realize that they are nothing of the sort. More times than not, what we are seeing – what you see when you read through a Mintel report, or the findings of a Mori poll, or the latest offerings of Nielson or YouGov – is at best information, at worse data. The former is data arranged sequentially, or grouped in some way that makes it more than the sum of its many useless parts, and at least logical although not always sensible. Data is the many useless parts arranged in no particular order, which is hardly ever logical and even less sensible.

### ■ Information isn't knowledge, just data with a better brand image

We are stating this not to be contentious, merely to be accurate, and to remind you that in itself data is nothing more than the bricks and mortar of the information walls we all chip away at on a daily basis. And these walls – as anybody who has ever worked in planning or analysing markets or understanding shifts in tastes, outlook or social or cultural mores will tell you – are only as useful as the broader cultural perspective that those attempting to use the information bring to the process. This is why we distinguish between 'information officers' – those who corral information or house it in some way or another (in reports, in their hard drives, in libraries, online, in books, documents, in their heads) – and 'knowledge officers', or insight analysts – those who take what data and information are available and use other ingredients or factors to add value, substance, depth or a much broader interpretation to the material collected than is contained in the material itself.

The difference between information and knowledge is simple – information speeds up the processes of production (or at least it should do), while knowledge makes more of what we produce – which is why many brands now exceed the value of their tangible assets, or use 20 per cent less assets to produce one dollar's worth of sales than they did 25 years ago, according to *Fortune* magazine. In other words to do what real forecasters and futurologists do – take what we can record and what can be measured, and transform it into 'things we can know', and 'things that sometimes cannot be measured' – as in ideas, culture, art, literature or speculative but useful forward projections such as long form narratives, predictive story models and future-faced scenarios.

Knowledge then, to borrow Alan Burton Jones' definition, is a cumulative stock of information that brings us to a higher and more self-aware level – a level at which forecasters, futurologists and future-faced brands and corporations need to work from 24Seven.

In other words, knowledge is about knowing more than can sometimes be rationally articulated. Why one person looking at an open section of ground marked off with thin white lines and boxes sees it as that (data); why another will see it as a car park (information); and yet another reading these lines with previous skill sets (knowledge) and using cognitive processes along with them, will see it for what it really is, a football pitch (insight).

Knowledge then doesn't just require more data or more information – although both help – it requires lateral information and interdisciplinary data from many fields rather than a single specialized one. It also requires experience, or previous knowledge of the thing being viewed or of similar things which, when the brain gets to work, is processed in an odd and uniquely human way.

This is why innovation – the product of knowledge and insight – happens in clusters, and why change or shifts in the culture come in peaks, or movements, or periods in history (the Dark Ages, the Renaissance, the Enlightenment, the Modernist Movement, the Consumer Society, the Information Age, the New Economy, the Knowledge Economy, the Creative Economy) because knowledge, once unleashed, acts likes a catalyst firing and flinging other ideas together, thus creating 'bridge moments' or fused opportunities that create new levels for new but associated ideas to grow. It is also why we find the same developments in parallel fields – functionalism in design but also in building, politics, art and technology.

For what we all know, and what scientists are just getting to grips with, is the way in which we take such experiences and jags of data and interpret them at a higher level – in our limbic centres to be exact (that bit of the brain that gives vent to our emotions and to the non-linear, non-lingual aspects of our thought processes) and in the prefrontal cortex (that bit of the brain that neuroscientists credit with our ability to rationalize and contextualize) so that the collaborative effect is one of greater awareness.

## ▓ Knowledge needs to be combined with emotion

In other words, the process of combining data and information with emotion and experience, and our ability to use existing experiences and knowledge raise our overall awareness of the situation, and allow us to make the kind of cognitive or intuitive leap that converts the information gathered into something far more profound – a kind of raw fuel that converts knowledge into insight.

This is what many neuroscientists and sociobiologists believe happens when we see these sudden sea change shifts in how man stopped being a hunter gatherer and moved down into the savannahs to become a farmer; how minds like Galileo, Newton, Darwin, Einstein, Tim Berners Lee, or James Watson and Francis Crick (the codiscoverers of DNA) took what was there – information – and in the process of applying knowledge from many fields and observations (Crick for example came to DNA via designing naval mines, Watson via ornithology) made a leap – the Great Leap, as anthropologists call this sudden shift from one level of skills set usage to a higher more profound one – and in the process gained insights into new and unique areas of research.

This perhaps is what Newton meant when he claimed that his own insights were only possible because he was able to see further by standing on the shoulders of giants like Kepler, Galileo, Descartes, perhaps even Robert Hooke, his sworn enemy – not that he was standing on other men's shoulders literally, but that he was using what they had achieved and what they knew to help mankind scale greater heights and see even further into the future.

And this is what we mean when we say that intuition is all when it come to reading trends the way we need to read them. That the processes used to make this reading of trends possible has to be understood in context and that the facilities and technologies to make this context possible – networks, observational hides, ethnographic field study procedures, cultural braillers – need to be at the heart of your company.

> **❝ And this is what we mean when we say that intuition is all when it come to reading trends. ❞**

And this means creating a company that works and is structured along the lines of the human brain – a federated, integrated connected web of people and strategies. One where tacit knowledge (where we can know more than we can tell), explicit knowledge (knowledge we can pass on), and implicit knowledge (knowledge that we possess without knowing how and why) is found coursing through it at every level.

A company where, like the brain:

- nodes, or departmental 'hubs' are linked and feed constantly one to the other;
- where information is collected and processed in real-time;
- where the very areas companies and brands tend to keep apart (research, development, marketing, PR, customer intelligence, management, design, manufacturing, distribution and post sales monitoring) all work and function separately not just together;
- but in the SAME place;
- in the SAME room;
- with the SAME knowledge-sharing continuum;
- and with the kinds of people and areas of interest you hitherto wouldn't consider useful, or indeed allow into your building!

Already some brands are beginning to do this – Nissan, Philips, Nestlé, Canon – but it is usually for the creatives or, as Nestlé has done, for the 'soft' sectors of the business, their customer service departments, a kind of integrated consumer relationships hub run not by Nestlé but by the brand's French advertising agency (McCann Relationship Marketing, Paris) where marketing executives, PRs, new media, branding, consumer intelligence and management consultants are housed under one roof.

The right idea, but the wrong way of running it – as a carapace, as an outrider hub that still doesn't engage with the brand in the way it needs to. Imagine your brain operating like that, the prefrontal cortex in your head, the limbic centres in a bag, dangling somewhere by your side! Not a good look, and not good for where you need to take things if you are to become the tactile company reading the future. It doesn't work because it can't work. It separates the 'soft' from the 'hard', the sections designed to hardwire consumer knowledge or insight into the company or brand from the sectors involved in that process of brand or product creation – the designer, the planner, the manufacturer and the creative, but also the prosumer.

Which is what tactile corporations or future-faced companies are really about – hardwiring the prosumer into the very heart of the creation process. Or rather, building the brand and the company around the prosumer so that they are its heart, the very engine that pumps the blood of creativity through your corporate network, into your brand, making it live, vital, emotional and engaging.

And in this kind of company, the only thing that kills profit is departmentalization, cultural chauvinism with consumers being kept at arm's length from the creative process – from marketing, R&D, the way you sell, manage or broker your relationship with them. In the tactile world, in our tactile futures, only one person matters, only one idea sells – that created by your customers.

## ▓ The future is consilient

The future then isn't about the specialized, or those with specialized skills sets – this kind of myopic autism has crippled companies, neutered their creative edge and ability to envision. It is about the fluid, the integrated, the consilient – as the sociobiologist and writer Edward O. Wilson explains.

The notion that knowledge works better when it works in harmony and across seemingly unrelated disciplines – art, biology, psychology, anthropology, philosophy, neurobiology, sociobiology, marketing, distribution, manufacturing, design, retail anthropology – all running in concert. Much like the brain runs many disparate and, on face value, totally unrelated facts, ideas and fragmented knowledge pools together, shuttling them between limbic and prefrontal centres until something naval radar operators refer to as 'on the bubble' happens – a point when all the many tasks, vectors and on-screen images they are attempting to plot, juggle and direct come together in a moment of supreme beauty, of startling insight.

And startling insight is what the true tactile company is about – using information and data to do something more than becoming a Gradgrind, the character from Dickens' *Hard Times*, who asks one of his students to explain what a horse is when another, Sissy Jupe, tongue tied, is unable to explain it in the way she knows Gradgrind wants. 'Quadruped,' the boy replies to Gradgrind's question. 'Graminivorous. Forty teeth, namely twenty-four grinders, four eye-teeth and twelve incisive. Sheds coat in the spring; in marshy countries sheds hoofs too. Hoofs hard, but requiring to be shod with iron.'

How we snigger when we read this. How we applaud Sissy for what we know she really knows about horses, their spirit, their poetry. Yet look at how we audit consumers, measure them, break them down, segment them off – the term 'audit culture' is now part of day-to-day usage.

Our obsession with measuring without garnering insight from the process has turned us all into Gradgrinds. Blinded us, and in doing so prevented us from seeing prosumers as they really are, and thus the future they are already carving out for themselves. Even the man who many blame for the current 'profit over poetry' world we live in, spotted this. Maynard Keynes who kick-started, at Bretton Woods in 1944, what was to become the IMF, always believed that the sole purpose of economics was 'to increase the pleasures of human intercourse and the enjoyment of beautiful objects.'

Indeed, at a now famous lecture at the University of Dublin, in the fledgling years of the Irish Free State, he went further by saying that once we allow ourselves to be disobedient to the test of an accountant's profit, we have begun to change our civilization. That and the way short term profits prevent us from seeing long term truths.

This is what true tactility is about – knowing the culture and the future well enough to be able to let go. But before you do, you need to know why the very things marketers and economists have embraced are the very things they now need to bury and forget about.

# Irrational exuberance –
## when nonsense makes cents

Inside every consumer there's a Sissy Jupe trying to break out. And inside every Sissy Jupe there's a model of the world many companies and more economists are unwilling to accept. This is a world where the emotions reign, where the irrational makes sense, where the logical is tedious, where needs, desires and hungers are not only childlike and beautiful, but essential and impulsive.

This is the world as it is. Yet this is the world that has been supplanted by a version handed down from Malthus to Smith, to Keynes and the many Gradgrinds that have come tumbling down through history in their wake. A rational, linearly regulated, easy-to-measure model where everything has its place – or at least its place in a formula where X and Y can be factored into an equation that allows analysts to map rational expectation against project growth and come up with a figure somewhere between accepted profit and sustainable loss. A meaningless and easy to measure piece of gibberish, but a way of reading and regulating markets that depends on everybody buying, more or less, into the same things – that the world, or the markets governing it, is, as the economist Paul Omerod wryly explains it, 'a machine', that may be very complicated, 'but in principle it can be understood completely, and the consequences of using it in various ways can be predicted. A lever pulled here or a button pushed there will have entirely predictable consequences.'

It is also the kind of world in which we obsess about the wrong things as in Mike Hammer's famous ETDBW (easy to do business with) rule – a subjective abbreviation that became the catch cry of businesses which not only measured the wrong things, but forgot what it was they were measuring in the process.

Hammer's rule was simple – make things easy, smooth things out, shed the middle men and the muddling forms, and profits follow. In essence he was pointing out the blindingly obvious – the more tiers, or links in a supply chain you have, the longer it takes for things to get through that chain, and the more chances there are to make the kind of mistakes that cost you money.

He found, for instance, that most orders went through 15 to 20 departments in the average American business before they were actually fulfilled, one company discovering that it cost $97 to process an order for batteries that cost $3. So his solution? Strip things out, pare things down, make things simple.

But how about this? Asking the question that company should really have being asking – how come so many of our employees are happy to waste their time doing that kind of drudge-job? Form filling? Line toeing? Drawing breath instead of drawing inspiration?

Hammer knows this better than most, employees are only as good as their employers – and to cut costs is as much an admission of failure as it is a sign that a company has already become too fat, strayed too far away from its founding principles. Or rather what its principles should be concerned with – not measuring, but inspiring; not cutting but being cutting edge. But cutting edge isn't so easy to manage, or for that matter measure. Nor is originality, innovation, risk, daring,

> **Cutting edge isn't so easy to manage, or for that matter measure.**

doing, creating and all the dramatic adjectives that usually come packed with these very words.

Omerod and a growing number of economists, forecasters and trend analysts on both sides of the Atlantic would say, however, that these are the very things we should be looking at. And that far from being a machine (which as Hammer suggests can be made simpler, cleaner, more efficient) the world, the markets, the trends and processes these markets throw up (or indeed the markets trends throw up) are really highly complex, interconnected webs that are governed not by pat and easy-to-trot out or regulate linearities or laws (ETDBW? Yeah but you're boring so I'd rather not bother thank you) but the very things the Gradgrinds of this world refuse to measure, and the Sissy Jupes live and think by all the time – it is the tactile, engaging, ever shifting and irrational world complexity that 'butterfly' economists like Nobel prize winner Daniel Kahneman and Omerod, and Berkley's Matthew Rubin are now beginning to understand and explore.

Kahneman, a psychologist by vocation, is among the best known and the most often quoted, although his name is hardly known to city suits and desktop actuaries and statisticians. Kahneman's work can be summed up simply – through experiment he discovered that people use information at hand, or information easy to get at, or tacit knowledge to understand how the world works, rather than make long-winded incursions or investigations to find out more, or to seek out objective or definitive truths – the thing neoclassical economists say most of us do. In other words when confronted with a problem, we seek out all there is to be known before making a rational and calculated decision.

Kahneman also discovered something that most clipboard marketers and focus group researchers would rather their clients didn't know – answers to surveys or controlled questions depend greatly on how they are phrased, and not necessarily on the calibre of the people being questioned. Poor questions not only lead to poor answers but, since they are being asked of people drawing on understanding that may be incomplete anyway (his primary observation), they are doubly flawed, more specifically skewed, and more times than not downright inaccurate and ill-informed.

His third insight to how we behave is equally damning for the Gradgrid school – that people are not always good assessors of risk. They tend, for example, to overestimate the probability of a nuclear power disaster, but underestimate the risk of being in a car accident. All blindingly obvious to the man in the street but not to economists who tend to work to the following rules when assessing the future, or rather how they think the future will shape up based on their understanding of how they think people see it shaping up. In other words, if they warn us about recession, they assume we pay attention.

For them (more maths) human decisions are made in terms of expected utility. As the *Economist* puts it, that is 'the sum of the gains or wealth they think they will get from each possible future scenario, multiplied by its probability of occurring.' So the problem then is obvious – since people assign greater weight to some scenarios than others, their decisions are flawed, or rather not flawed but irrational – or to make it simpler still, all too human.

## ■ Economists are full of hindsight

This is why stock market analysts, for all their benchmark measuring and rational expectation theory, never get the big one right – long booms, and they continuously predict downturns; rallying markets and they come over all optimistic and gung ho, as they did during the great dotcom scam. Butterfly economists, as their name suggests, are far more flighty and, as a consequence, a tad more accurate.

Butterfly economics, or as Rubin calls it 'gratification economics', is a complex system that looks not to measure the very things that make us WHAT we are, but to observe HOW these things impact on the market – things like emotions, fears, cravings, needs, desires, dreams, poetry, pleasure and spirituality; urges and actions that we all like to satisfy today or now, rather than next week or next year. Try running those through your ETDBW model and see what happens!

'Economists have historically assumed that people are 100 per cent rational in their choices, but if you ask someone if they would rather have $10 now, or $15 in a week from now, a lot of respondents would say they wanted the $10 now,' explains Rubin. 'If you ask them if they would rather have $10 50 weeks from now, or $15 dollars 51 weeks from now, they would say $15 51 weeks from now.

Rubin continues, 'In other words, when you make a problem abstract or notional, people (like economists!) are happy to apply logic and rationality to solving it, but when you shut the problem down to a point that makes the possibility of having the cash more immediate, our emotional side kicks in and logic is moved to the background.'

Economists and marketers don't like this, says Rubin, so they don't factor it in. And yet whether you are dealing with pork belly futures in Minnesota, or the GDP of France, or attempting to address a new consumer demographic, that's really what you are asking someone to do – to gauge or predict human behaviour, to measure abstract and logical need against everyday but potent desire and emotion.

Yet this is seldom owned up to, or even talked about by old-school economists, argues Robert J. Shiller, whose book *Irrational Exuberance* described those heady dotcom years of the mid to late 90s as 'an irrational, self-propelled, self-inflated bubble.'

## ▧ When the bubble bursts ask how, not why

Few saw the bubble or how it was about to burst, he says, because they were still looking at 'the data, the numbers rather than the emotions, the psychology, the zeitgeist – the prevailing trend or driving emotional, or irrational force dominating the cultural consciousness at the time.'

This is what the dotcom phenomenon was about – what all market and cultural shifts are about. Human behaviour. The thing that kept US and UK consumers spending during 2002 when economists were saying that we were in recession post-September 11th, about to experience a downturn in trading – the double dip thing.

But if we were in recession, shoppers continued to shop, house prices continued to rise, and credit lines continued to be used and extended as consumers ignored what the business pages were telling them – that things were bad, it was time to pull back, pull in. Why? Because post-September 11th, if people were worried they demonstrated their worry in a wholly human and understandable way (if you're a person and not an economist that is) by enjoying themselves, partying, living for today rather than saving for a tomorrow they may not live to see. This, says Shiller, has always been the case, 'When something major happens, it's because . . . a lot of factors are moving in one direction. One of the criticisms that I have of economic departments is that they like to emphasize rigour to the point where they feel they can't rigorously handle so many different factors at once, and so they just focus on the one.'

An example – in the area of financial forecasting, specifically in the area of attempting to predict risk, numerous types of computer-based spreadsheets, or regression analyses, or so-called system dynamic models are used. And many, in the wake of financial mistakes by financial organizations like Daiwa, Sumitomo, Barings and Kidder Peabody, are called on to predict or run 'what if' scenarios – as in what would happen to the market if, say, an accounting fraudster or rogue was at work in the system, or a simple mistake was made during the addition or subtraction processes?

Rounded factors are also programmed in – current economic figures, incomes projected against rates/goods/house price increases over the next year, the company's value on the stock exchange, its position against market competition, the strengths, weaknesses of its investors, the strengths, weaknesses of competitors, and so on.

## ■ The deeper the narrative, the better the tale

Obviously, the more factors you put in, the more accurate the outcome, but how much does one need to put in? How much information or data (as opposed to knowledge) is required? And more importantly, what do we need to put in? Details on weather patterns? On annual holiday trends? On seniority or analysts and clerks working within the company? And what about their love lives, their emotional states, where they shop, what they eat?

At this point the neoclassic economist (or brokers if we are dealing with stock market predictions) will have hit the 'run program' button, two phrases perhaps cascading about their ears as they do – 'too much data' and most of it 'too irrational, too inconsequential'.

There is the belief that in such programming or prediction models, things should be kept simple, that linearity is all. That these kinds of models – stock market, online – if they are rational and handled by experts, will somehow sort things out. Remove the anomaly the human aspect of the model or program and you sometimes remove the very thing that makes a forecasting model all that more accurate.

> **There is the belief that in such programming or prediction models, things should be kept simple, that linearity is all.**

Weather forecasters find this all the time. In the US in March 2001, the best were saying that bad weather was imminent, snow expected but nothing as bad as the 1993 storm of the century that brought much of America's east coast to a standstill due to three-feet-deep snowdrifts. Some of the more powerful weather supercomputers begged to differ however – for March 2001, big drifts were expected, storm warnings issued and emergency services put on blizzard alert.

Old-school meteorologists weren't convinced but the data said it all, so the forecasts were presented to the public as fact, a given. March 6th arrived and the snow came as predicted, but by US standards it was nothing more than a flurry, something for the kids to sledge in. And the reason the computers got it wrong? They couldn't crank through the calculations fast enough or fluidly enough, or they had too much anomalous data – factors deemed by programmers to be irrelevant. So they did what most linear or rounded model prediction programs do when confronted with too much data – uses clever algorithms that gloss over certain details, and in the process gloss over what, in essence, is the very thing likely to influence the final outcome of the exercise.

This smoothing, or algorithmic jump, is common to most prediction modelling methods in biology, physics and chemistry and because of this, all have moved over to more complex adaptive processes or processors. The money markets however continue to run such models and depend on experts who think in very much the same way – rationally, appropriately, smoothing certain jagged edges out, factoring only logical things in. Yet as online games or virtual stock markets are showing us, amateurs drawing on emotional and irrational but perhaps more intuitive and realistic approaches to reading markets are beating the experts more times than not.

The Hollywood Stock Exchange and the Iowa Electronic Market (or the Foresight Exchange) are both testament to this. Each trades in predictions, virtual stocks or toy money and each has proved time and again to be more accurate in their predictions of how a market will behave – which stars will get the most Oscars, or how stock will perform – than their real life counterparts.

Collectively it seems people can work together using their intuition, their emotions, their sense of risk or censure – if they don't want to embarrass themselves online or in front of their peers – to analyse and gauge markets based on what purely observational and emotional knowledge of the world tells them.

In 2001 for instance, the Hollywood Stock Exchange was so much more successful in predicting Oscar wins than industry panels that studios are now paying it for detailed trading information. Likewise, the Foresight Exchange is now used by brokers, investors and an increasing number of Wall Street analysts to help them gauge more accurately when breakthroughs in key areas of the biotech sector or in Aids and cancer research are likely to happen. This is what gratification or emergent economics is about – using the irrational, the emotional and the illogical to create a framework or an emergent network within which it is possible to read and understand people and the future.

Some, like Eric Bonabeau (a forecaster at ICosystem, an emergent predictions consultancy) are doing just that – using our very idiosyncrasies to tell us why, for instance, most of the profits lost annually by the French and Italian banking systems are lost during the month of August; why a slight increase in the number of shoppers in a supermarket leads to a fall off in wine sales; why microscooters become a 'must have' urban transport toy for the latte and Carharrt generation, but miniscooters (or the equally odd-looking Sinclair C5 type products) bomb without trace?

The stuff Bonabeau and his kind are computing or the stuff they are working with, is of course the stuff of our irrationalities, of our dreams. And yet, like our

Hollywood Stock Exchange players, these too are proving more accurate than traditional models which work from the top down, taking global equations and frameworks and applying them to a local situation in a way that imposes the bigger picture on to the little one – making the little one, in effect, null and void, or rather swamping it in a way that disguises its true impact or consequence.

## ■ Use the micro to evaluate the macro

Emergent models do things in reverse. They take the micro factors and see how they are likely impact on the macro ones. Thus 'emergence' is a bottom-up system or philosophy that starts with the little person, the individual, and looks at how they might interact with the people immediately around them and what the consequences of these interactions are likely to be.

And what emergent modelling systems are showing us, and what emergent economists are finding out, is that markets or trends aren't just complex, they are also contradictory.

Imagine, for instance, a two-lane highway and that this is blocked by traffic. Logic and economics (since there is more instant profit in this) would dictate that if you build another lane with appropriate exits and ramps, this would speed up the traffic. Bonabeau and his associates would say no – and they'd be right. If anything, it just causes more congestion, attracts more traffic to the lanes and causes even more heartache and aggression for drivers.

But before Bonabeau, before complexity and before butterfly economics, as far back as 1968 a German operations research engineer noted this conundrum and it has since been named Braes' paradox.

It is the kind of paradox, or irrational but perfectly understandable consequence, that you need to see as the norm if you are to abandon the staged linearities of how we read things in the past, and embrace the kind of looking-glass irrationalities that will allow us to better view and harness the future as it should be harnessed.

# Beating the system –
## by playing with new ones

Braes' paradox identifies a phenomenon we are all familiar with – one that intuitive forecasters notice without necessarily knowing why they notice it all the time – that drawing attention to something, in a negative or positive light, only makes more of the same thing happen not less as the case should be. This happens especially if we are attempting to dampen it down, or stamp it out – for instance, drug use, people smoking, road rage.

Prior to the racist killing of Stephen Lawrence, for instance, race attack figures ran at about 1149 per year, but after media coverage of the murder, attacks shot up to 7790. Sex abuse statistics echo similar patterns – in 1984 there were 1500 a year, but then media coverage and questions asked in the House of Commons and a raft of sensational TV programmes sent figures rocketing. Cruelty to children figures also show that when the issue crept into public consciousness between 1984 and 1985, instead of reducing incidence, the NSPCC reported a 90 per cent increase in the number of new or reported cases!

## ■ Don't flatten contradictions, embrace them

Like Braes' paradox, none of this makes immediate sense if we try to use standard ways of reading and interpreting the culture on how the public are likely to react when an existing trend is spotlighted or a new one uncovered. But if we accept that things do not work on a collective basis and then spread out into the culture (how many viral marketers or advertising agencies see trends spreading?) but on a single and individual basis and then spread up and out, we have a better understanding of how and why these things 'appear' and happen as they do. Why one suicide triggers a spate; why, when faded jeans with a striped or faded effect on each leg are worn by a certain group we all wear them; why when the economy is doing badly, people spend.

> **A better understanding of how and why these things 'appear' and happen as they do.**

The reason is simple. Like our brains, we interconnect and interrelate. We are networked up, and the connections and the relationships established, or the tactile and emotional networks that bind us together, also compel us in ways we ourselves may not even be aware about or indeed fully conversant with.

Some blame this on the butterfly effect, others on the symbiont nature of the close urban networks we live in (where when any idea spreads, it spreads ubiquitously) because we are all connected in one way or another or rather, as we shall see, thanks to technology no longer separated by six degrees but by a hell of a lot less. We are of, in many ways, a hive mind – a highly sensitive and intuitive one at that, as sociobiologists, urban planners and irrational expectation economists are beginning to find out.

And much of it has to do with how those slimy bits gather in your garden when things are a bit damp and overcast; how ants collect their food and bury their dead; how viruses spread; how ideas communicate; how city neighbourhoods like the ones we've located our offices in come together and create dense, intelligent networks that demonstrate consilient properties which begin to tell us how tactile companies should work, and how insight networks and consumer reconnaissance units can be formed.

These things have nothing to do with data or information or structured linearities, but are to do with random happenings, irregularities, the individual and how each impacts on the other.

In August 2000, a Japanese biologist Toshiyuku Nakagaki, while studying slime moulds noticed something that tells us a lot about these processes and something that teaches us how to harness them in ways that make us better forecasters and future-faced companies. The slime he was working with could find the shortest way though a maze he had built for it, and feed itself in not one but two places, despite the fact that it didn't have a brain or a central nervous system.

He was puzzled and intrigued. How, since it couldn't talk or communicate in the way we understand, was it able to do what it did? Nakagaki wasn't the first to notice this, however. Similar experiments had been carried out by Evelyn Fox Keller in the late 60s. Keller and a colleague Lee Segal (an applied mathematician) were equally curious about how slime mould could move and interact with its environment without having a nervous system or any obvious means of communication. They also noticed other peculiarities about the mould – it seemed to appear out of nowhere, do whatever it was attempting to do and then dissolve back into the woodwork without trace.

They knew that the mould was made up of thousands of small, single cell entities and that these could move separately from other cell mates in the immediate vicinity. And most did, randomly going about their business. When the weather was hot, cells were invisible to the naked eye but once temperatures cooled and the terrain grew damp, cells came together to feed in the form of a jelly-like lump.

But without a brain how did they know where the food was located? And how, without consciousness, did they know where to find their colleagues or to lead them to where the food source was located? You can see then why Keller and Segal were puzzled, why Nakagaki was ecstatic when his mould located not one but two eating spots.

Most scientists believed that these behavioural changes were 'communicated' at some microscopic level – the way that many think trends are spread – and that some kind of shared intelligence must surely motivate these cells to form larger, more powerful bodies. Something was triggered okay, but not a circuit command from a lone leader cell as many had previously theorized.

What Keller and Segal discovered was much more significant and momentous. Single slime cells could orchestrate other independent cells to work in concert simply by altering the amount of a substance called acrasin they secreted from their bodies. If enough was pumped out – which was the case when food supplies were plentiful – others gathered, following the trail laid down by previous cells until a thick glut of cells was visible. No single cell however had intentionally or consciously followed another, nor indeed had they intentionally clustered in the manner they did. Nor for that matter if they could speak, could they explain the rationale of the cluster, its raison d'être.

Forecasters are forever encountering this when they note a trend – for experience holidays, risk culture, having botox parties – and ask those carrying it into the mainstream what it is that makes it unique, different or, indeed, a trend.

In many cases those who 'do' the trend, don't see it as a trend, but something that makes them unique, different, individual. Or more particularly, part of an elite group, crew, posse or movement. Others, the late majority, do it because it seems to be the thing to do – buying a Smart car, drinking chardonnay, using phrases like 'thinking outside the box'. Few can articulate the reason for buying into a trend however because in many cases it isn't a conscious decision to do so – which is why focus groups that are used to determine trends seldom offer up anything except answers we already know. Because what we are attempting to uncover or 'measure' is part of the irrational world, a world that hotwires itself in to a network that has other ways of working, thinking and influencing us.

This is what the slime mould was doing – acting alone, or seeming to act alone in a way that motivated other cells to act alone or seem to act alone when each, in reality was impacting in some way on the other. In the slime mould's case by laying a trail that others followed – so that the one became two, the two three, the three a movement . . .

## ■ Emergent forms

This is emergence at its most basic level and is the first thing you need to know about observing the future. That through watching and following and mapping the moves of the individual, the greater movement or cultural shift is made visible, not the other way round. Individuals influence the future, not majorities as we tend to believe.

Like a disease, it is the latter that infects the former. The anomalous that carries the spores for our collective tomorrows, the individual that infects the mass with the pattern all others will inevitably follow in the future.

The biologist and philosopher Edward O. Wilson noted a similar activity in his now seminal work on ant societies with Bert Holldobler. In *The Ants*, contrary to the long-held beliefs of the time, he demonstrated that an ant's ability to built its colony, bury its dead, create food middens, locate new food sources and regulate its society in a highly efficient and specialized way, had nothing to do with the queen and less to do with organizational intelligence or structures in the way we understand it. But it had all to do with the way the individuals (cells) in the colony recognized patterns in pheromone trails and acted on these patterns accordingly, each ant on its own laying more trails and alerting more ants until the activity snowballed into one of the many ant trails you see in the countryside on a lolling, lazy, hot summer's day – a trail with a stick across it perhaps that you remove and reorientate, only to watch over time the line of ants reform and get on with its collective business.

If you were to take one of these ants and ask it why, like the slime mould or our new and emerging social tribe, it wouldn't know, or indeed wouldn't even be able to articulate the why. This is a singular act, an event from the bottom of a group, movement or social shift that causes things to cascade up so that the whole becomes the product of the part.

> ❝ How can we harness them to improve our ability to read the future? ❞

This is the basis on which emergence or complexity theory operates, and the basis on which many emergent or agent-based prediction networks function. Still in their nascent stages, they are, however, proving more successful in many areas of business, science, the arts, retail and life trend analysis and prediction.

At the Sante Fe Institute, one of the most advanced study centres for complexity theory in the world, its BiosGroup uses emergence modelling to look at everything from predicting the effects of reducing the tick size of trading on the Nasdaq to how a sexually transmitted disease spreads through the population. Other systems have been used to investigate better store design layout, or for companies like Hewlett Packard to predict how changes in recruiting policy would impact on its corporate philosophy.

But what do these systems look like in the flesh? And how can we harness them to improve our ability to read the future? Let us take you into one – the area we work and live in. It is an area that has already created some of the key trends and cultural shifts impacting on the way we work and live, but also one that continues to create ideas, outlooks and brand strategies set to influence key areas of business, design, fashion, retail and corporate and organizational strategy for some time to come.

# Real-time emergence –
## what observing the anomalies can teach us

Imagine then you're in an area of East London – Commercial Road lies to the east, the Highway, Wapping and the Thames to the south. Imagine you are a member of a network instructed to do nothing but observe. On first reading, the area you are in is very old and very run down. Post-war tower blocks abound and in the spaces cleared by German bombs during the Second World War, poor quality four and five storey brick flats with hard edged façades, uncompromising balconies and empty stairwells have appeared.

Some of the windows are bricked up, but in other dwellings, built in the 60s and 70s for old East End families and the growing number of Bangladeshi immigrants who flocked to the area, there are signs of poverty and people making do everywhere. In the darkened passageways to lifts and stairwells you can hear voices, occasionally see the flame of a match burn, and recall the flash of tinfoil in a beam of sunlight as you hurry nervously past.

Between these blocks there are older, more elegant houses, Georgian in appearance, rundown and dishevelled but with many of their original features still intact – hooded door canopies, sash windows – and through their dusty panes a slash of cornice work, a hallway with flagstones and ancient wood panelling.

There are shops along these streets. Some are doing well, most selling Bollywood videos, saris, jack fruit and vegetables on trestle tables covered in gaudy astroturf. Shopkeepers here wear traditional dhotis and kiafas, the women and girls pass you in saris, burkas and chadors. Between the shops on the streets you walk along are brightly lit walkways with fit-inducing strip neon lights leading to warehouses and machine shops above – most making dresses, blouses, ladies' outsize skirts and separates for the area's burgeoning wholesale clothing business. You're walking along curious, puzzled perhaps why many of the signs in the area are in Bengali and Urdu, but the older more faded ones in Yiddish, Polish and, in some cases, German.

You note this without knowing why, and you also note, both in chinos and tight, perfectly ironed shirts, two men walking down a side street with a pair of Dalmatians straining on leather leashes. It is a momentary vision, but one that jolts you so you now look around you in a more calculating and measured way.

Something about the area intrigues, something jars about the texture of the neighbourhood. And that's when you note the Japanese student with his bleach Mohawk hairstyle and 'look-at-me' shoes that remind you of platform trainers possibly sported by clowns in Covent Garden's open air market. His hair is cut into a fin and he carries one of those odd looking, courier-boy rucksacks with one shoulder strap. Whatever it is, it's got your attention.

And now that you're noticing things, you see other people who don't quite fit among the saris and Hindi videos and halal chicken takeaways – a girl in hipsters with tattoos, eye bar piercings, cropped white hair; a man-child type in feather haircut, about-the-hip jeans and old skool trainers gliding past you on an aluminium fold-down microscooter; a tall thin woman with long sleek hair carrying a portfolio under her arm; a courier delivering padded envelopes marked 'fragile'.

You turn a corner now and enter a road that looks the same as the last – shops, trestle tables, astroturf, a run of crumpled looking Georgian houses, only one or two of them looking freshly painted and because you've started to notice things you give them a second look.

The doors have been redone. Inside one, the hall panelling stripped back, waxed. Inside another, through a window with painted shutters folded back you see a tawny light room, large and spacious with a long polished table holding a G4 Apple notebook, an iPod and a Treo. In another there are trestle tables, old armchairs, people huddling over computer screens, some throwing a ball into a basket mounted on the back of a door . . . You walk on to a warehouse, rundown but inside are uplighters, a rickety but artistic display of old standard lamps, a suburban dining table but the man working at it is far from suburban, he is on a mobile and wears a Moldy Peaches T-shirt, oily denims and a T-bar flatlink neckchain with a fin hairdo, a bit like the one sported by the Japanese student.

A coincidence? A connection? A sign? A new social class emerging? A new way of doing business? A trend towards alternative ways of living one's downtime? A way of merging downtime with career time? Of moving Asian families out and the creative classes in? Something to improve Mac sales over PCs? To make people buy more organic foods, take more recreational drugs, create new brand types and product streams?

The answer of course – if you've been paying attention and if you are part of the kind of power curve network you should be a part of – is ALL of these.

## ▧ Observation suggests ways forward, new narratives to think about

This is 'emergence' in the flesh, in the life, but if you asked any of the people we've just seen, the Bangladeshi shopkeeper, the girls in their burkas, the Japanese student, the two men with their Dalmatians, the man on the mobile in his Evisu jeans in his pared down Georgian front room, they may not be able to fully articulate this.

Each has their own reason for moving to the area. The Bangladeshi shopkeeper and his family moved because other members of his village were originally relocated here in the early 70s – they were involved in clothing and this area, before it was a enclave of Bangladeshi clothing wholesalers, was an old Jewish rag trade district, hence old Yiddish signs. The two men with the Dalmatians, gay, self-employed, moved here because it offered them the kind of low rent loft spaces they could live and work in – one is a TV agent, the other an accountant for the music industries. The Japanese student is studying art at Central St. Martins, he likes the area because it has a buzz, a feeling in the air of raw, unexplored creativity . . . he's an outrider, an explorer in a culture that seems odd, intriguing and exotic. The man in the Georgian house is a photographic agent, there because of the 'atmosphere' but also because two of his clients – photographers for microzines like *Tank*, the *Shoreditch Twat*, the *Stealth Corporation*, *Pop*, *Dazed* – have studios in the area, while two of the stylists he represents are now looking for flats there. A buzz in the air, something on the move, on the 'up'.

> **❝A buzz in the air, something on the move, on the 'up'. ❞**

## ■ Trends are the threads that link lifestyle narratives together

Imagine now travelling into the future, on that machine used by Rod Taylor in George Pal's original version of H.G. Wells' *The Time Machine*, so that everything around you speeds up and becomes a time-lapse picture of things to come. What will you see? A clear and particular pattern emerging: the arrival of certain types of people into the area – creative types, gays, dotcomers, graphics designers, DJs, MCs, stylists, artists, photographers and agents – all lured there by a certain kind of building – old, large and with character.

They are there also because they can't afford the going rate in more salubrious areas – Notting Hill, Portobello, Hampstead, Clapham, Hoxton – but also because these areas are past it anyway. They lack buzz, edge and vitality.

Now imagine your machine can travel in space as well as time – along a street, past a warehouse allowing you to look through windows, into rooms. Over time you will see strip neons being replaced by halogen spots, downlighters, low ambient lamps and floor spots that transform high empty rooms into warm minimalist grottos. Skips will appear, builders' palettes containing glass bricks and reconditioned wood floors.

You will see bars opening – wide, open plan, open space affairs with windows you can look through with everybody in them dressed in T-shirts, cropped jackets, about-the-arse jeans and trainers; and all with bottles, glasses, Rizla rollies and Marlboro Lights in their hands instead of flat pints and dodgy Silk Cuts.

Just as the old Yiddish signs in the area were replaced by Bengali ones, so are the latter replaced over time by ones for design consultancies, ad agencies (in sharp no-

nonsense Helvetica and Futura), architectural practices, indie music shops and magazine publishers; also clothing shops, furniture shops, kooky, cutesy, kitschy, cooing whiteout spaces with 70s chandeliers, Eames desks, Panton chairs, Paulin lamps; and small, sandalwood-oozing clothing boutiques with bead curtain changing rooms, seams on the outside jumpers, slash and burn tops, and formica tables resplendent with bottlecap handbags and boxed sets of obscure one-off vanity press art books. The assistant, if you can find her, reminds you of Velvet Underground tracks and Lou Reed album covers. Coouulh!

Smart cars will appear, mountain bikes U-locked to freshly painted railings. For sale signs spring up, once selling whole houses or 2000 square foot warehouses with 24-hour access for next to nothing, now offer luxury apartment and live/work units with Smeg kitchens, Bulthaup steel surfaces, and exposed brick walls for prices the local Bangladeshi traders will have a good laugh at.

Creatives still live there, but now they are joined by people called creative professionals, or professionals with weak tie associations to the creative community – lawyers, marketers, advertising executives, estate agents, hip city brokers, his and hers marketing couples with off-road prams and off-road sensibilities, urban, urbane pilot fish that live off the legacies and Bobo credentials laid down by the early settlers.

Then you see it. Fewer and fewer Bangladeshis, more and more Patagonia sports clothing, Acupuncture trainers, Quiksilver tops and Gucci and moccasin-clad creative professionals. A shift has taken place, a new point in the emergence game is reached. One group, one trend, one mood, movement, look or ideology has been usurped, absorbed or repelled by the incomer. The old replaced by the new, the old transformed, infected by the neurotic, the anomalous, the odd – or worse, pushed out or aside by these newcomers.

## ▓ Future tales

And this is, more or less, how all trends work, or come to pass. The new infect and impact on the old world, or the status quo, and by being there, by being close to others who share similar ideas and outlooks, hook up to them or are drawn towards them – sometimes knowingly, sometimes unconsciously – so that alliances are formed, patterns created, opportunities and creative and cognitive leaps made. In the past we sensed these things intuitively, now we know them for what they are – hidden but compelling rules and laws that can be mined and used to incredible and creative effect.

# The new rules of engagement:
## network laws and how to harness them

# New cults rising –
## to the outer edges and beyond

This cultural shift – the point at which an influx of people into an area becomes visible and starts to have significant impacts on others in the area – has already been noted in other fields. Mathematicians refer to it as a giant component or cluster. Physicists call it a percolation or a phase transition – when something transforms from an ever shifting fluid to a highly visible solid, like water turning to ice. Sociologists recognize it in the formation of a community.

For trend forecasters, it is the point a which a trend goes 'viral', or becomes 'visible'.

What you are witnessing is a spread of ideas, or attitudes or product sensitivities via the kind of 'emergent' or 'organic' networks which physicists like Albert-László Barabási and his team at the University of Notre Dame are only just beginning to understand and decode.

If you mapped, or modelled on a computer, the process described in the previous chapter, you would see it something like this – a random arrangement of dots (our edge dwellers) scattered along streets, or computer grids, in no apparent order.

Now imagine these dots moving. Let's say they are people and imagine that as they 'touch' (when they talk, do business, see each other on the street) links are formed – lines that connect each to the other. These could represent physical connections (partnerships, friendships, casual meetings in bars) or verbal ones (conversations via mobile, SMS texting, online).

The oldest dots, the community's earliest settlers, they have been there longest and so connect first and extensively – more people know them so they have more opportunities to connect. As more and more dots appear more and more links are forged, but again the older dots attract more links than the newest because they have been around longest and, as a consequence, are better known and more useful.

In other words, older dots function a bit like those people in a room or society who, by virtue of their longevity or sociability, know and meet more people just because they have the advantages of age, experience and knowledge.

Because they have knowledge (they may know the nearest internet café, photocopy shop, underground bar, club; they may know where the best bars are; the warehouses doing the best deals), so they become fixers or connectors – people to be sought out. So lots of links connect them to other people and, in our model, they are the dots with many links.

But there is also another kind of dot in our model – early settlers (our 'creatives') who tend to have weak ties because of the kind of work they do and the fact that their work requires a high input of ideas, a high degree of collaboration and reciprocity. By 'weak tie' we mean the kind of relationship we have with friends of friends, rather than friends themselves.

These individuals, because of their jobs or their outlook, will have 500 or so useful contacts compared to the magical number of 150 that most of us have in terms of acquaintances who we can all speak to and interact with in ways that are human, sociable and non-threatening.

Our edge dwellers or creatives, on the other hand, need more contacts to further their cause and so their network proliferates far more quickly. It does so through strong tie associations and also weak ties, the number and 'nature' of the people who their strong tie friends eventually plug them into. Not friends as such, not even colleagues but many times removed acquaintances that networks guru Mark Granovetter believes are far more important to the spreading of ideas or trends throughout the community – PLUs (people like us); people we don't know personally, but those who are connected to us in a way that makes them want to imitate us, or us them. This is because each subconsciously recognizes the other's importance in this connected web and how, by working it, they can use it to better their own ends – and in the process help others better theirs. Imagine them on our model – all connected up, all linked by weak ties, and among them other dots with many links and connections running to and from them – our early settlers, the knowledge holders.

> **Each subconsciously recognizes the other's importance in this connected web.**

## One man's network is another man's periphery

This network, our edge dwellers network as we shall call it, is only one of the many networks that could be shown on our East London map. What about the one with the Bangladeshi trader with his family and their weak and strong tie connections? Or the old white East End families with their weak and strong tie connections?

They are all there, of course, and all connect up in the same way and all interact and overlap, but these are what we call background or 'shadow' networks in that they are not the networks of our focus – since our focus is on the new or the emergent, or the edge – but their presence is vital not just because they are one of the prime reasons why the edge network has located itself in this area (or those like it across the globe), but also because they are connected to our edge network in ways that bring new ideas in and carry new ideas out. Again, this may not be articulated easily but if you observe it, you can measure it – as researchers have done.

## Reciprocity generates network capital

All networks, our shadow ones, or our edge ones, operate on a thing called social reciprocity – the implicit understanding that if I do something for you, you will return the favour. We never articulate these things, except perhaps when it needs to be stated in a contract or written agreement, but the understanding is there nonetheless. Without it networks would not exist – why should I connect you to

A, who might help you with B, if down the line you will not connect or help me with something else?

Even if we do something altruistically, conscious of the fact or not, the goodwill or social or creative capital generated makes the gesture more likely to be reciprocated. Tight and focused edge networks have high levels of reciprocity because those plugging into it understand implicitly what is required. That contributing to the network not only improves the overall value of the network but their own stock in the process – few say this but most know it, even if they don't know it.

This process is especially familiar to those creatives who live in the area we have described. It is also familiar to medieval scholars – when guilds, religious brotherhoods, tower societies or quasi-religious organizations were used to generate social cohesion and also to carry implicit knowledge or information from one part of a community to another, or to house it in one bit of that community. The more involved you were with a group, the more involved or plugged in you were with the wider culture or society you lived in because all were interconnected.

The Catholic church, from medieval times to its greatest moments during the high points of the Renaissance, understood this implicitly using its network of monasteries, papal nuncios, convents, priories and 'God's own foot soldiers' – the humble parish priest – to weave a web throughout Europe and parts of the near and far East that was one of the most effective and secretive listening stations for tracking shifts in how ideas were spreading or groups were thinking and conveying them back to the Holy See.

Such networks were the reasons why the British Empire, at its most expansive, was also at its most prosperous and proactive. Not an empire of governors and narrowcast regional despots – although undoubtedly this existed – but an empire of little people, of regional administrators, officers, officials and rank and file civil servants that were far more effective at holding the empire together and running it than any number of armies. This was because the network they created was one held together as much by schooling, background, shared social philosophies and traditions, as it was by the official bureaucracies that sometimes disguised the empire's real power base.

Social, business and trend networks continue to function like this – as do class and business networks. We attack them, argue for or against them, demand entry, ask that they be dismantled, say that they are antiquated, exclusive and snobbish, but few will say that they are totally powerless, or indeed useless, except for the excluded.

Which is a fair and simple way of thinking about networks, or at least understanding them – that they are powerful and that their power comes, as you suspect, from the very fact that they are designed to connect some people together and keep others apart or out. This is what we call the discretion of networks – and discretionary networks are among the things you need to cultivate and build if you are to become a future-faced, tactile brand.

# Gilding the net –
## new communities offline

Discretionary networks were the kind of networks found in the old guild cities of Florence, Genoa, Venice and Bologna. They were networks made up of vested interest groups and are the kinds that we find in creative or hub groups, in new and emerging edge communities, in cities like Singapore, KL, Barcelona, Atlanta, Edinburgh and Dublin – international cities but with strong local, regional and partisan ties that are not always visible to the outsider or newcomer.

In Tom Wolfe's book *A Man in Full*, the processes, potentials and dangers of discretionary networks are made clear. By explaining how black Atlanta lives inside white Atlanta, how old money connects to new, and how one feeds off and needs the other, Wolfe shows how all these seemingly disparate characters with such diverse social backgrounds are all connected in one way or other. Because of these connections they are tied into other people's communities or destinies whether they want to be or not.

This process of discretionary networking, or rather of flocking and connecting with like-minded people, is how areas such as Silicon Valley are created – why Cambridgeshire in England has become a tech centre; cities like Berlin, Austin, London, Lisbon and Marseilles centres for fashion, music and emerging street tribes; why the Prato region of Italy is one of the most successful and connected textile centres in Europe and is such a good example of how discretionary networks can and should work.

> **A good example of how discretionary networks can and should work.**

It was instigated by one man, Massimo Menichetti. He was a textile manufacturer who, in the early 70s, inherited a large textile mill facing hefty financial losses. Instead of closing it, he broke it up into eight functionally separate companies – our slime mould principle in reverse. Of each of these, he sold 30 to 50 per cent of their stock to key employees (thus creating cells within cells and the beginnings of a very neat and potentially useful emergent system or network in miniature), allowing them to pay for the stock out of their own profits.

So successful was the arrangement that other mills faced with similar problems followed his example. By the late 80s, when we ourselves were working in the fashion and textiles sector, there were 15 000 small cell-like mills operating in the region, all with an average of five workers and all interconnected by family, friends, stocks, shares, suppliers and highly flexible distribution networks.

All were in competition, but all were plugged into the same distribution networks, buying cartels, trend forecasting groups and the newest, most advanced technological innovations. This meant that costs could be kept down but maximum advantage gained from all the reciprocity.

Connections, ties and associate arrangements were further encouraged at all levels. Each mill was connected to all others in the region via a network of impannatori – textile brokers or middlemen who ensured that everybody benefited in some way or other from group or individual deals struck in the bigger fashion and lifestyle landscape.

In this way, a mill that had produced a unique fabric, or a high grade cloth which many designers or retailers wanted to buy, could accept orders way beyond its capacity, knowing that the impannatori would pull together a federation of smaller mills – a network within the network, which could act as an entity to deliver all orders on time and to spec.

The benefits of this system are obvious – it generates high levels of social capital, or reciprocity, and also of knowledge and exchange of ideas. More and more social and venture catalyst networks and networkers now operate like this – connectors like Nick Golfar, Los Angeles' self-proclaimed 'social hubsta', who says he can plug you into a network of 9000 freewheeling (some would say freeloading) creative souls who will help you 'get what you want, if you help them get what they want'. Another is SenseWorldwide which connects you to people who connect you to ideas and new ways of brand building and brand deployment. The tomorrow project.com and Worth Global Style Network will connect you to style setters and trend starters. The Global Business Network connects you to people who connect you to the future – and so on.

The point about these connective clubs is that they are there to do just that – connect – and in doing so enhance your weak tie possibilities. In the process of doing this, they create a mesh or a grid along which, if all are participating in the connecting and passing-on process, ideas flow and fertilize others.

Because such networks are not organic, because they have been deliberately engineered, or brokered, they come with many riders, provisos and problems. We know this from studying the histories of royal households, of dynastic marriages, or, more recently and appropriately, of business mergers. All these are about plugging one discretionary network – a brand or corporation – into another.

Research by KPMG into the effect of mergers on companies shows, for instance, that less than one third of all mergers adds value to the combined assets of the new company, whereas 31 per cent actually destroyed shareholder value, and 40 per cent of the deals hardly made any difference at all!

Worse still, previous experience made no difference to the outcome of mergers. Despite the evidence and the obvious employee discontent (not to mention the number of jobs shed during the process), 75 per cent of company directors involved in mergers saw them as being successful.

The reason they don't work is fairly obvious say KPMG analysts – a clash of cultures; an attempt to merge things that are not at that point compatible; the blindness of those who buy new companies or brands in attempting to splice them into their own (splicing isn't the same as merging). But the main cause is the problems which arise in trying to map a company's soft cultures – its people, culture values, communications and language strategies, or networks, into those of another culture. Worse still, trying to map or network a company's 'soft' centre into the hard assets of the new one – THEIR philosophy, THEIR infrastructure, THEIR way of doing things.

What we are seeing here isn't about merging or mapping like into like, or left into right, or 'dovetailing' as many mergers and acquisitions personnel describe this all too painful process. It is a case of taking a discretionary network from one culture and attempting to hardwire it into another.

Imagine our East London street again with its edge and shadow communities. Now imagine forcing one to be part and parcel of another – our Bangladeshi trader say, a devout and strict Muslim, now has to live with our two gay creatives and their dogs – animals described in the Koran as being unclean.

Think of the problems here – the misunderstandings and resentments! From both sides. Well, this is what happens when you try to force networks together – resistance, dispute and eventually a shedding of the old, not always the worst, staff or networkers.

Networks, like Royal houses, carved or crafted in this way seldom stay the course, or stay healthy and fit in the long term at least. They are not organic, or emergent or responsive to the emotional or physical and tactile needs of employees or consumers. This is why they peak and trough, come and go, like the Egyptians, Greeks, Romans, Mayans, Aztecs, and 208 of the companies McKinsey once studied over an 18-year period to see which would be the most successful and why.

Only three lasted the whole 18 years of the study; 53 per cent managed high levels of productivity and creativity for a mere two years before dipping, before the rules that gave birth to them – the networks they worked to and through – brought them to their knees. Or worse, made them into something that all companies fear – an institution, a global behemoth.

Yet these blinkered networks – or, as they are better known, hierarchical networks – are the very networks that most of the companies we work with continue to cling to. Or if not this then a variant of it – the global grid or decentralized network where there is a sense of autonomy, of independence, with branches or semi-independent offices scattered about the globe, all with their own MDs, marketing departments, distribution systems, local ears and eyes on the ground. Like IBM, McDonald's, Microsoft, Ford, Levis, Coca-Cola – all still adhering to a single rigid mission statement, a core philosophy, and still reporting back up the line.

> **ff They are connected but not interconnected; networked but not networking. 55**

They are connected but not interconnected; networked but not networking; in the field but not on the ground; listening but not learning; watching but not observing. Rather being told and passing these things on, tuning them slightly for the local palate – as if the local palate has no say in the matter, as if consumers still consume.

## ▓ Being linked keeps things in, but it also keeps things out

These kinds of networks do well – in the short term at least. If you look at them on a localized level they actually generate good returns. According to a recent report by the Institute of Social and Economic Research, Britain's new middle rich are particularly good at recognizing the value of semi-distributive or face-to-face weak tie networks to help improve their own or their children's finances.

Further studies show that men who enter the same profession as their father – where weak tie networks are in operation ('ah Tom's son: I didn't know your father personally but knew of his reputation') – earn 5 to 8 per cent more than those who enter the profession on the same level but with no previous connections to it.

Decentralized or semi-fragmented networks are difficult to break, but relatively good to use because they have about them the semblance of being organic – for that read independent as in connected but not controlled. They allow people using them to believe, because there is no single person driving them, that they work a bit like our slime moulds or ants – collectively and collaboratively towards a common purpose. Each feels independent, but that what they do profits themselves and others – rather like one of those pyramid selling schemes.

This is why terrorists – Al-Qaeda, the IRA or members of the Zapatista movement in the Chiapas region of Mexico – favour decentralized networks as a way of functioning. There is no one leader, no centralized hub from which all other links extend (how most hierarchical brands or businesses work) so it is very difficult to shut the network down, or truncate its actions by removing one hub or by knocking one link out.

However, these networks, as we've explained, offer only the illusion of independence, the idea of emergence. They are still vulnerable, still open to decay, attack, atrophy and decline because they are still semi-rigid, still semi-controlled by hierarchical systems and notions. If we are to create networks that find ideas or trends and plug us into those generating them (or help us to generate them), we need to evolve networks that are truly edge, emergent and future-faced.

# Organic networks –
## every brand should have one

The best and most successful kinds of networks are the ones that form and grow organically – networks that imitate our slime moulds, networks that imitate the emergent properties of the streets we've located our offices in. Networks structured a bit like the human brain in fact, where it is possible to lobotomize sections without shutting down the entire organism. Or indeed networks with the shape and strength of a Buckminster Fuller dome, which uses a simple pattern of weak tie links or struts to create a dome that is among the strongest structures ever made.

These weak or loose tie patterns or networks were first identified by Paul Baran, a pioneer in network mapping and visualization, while working for the Rand corpora-

**A distributive network is a network that allows ideas, innovation, change and newness to flow through it in a way that encourages creativity and promotes an atmosphere where the best kind of cognitive leaps can, and usually do, take place.**

tion, a US military think-tank established after the Second World War to advise the military and the US government on future-faced strategies.

Attempting to design a communications systems that could survive a nuclear strike, he suggested that existing systems – the hub and spoke network (used by traditional companies and corporations), or those that were more egalitarian, or decentralized (design studios and advertising agencies) – were still vulnerable to attack. If you strike out a few key branches or hubs then the rest of the network soon loses its energy and vitality.

A distributive or conversational network, on the other hand, would be the strongest and most difficult network to breach. They are the most powerful type of network to establish when listening to the culture, or exploring the market for new ideas and shifts.

Because they are distributive and held together by weak ties, they extend out into the culture in a way that is casual, conversational and non-directional.

In other words, they are not targeted in the traditional sense – they float or 'hang out'. Think of the Puerto Rican neighbourhoods of Brooklyn, the Irish neighbourhoods of West Kilburn, the North African enclaves of Barbes in Paris and how culture is communicated via the street, by word of mouth in organic and highly federal ways. They are buoyed up and taken where the culture is going to, and not just where it is coming from.

And because they are federated, or flat rather than hierarchical or decentralized, they are not likely to be dominated by a single – controlling – voice but by a more egalitarian one, one that reflects the sum of ideas collected by the network's many parts or hubs, rather than a single idea promoted by the dominant, but not always right, part.

These networks, however, contain certain peculiar properties which Barabási and his researchers discovered, and as we have already explained.

> **And how culture is communicated via the street.**

Some of the dots in our model have more links than others – our early settlers and edge dweller creatives – while many of these types of links seemed to group together. In our East London neighbourhood terms, you could see this as a cluster of creatives in the same street, in the same warehouse, or they could be a group that meets regularly in the same bar or club.

## ■ Hubs and supernodes

Barabási calls these nodes which hang out in clusters, hubs. This is because they were more connected than other dots or nodes and thus allowed more movement through them.

We've already described this process – how people connect, interlock – but Barabási and his researchers modelled and mapped it. In the process he discovered that the surface randomness of these connections or encounters were nothing of the sort.

Networks grew when people or 'nodes' met and connected – our gentleman's club, royal families, our group of East End early settlers. This much is obvious, but they did so in a particular and peculiar way. Imagine our dot or edge dweller again – single, alone. Then another appears, and connection is made. Two dots are now joined by a single line.

Now a link has been formed, another person, perhaps known to dot A, who introduces them to dot B, so now there are three dots on our map, which creates three links.

The same procedure may be repeated – another dot is introduced and another link is formed. Now there are four dots, which creates five links, and if another dot is added, six links are formed – and so on and so forth.

Barabási calls this his growth rule. The idea that networks, far from being random or chaotic in structure or formation, are created one link at a time, as a dot – node or person – is introduced. This seems obvious when you think about it, but what Barabási has done is show that there is structure to such formation. And where there is structure there are highways along which information passes, roads along which knowledge flows, which means there must also be places to where this information and knowledge are flowing. They were of course flowing to the points where these links met – points Barabási called nodes. But he noted something else – that information and knowledge tend to flow along lines towards nodes that had more than one link in and out of them.

What he noted about the nodes however is that they always linked to those nodes which had more links running in and out of them (i.e. the nodes that are the oldest ones in the network). He called this his 'law of preferential attachment', and this, if you unpack it, explains much in the way of why some restaurants are overflowing while the one next door is empty; or why one brand has a large number of devotees – Hermès, Gucci, Louis Vuitton – while others – like Joop – regardless of the amount spent on them attract a low following.

Newcomers (new dots), he observed, are attracted to those with the most links to and from them because they are more likely to offer what they need in terms of connections, that is their ability to fast track the newcomer to a network's inner circle. Also, because of their connections, they are more likely to transform the newcomer from a lowly node into a hub or superhub in their own right.

In other words, reciprocity. Or as *Selfish Gene* author, Richard Dawkins, sees it, an almost genetic urge to gain an advantage and a lift up the evolutionary ladder by locking onto a person, cell or gene likely to improve your stock.

This is why older men, or women, because of their income and social placing, successfully attract younger partners, why establishment clubs have greater cachet than their upstart newcomers, why certain brands that plug into the right social trends become consumer magnets – not just because of what they are, but because they are offering the right connections for their customers to plug into and benefit from.

## ■ Connectors may be talkers but they are also good listeners

In life, these hubs are known as connectors – people, brand or organizations situated in key areas of the culture that make them conduits of new ideas, and also listening devices for new ideas about to bubble up to the surface.

If we were to map this flow of ideas, it would look a bit like a bell curve – the idea is created or designed or instigated by our edge group, who in turn infect the mainstream along the following routes or channels:

■ Receptors, or our strong tie prosumers who are keen on new things and live cheek by jowl with our edge group or community.

■ Reflectors, who are keen on things bought only on personal recommendation, things that are new and different and passed on and out from our edge groups via weak tie colleagues they come in contact with.

■ Absorbers, who take ideas and modify them in ways that appeal to the late majority.

■ Latents, or the late majority – those who are pulled into the network because they are 'touched' by more and more weak ties and therefore find it increasingly difficult to escape their influence.

■ Laggards, those bits of the network that are drawn in because the law of preferential attachments makes it more and more difficult for them to remain outside the network's influence.

> ❝ **Hidden factors that will help us make our own networks 'superboosters' and superbraillers.** ❞

■ Resistors, our *Daily Mail* readers – entrenched, backward looking, ever suspicious of the future types who are drawn in whether they like it or not but hold out until what seems to be stubbornness is viewed as social awkwardness and they comply, but only just.

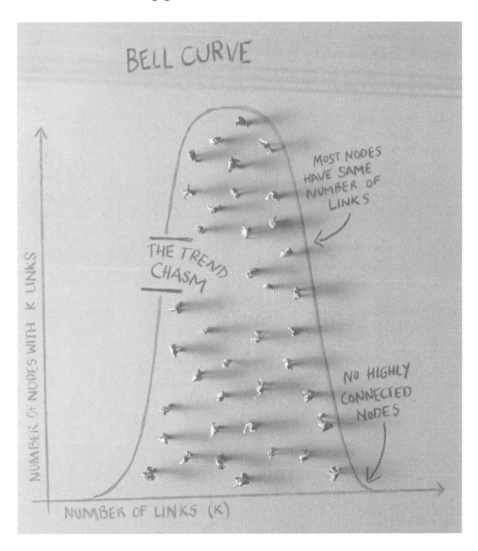

The bell curve theory promotes the idea – not entirely correct – that trends sweep in and through the population in the manner of a curve or wave.

This is how Barabási observed his networks functioning, and how sociobiologists tell us our own human networks function. And they do, but with certain important twists that we need to note – hidden factors that will help us make our own networks 'superboosters' and superbraillers when it comes to taking things out of the culture or seeding back into it.

The bell curve theory of trend dispersal was first noted by Bryce Ryan and Neal C. Cross when they investigated the uptake of hybrid supercorns among farmers in Iowa in 1943. Initially only a few adventurous or edge dweller farmers braved the new supercorns they were being asked to pilot. Most resisted, but a few listened, learned and attempted to plant the seeds accordingly.

The seeds grew and did well. Those early adventurers (Receptors) passed on their knowledge to other associates in their network, their strong tie links, until more and more farmers began to plant them (Absorbers). When yields were seen to be high and the stalks stronger and more resistant to disease than older stocks, those who constituted the larger swathe of the network (Latents) began to buy into the seeds and use them, and so on. So the trend spread and most farmers in the region, even those who had doubted the supercorn's abilities (Laggards and Resistors) were persuaded not just by the others' success but their own growing sense of foolishness and isolation – and also by their falling profits.

This is how many trend forecasters see a trend's path, how many viral marketers see it – as a bell curve where the trend passes through the population in a bow-shaped manner, from fringe to mainstream in an easily segmented and visualized curve. The trend arc as some call it, or trend vector or trend trajectory.

Some even show a dark area on the left-hand side of the curve that looks a bit like a breach or break. In his book *Crossing the Chasm*, viral marketer Geoffrey Moore calls this a trend chasm, or trend wall – a black spot where Reflectors live, and where most trends die because they are far too new for the mainstream to bother with.

As futurologist Zeth Godin puts it, 'pre-chasm people want things that are cool; post-chasm people (those on the other side of the curve – the Absorbers, Latents, Laggards and Resistors) want something that works.'

Some marketers concentrate on bridging this gap, on forging links across the chasm – that guerrilla and viral marketing thing – while others talk of 'trend sneezing', or 'spraying', and in their presentations use graphs or animations to show such a happening taking place. Enter Powerpoint displays of trend molecules shooting out and over the chasm, all spreading, settling, sticking, infecting – trend molecules called Hotmail, eBay, Amazon, GeoCities, Wallpaper, Big Brother, Miss Kitty, Smart cars. Names we all nod at and say, 'Well if they've used that trick, followed that trajectory, then it must work, must be like that.'

The notion that a trend map looks a bit like a bell curve sits easily with the rational economist's sense of simplicity and order. Borrowing from the worlds of sociology and virology, they can even use rules or 'assistive laws' that help explain, plot and predict the path of a trend through the culture in the form of an easy-to-understand threshold model – a mathematical proposition used to calculate the speed at which a disease or a new idea spreads through the population. Until now, however, even viral marketers didn't know how this process worked, or how trends which started in one area or part of the culture appeared in another almost simultaneously.

# 80/20 networks –
## booster hubs and trend wormholes

These kinds of happenings can't be explained by the bell curve theory alone, but they can be explained if you turn the bell curve theory on its head. Literally.

Imagine our bell curve turned upside down and tilted on its side so it looks a bit like a slouched bow. At the top end of the curve there are lots of nodes with only a few links. At the bottom there are a few with lots of links. This is a mathematical plot of how a network looks, but it is also how a room with lots of people looks, or indeed an overcrowded brandscape or retail environment – some stores with a few connections, another set (superhubs) with many.

What you have then is a lot of nodes with lots of connections at the top end of the curve, but so scattered are they and so spread out that their power to transmit data, carry ideas or influence other nodes is pretty limited.

In contrast, those at the other end of the curve, the few hubs with many connections, are veritable powerhouses, each hub in itself brimming with life, but each in turn pumping data, information, ideas and knowledge through similar hubs with an equally high number of links. This is why this end of the curve carries most of the traffic, despite the fact that it contains fewer nodes.

## ■ 80/20 networks

Sound familiar? It's called the 80/20 principle, or the Pareto rule after the 19th-century Italian economist Vilfredo Pareto, who first noted that, no matter which country you looked at or which economic model, 20 per cent of the population controlled and were responsible for generating 80 per cent of the wealth.

Darwin, in his own way, recorded this in his work on the origins of the species – that 20 per cent of the changes in the flora and fauna of the earth were responsible for 80 per cent of nature's bigger evolutionary shifts. The same pattern has been noted in team work, ideas creation, innovation, and in political, social and environmental change.

And this is what Barabási and his team were seeing in their studies of networks – a small but potent group of hubs was responsible for most of the network's activities. They called these power hubs. This kind of activity is governed by a law known as a 'power law' – one that exponentially demonstrates the fact that in most real networks 'the majority of nodes have only a few links,' explains Barabási, 'and that these tiny nodes coexist with a few big hubs – nodes with an anomalously high number of links.'

He continues, 'The few links connecting the smaller nodes to the bigger ones are not sufficient to ensure that the network is fully connected. The function is secured by a few, relatively rare hubs that keep real networks from falling apart.' These are

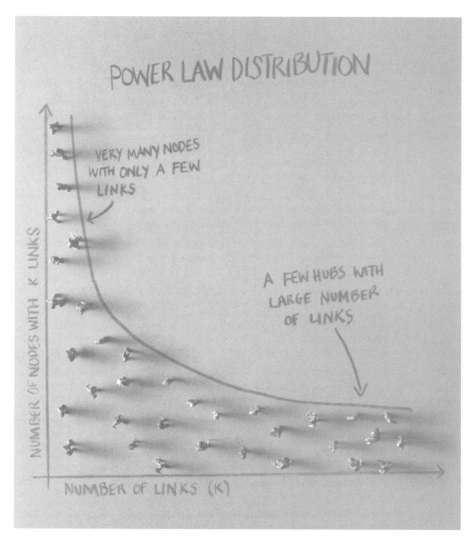

The power law explains why there are key players or superconnectors in any room, restaurant or consumer group. By identifying them, you can 'wormhole' your message in all parts of the group via the 80/20 principle.

the people that hold clubs, organizations or trends together, but also connect them to other people and other areas of the culture.

This is why some products succeed even if they come with high critical thresholds attached. Their time may not be right but, because they have managed to plug into the right hubs in the network (those significant but all powerful few), they can by-pass the normal laws that govern such things (the bell curve process) and find themselves being booted through the network at high speed and with such force and ubiquity that resistance is futile!

Ideas can be boosted in the mainstream by finding where your superhubs are located. But this doesn't mean that the idea will definitely succeed. If the idea itself is weak or 'off trend' it will develop into the worst kind of idea – a fad, something that lasts a season, leaves little or no impact on the cultural landscape and even less on your long term profits.

**ff 20 per cent of the population controlled and were responsible for generating 80 per cent of the wealth. 55**

Understanding 80/20 networks and realizing that they work to specific rules and contain certain internal rhythms that we can harness underscores what we've always believed. Networks have the power to influence and more importantly, the power to plug into the culture and become our ears, our eyes – seismographic nodes that can be used to read even the most subtle shifts in the world or markets around us. They may be situated along cultural fault lines – like the one that runs from Hoxton to Shoreditch to Wapping to Stepney (where we've chosen to locate the Future Laboratory's office) – in clubs, bars, bands, cities and countries or areas of academia, art, design, graphics, film, video and science where shifts in the tectonic plate of the culture can be read and registered more speedily.

There is no point however in carrying out your research in areas deemed to be 'average' or representational of the 'mainstream' in the way that many market research companies do. This will only tell you what people are doing and thinking now, rather than what they are likely to be doing or thinking in the future. Edge groups or creative types, because they are networked into the 'new' (or indeed the deviant), are more likely to hold the ideas and outlooks set to impact on our collective tomorrows. This is what regional strategist Richard Florida believes and why he calls them his creative class. He estimates that they make up 30 per cent of the US work force, and are highly connected, hugely interactive and influential men and women. He claims that these people not only drive cultural change in the United States, but also make the places they live in magnets for like-minded firestarters and innovators.

Florida first noted this phenomenon when he met Gary Gates, a doctoral student at Carnegie Mellon University in 1998. Gates was exploring the distribution patterns of gay people, looking at where they lived and why they wanted to live there. Florida, as it turned out, was doing something similar in his own thesis on the location of high tech industries and talented people. As he explains in his book, *The Rise of the Creative Class*, Gates' findings on how and why gay people became concentrated in particular areas and how this subsequently impacted on the culture around them, overlapped and in many cases mirrored those in his own high tech investigations.

So too did the findings of another project Florida was working on. His 'bohemian index' set out to map the density and location of artists, writers, performers and musicians in a particular region. As before, the idea was to assess how this spread impacted on the region in terms of culture, but also in terms of the profits generated by their work and business.

## ■ Creativity hubs

All in all, what Florida and Gates uncovered was a nexus of types, or a network of types, that seemed not just to be a factor of innovation, diversity and creativity, but the driver of it. In essence, this research confirms what we have known anecdotally – that the creativity, diversity, excitement, buzz and vitality needed to make these areas happen are caused by the very people and cultural activities that organizations and Laggards shun or are suspicious of. Immigration, ethnic diversity, sexual possibility, new ways of brokering and binding families that have little to do with biology, even less with marriage but more to do with like, love and polymath desire.

As Florida discovered, communities with a high density of gays or a bohemian 'alternative class' tend to be more radical, cutting edge, risk taking and creatively affluent than their white, middle class, middle American counterparts.

Incomes in these 'flashpoint' areas tend to be sporadic in the short term, but high over longer periods. His creative class warrior earns on average $48 000 compared to the $28 000 of his blue collar counterpart. Also, the creative texture of the area is more likely to throw up new ideas, new clubs, music, social scenes and ways of doing business or running companies than those located in more sedate white or blue collar areas.

Separate studies into the social and lifestyle patterns of the inhabitants of Austin, Texas produced similar findings. In a city that went from zero to a creative centre and cultural and social hub in less than ten years, the only things measured that could account for such a transformation, says sociologist Robert Cushing who carried out the study, was the influx of gays to the city, the rise in its creative, media and alternative music and leisure populations. 'When you hear about cities that have gays and bobos, it doesn't sound very scientific, it sounds gimmicky . . .'

It does sound gimmicky but, as Florida says, more and more diversity is what makes cities more profitable and communities more vibrant. Diversity, difference and the encouragement of those factors that make these things happen – tolerance, 24Seven culture. 'As a group, the creative class favours active, participatory recreations over passive, institutionalized forms; they prefer an indigenous street level culture – a teaming blend of cafés, sidewalk musicians, and small galleries and bistros where it is hard to draw the line between performer and spectator.'

This is not unlike what Jane Jacobs concludes about the perfect American city in her 1961 classic *The Death and Life of Great American Cities*. She rightly argues that cities are killed not by people but by planners, or rather the use of zones that create culture deserts and business ghettos, residential enclaves and shopping precincts that legislate against the very things needed to make communities thrive, streets diversify and ideas flow. Our forced mergers again!

In the majority of cases, cities or areas with unplanned, spontaneous, bottom-up outbreaks of energy thrive, or show all the indications that they are about to. Those with populations in their thirties or forties, predominantly white and settled, show increased signs of languor, social torpidity and a cultural vitality in decline.

'Cities don't need shopping malls and convention centres to be economically successful, they need eccentric people . . . Without diversity, without weirdness, without difference, without tolerance a city will die. So too, it can be said, will companies, or indeed networks developed to flood your organization with future-faced ideas or intelligence on upcoming trends,' argues Florida.

Of the 26 cities he studied with large working class populations, only Houston, Texas ranked among his top ten creative cities, while the rest didn't feature, suffering instead from what economist Mancur Olson refers to as 'institutional sclerosis' – a hardening of the cultural and creative arteries because little in the way of newness, innovation or diversity now courses through them.

Despite this, as Florida, points out, cities (and brands) still attempt to court and attract MBAs, or married (as in stable) couples in their mid-thirties. They build sports facilities, business parks, bland 'silicon somewheres' in the hope that this will kick-start the upturn in the local economy that continues to elude them.

## ■ Creative networks require creative players

And continue it will, he believes, because politicians, architects and town planners are still building the kinds of cities and communities that few creatives are keen to live in – cities that have sports facilities, shopping centres and well-planned, neatly laid out family houses but little else. 'Creatives,' he says, 'require 24Seven stimulation, round the clock access and mixed usage zones where bars, offices, clubs, workshops and live/work apartments can be found along the same street and in the same zip code.' In other words, a single area in which they can work, rest, play and plan – an area within which new ideas, products, insights and technological innovations explode into the culture as a consequence of their presence and the creative energy they generate by being there.

In establishing the kinds of networks you need to create, or the kinds of future-faced companies we are looking at, you need to locate outlets and members who are living, working, breathing and participating in the growth of these creative and innovative nodes.

Florida continues, 'Take Minneapolis, which has long been a centre of musical innovation. Prince, Bob Mould, Jimmy Jam and Terry Lewis and the Twin Cities Gay Men's Chorus are far more important to that area economically than a new shopping mall or convention centre.'

Better, Florida shows how his creative class (creatives and the creative professionals that thrive alongside them) are behind many of the trends we've documented – dotcom culture, flexecutive work patterns, dress up Friday, 24Seven living, hypermobility, boutique hotels, 'experience culture', Samurai Man, the Bobo, even Linux and open source networking.

Florida says it is the rule, when applied properly, that revitalizes cities and kick-starts dying and flatlining cultures or companies by plugging them into the kinds of people that hitherto most cities, communities or cultures didn't want – gays, blacks, Puerto Ricans, refugees, musicians, artists, dancers, performers, programmers, DJs, A&R people, microzine publishers, graphic artists and the kinds of people who want to do the kinds of things that don't pattern into the norm.

This can range from people trying to open clubs, bars and shops that run 24Seven in hitherto moribund neighbourhoods; a black man and a white woman who choose to marry and live together in an ultraconservative postcode; couples who decide to build their own suburban or inner city houses to plans that defy the 'retro' planning styles sometimes favoured by short-sighted local councils; people generally who prefer to see cities, or the places they live in, as living, breathing, complex organisms – where people rather than businesses matter, where roads are designed as much for pedestrians and bike usage as they are for cars.

## ■ Think creative capital, not just social capital

Florida's creative class is made up of, in essence, the kind of people who see cities, places and products differently. People who see that 'place' works not because it is about stability (stasis), or about white, middle class homogeneous centres for white, middle class homogeneous families to do their thing in – which in many cases is very little, merely about being white and settled and middle class! It is places which encourage experience, doing, going out, engaging, creating, challenging and making connections that make for more creativity, and in the process generate creative capital and not just social capital – that thing Robert Putnam strenuously favours in his book *Bowling Alone*. This shows how the membership of clubs, or the kind of strategic social networks that traditionally held communities together in the Golden Age of the nuclear family, have declined severely since the 50s.

Accepting this, Florida, rightly asks 'So what?' These things are in decline, he believes, because they no longer suit the lifestyles we lead today. A lifestyle that requires us to work longer hours (47.7 a week), travel further and further to get there (we now spend 3.4 hours a day travelling to and from work) but also one that allows us to create our own work patterns (1 in 14 of us works from home) and be less prescriptive about our relationship types. We are also more mobile, tending to move from one community or city to another, and for cultural, social and experience reasons rather than just for work.

## ■ Experience culture and increased sociomobility

Despite what the media tells us, we are more tolerant of 'difference' and keener on ethnic, social and sexual diversity, keener on trying new foods, new holiday destinations and experiences.

A far cry from the closed, socially constrained and constraining worlds of our parents and grandparents. Over 50 per cent of them lived and died within five miles of where they were born. They knew, perhaps, many strong tie associates but few weak tie ones, which kept their circles closed to newness and isolated from greater cultural changes.

> **A far cry from the closed, socially constrained and constraining worlds of our parents and grandparents.**

And in many ways, if we think about the institutions they cherished – the golf club, the Women's Institute, the British Legion, working men's clubs, the bowling club, tennis and cricket clubs, preserved in aspic – all that should be left behind.

As Florida points out in his bohemian index, the cities that most encourage this kind of nostalgic view of what makes a community or a city, are those that have lost out to creative hubs, or centres of creative networks – cities like Seattle, Austin, Dublin, Berlin (where Norman Foster's Reichstag and buildings by world class architects like Frank Gehry, Oscar Piano, Helmut Jahn, Arata Isozaki and Jose Rafael Moneo have made the city a creative class hub for Germans and non-Germans alike) and Marseilles. Recently in Manchester, Salford, Walsall and Gateshead, creative hubs have been encouraged by bringing in the works and outlooks of architects, artists and designers that not only challenge the norm, but in doing so create a buzz or kick-start weak tie connection networks that will lead to greater shifts in this direction.

Indeed, if utopians like Prince Charles, who hanker after Poundbury-style villages with Poundbury-style people in them, are to be convinced by cash alone, Florida discovered that his creative cities earn 30 per cent more on average in terms of annual profits than their moribund counterparts.

These are the places then to locate our networks, and these are the kinds of people you want plugged in to them – running them, reading them, guiding them.

# Deviant strains –
## and the rise of edge marketing

In an article in *Fast Company* magazine, writers Ryan Mathews and Watts Wacker sum deviance up as follows: 'Deviance is the source of all innovation. It's the wellspring of new ideas, new products, new personalities, and ultimately new markets ... In its purest sense, deviance is nothing more or less than any one of us taking a measurable step away from the middle of the road.

> **Deviants are people who shun the norm, work against it and, in their own way, attempt to disrupt it and recast it.**

'Extend that step once more and you'll find yourself moving from the comfort of the accepted into the fast paced world of the trend setter. Take another small step and you'll land in the rarefied realm of the ultra cool avant garde. Venture one hesitant step further and you are in the sometimes seductive, more frightening world of cultist and fanatic.

'Dare to take that last step and you'll crash head-on into the heart of social darkness: the world of the naked, pure, unabashed and largely frightening deviance ... '

Replace the word 'deviance' with 'creative' or 'network' and you realize that we are talking about the same thing. Good networks should contain good deviants or creative types, and good deviants make for being good networkers! We can be more exact about this – networks are deviant strains or deviant organisms in everything but name, especially if we accept the notion that deviants are people who shun the norm, work against it and, in their own way, attempt to disrupt it and recast it in new and innovative ways.

## ■ Deviancy is really about difference

This can range from New York dominatrices such as Palagia, a curvaceous, olive skinned night dweller who organized terror sex orgies post-September 11th, to women like Lysette Butler, a 43-year-old nurse from Essex, England who, like one in five women born in 1960, happily chooses to remain childless thus deviating from the norm in a positive and challenging way.

Palagia, noticing an upsurge in the number of couples using chatrooms or advertising for 'no consequence sex' in the classifieds became the first of a growing number of sex industry workers, club owners or party organizers and lifestyle forecasters to allow 'terror sex' to go public, in the process reversing many of the legal or self-censoring prohibition that bars and swingers' clubs had introduced during conservative Mayor Giuliani's term of office.

In the process, terror sex has given way to 'hetrohedonism' – a trend towards promiscuity, open relationships and multi-partnering events hitherto associated with the more flexible lifestyle arrangements enjoyed by New York's gay community.

Lysette Butler, on the other hand, is part of a growing, guilt-free generation of heterosexual and same-sex couples who think that relationships and serial careerism are more important than having children. Child-free rather than child-poor, they are rewriting the rules of non-parent relationships, with 42 per cent of the female population across the world following suit – deviant, as Lysette and her kind seem presently. Tomorrow, as a group, they are set to become one of the most agile and self-determining consumers we will have to deal with.

But Butler and Palagia are only two of a growing number of deviant types your network must contain if it is to be suitably and profitably dysfunctional. If you look at the population base as a whole, you'll find that people like Lysette are not the only lifestyle deviants that should be plugged into your network. What about any one of the growing number of post-fifty women, part of our Rainbow Youth group, who have no interest whatsoever – despite pressure from daughters and society at large – in becoming grannies or looking after grandchildren? They prefer instead to concentrate on careers and their increased leisure options.

Here we are seeing the rise of bridge careerism (men and women in their late fifties and early sixties starting a second or even third career). They are burning their assets – houses, pensions, savings and investment portfolios – so that they can 'live long and die broke' rather than leaving their hard-earned money to bickering children and calculating relatives. The Jagger Generation – they know how to go on, rather than out, in style.

Then there are our Starter Marriage couples – men and women in their early twenties to late thirties (Generation Flex) who marry, divorce and then marry again. The second marriage always lasts longer that the first, which is viewed merely as a trial or a dry run!

You could include in your network one of our pro-protest-can-do Sunshine Teens – 11 to 19 year olds in the UK and US who see themselves as optimistic and inclusive, concerned and willing to fight for what they believe in, even if this means breaking the law. Keen on self-expression, self-learning, self-promotion and inclusive support systems for the less well off, they are also highly motivated, meritocratic and determined to keep things real.

## ■ Harness your own creative class

Network deviancy then isn't just about consumers who go against the grain. It's about harnessing key players from Florida's creative class. Architects like Zaha Hadid, Daniel Liebeskind, Nigel Coates, Coop Himmelblau, Frank Gehry, Peter Eisenman and Toyo Ito, who are creating an architecture of the ecstatic set to be every bit as influential as that of Le Corbusier and his machine for living contemporaries. It is about biotech artists like Eduard Kac who, with France's Institut National de la Recherche Agro-nomique, created the world's first transgenic rabbit that glows an alien green under blue light. It's cyborg specialist Professor Kevin Warwick who has implanted chips in his own arm and that of his wife so he could feel her stroking his fingertips as she opens and closes hers.

> **❝ Your network needs to be reflective of the key changes taking place in society. ❞**

Your network needs to be reflective of the key changes taking place in society. Not just those bits of society your brand or company taps into (that will only tell you things you know or things that are not worth knowing), but society in general, concentrating only on those bits that are about the now, the new, the upcoming.

On your shortlist of candidates I'd expect to see players from the world of artificial intelligence, biotechnology, nanotechnology, stem cell research and genetics. All of these are key areas set to dominate future thinking – from biotech brands to medicines, to foods, to cultured skins, organs and improved bodies and minds. GM foods, nano-medicines and zenotransplanting, despite current resistance levels, are the future and you need to be prepared.

## ■ Networks should have moral, ethical and social dimensions

But a future that tampers with the very fabric of nature itself is one that comes ready packed with its own moral, spiritual and ethical dilemmas.

This is why philosophers, ethicists and spiritual guidance counsellors should also feature in your network. They can look at how we can find paths through the moral and ethical mazes that these issues are creating, and ask the kinds of questions consumers themselves are asking – about safety, about 'Frankenstein foods', about the nature of clones (What are their rights? Do they have souls? Should they be told of their origin?).

To a biotech brand these questions sound whimsical and far, far removed from the world of white heat technology and genome science. To the consumer, the farmer, the ecologist, the ethicist or social philosopher they are concerns, founded or otherwise, that need addressing.

This is why Monsanto, Aventis and Norvartis are, in European terms at least, organizations to be treated with suspicion. They did not take the pulse of the world they were attempting to sell into. They assumed a position that was out of trend with how the rest of us were thinking.

And what of babies that carry animal genes inside them? Or animals that carry human genes inside them? Is the former lower down the bioevolutionary scale because of their adulterated genes? Are the latter higher up because they now contain a fragment of humanity within them? And if we eat them, does that make us cannibals?

Questions – quirky, gruesome, whimsical and trenchant – but how easy it would have been for a brand like Monsanto to think like this before planting GM crops if they had their insight networks up and brailling. Even if these things are inevitable, even if they are needed, it doesn't mean that consumers see it in the same light. Remember our critical threshold index – test GM foods against this and see what happens.

Sowing GM seeds has also put down seeds of another kind – a growing resistance to, or rather suspicion of, science. Again your network needs to reflect on this, as ours does. But let's pause here. Let's take you out of building your own network and into our Lifesigns Network proper. What is it telling us right now about the culture? Where is it up to? Where is it going? What's new?

The chapters which follow will also give you an idea of how networks operate, the kinds of insights to expect from them, and how these insights should be used and deployed.

# Brailling the culture:
## listening to the signals as well as the noise

# The science of unreason –
## why uncertainty is a profit margin waiting to happen

All networks function on the basis of each networker having their own contacts, their own points of entry into the culture and their own consilient sensitivities. They then report back to network coordinators regularly on new or noticeable topics they or the strong or weak tie associates are picking up on.

Some network coordinators stipulate areas of concern for their networks to focus on while others have priority lists for their networkers to watch and listen out for, which is less controlling but still leads to key or new cultural shifts being missed. In our case, the Lifesigns Network has a wide and roaming brief – what we call our creative's catchcry – listen, look, record, absorb, remember, report and learn, then extrapolate. This is the creative's catchcry because it is the fundamental and universal process adopted by creatives everywhere when assimilating and learning to work with new things, or engage in new experiences.

> **It is the fundamental and universal process adopted by creatives everywhere.**

We have our own areas of concern however – retail, interiors, design, architecture, innovation, graphics, packaging, lifestyle trends, music, social change, global activism, ethical and social responsibility, brand harmonics, corporate design, and key or interesting cultural shifts. Much of this is fed back into a biannual forecasting magazine we edit called *Viewpoint*. This is owned by Metropolitan Publishing BV, which publishes *Textile View*, one of the key forecasting books for the fashion and textiles industry, and, via its own colour and forecasting network, *Pantone Colour Planner*, the design- and products-sector bible for all the colours that every product, paint or magazine designer is likely to use in the near or distant future.

The underlying rule for all our networkers, and the networks they plug into, is to ask, what's new? Our network is a group of 2000 or so academics, DJs, musicians, designers, chemists, ethicists, architects, graphic designers, dancers, marketers, fashion scouts, journalists, cool hunters, poets, writers, geneticists, single mums, gay dads, straight edgers, nu-metal kids, structural engineers, retail anthropologists, ethnographers, photographers, video makers, economists, financial service providers, surfers, sonic branders, psychologists, regulatory officers in the area of in vitro research and cloning, cosmetic scientists, animal rights activists, environmentalists, social philosophers and so on. They all keep this question in mind wherever they are and whatever they are doing – What's new?

This is what they are reporting back to us currently.

The GM issue – big in Europe, certainly now that French and British chefs, as well as French, British, German and Italian consumers have called for a halt to

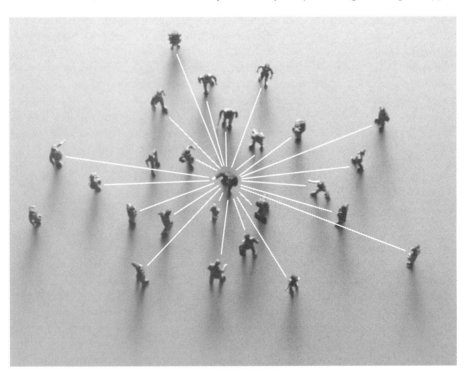

A central network is perhaps the most familiar of all networks and certainly the least creative. By nature and design it is inflexible, easy to dominate and depends on ideas being accepted by the top (or boss) before they are distributed throughout the network proper. This leads to ideas being corrupted or processes being polluted or watered down. It is a network of mean averages and average ideas and people.

what they describe as 'the pollution of our food chain' – is the tip of a very interesting and potentially dangerous iceberg. One that isn't just to do with the future of GM, but of science, knowledge and learning as a whole.

According to UK prime minister, Tony Blair, speaking about anti-GM protesters and anti-vivisection protests, 'There is only a small band of people who want to stifle informed debate.' According to our network, he's right – it's called the Government. Or at least that's how the vast majority of consumers see it – as do members of our own Lifesigns Network group.

## ■ Protests about one issue may be articulating fears about much bigger ones

As a nation, the UK (which represents about 1 per cent of the world's population) may have paid for 4.5 per cent of the world's scientific developments, produced 8 per cent of the world's scientific papers, and received 9 per cent of the world's citations (a measure of the worth of scientific research). But of late, science has figured pretty low in consumer estimation in Britain, the US and on the European mainland, where protests against GM, biotech, stem cell research and the seemingly exorbitant profits of pharmaceutical giants who refuse to engage with the Aids pandemic in Africa, have collectively fostered a climate of suspicion and a sense that people are anti-science.

And who can blame them? As our own Lifesigns Network groups show (as yours should be showing), there is the belief that research is done without considering the ethical, social and environmental implications of such activities.

## ▓ Government no longer of the people

In the wake of the foot and mouth outbreak of 2001 and the rise in the number of incidences of CJD and BSE, Professor Roger Morris of King's College, London suggests that there is a 'growing public mistrust of science.'

There is also the view that successive governments, research institutions and universities in the UK and US have, for too long, relinquished their roles as guardians of the public conscience in the face of party donations, the funding of academic research programmes, and approaches from vested interest groups who have managed to get their voices heard and strategies acted on over those of the ordinary man and woman in the street.

Sue Mayer of Genewatch UK writes, 'Critical questioning is not anti-science but is important for good, independent science and for a healthy democracy.'

It is, and even if biotech alone is set to make European companies a significant £62.5bn by 2005, people and brands need to know why science is so lambasted and how this can be changed.

As your network should tell you, it isn't just about being anti-science, but against the speed at which we are all being shuttled off into the future and the effect this has on our lives. Travelling faster than ever, perversely it now takes longer to get from Trafalgar Square to Brixton in London's southern suburbs than it did at the beginning of the 20th century. And networks are good ways of teasing out these contradictions, of using them to look at bigger trends, or to identify issues that are not being articulated in the press or public media because they are not tied into a particular news angle or event.

One of our networkers, for instance, uncovered a simple fact – that at any moment 360 000 people are in the skies overhead. This triggered a network debate that led to a bigger discussion on such ideas as hypermobility, connectivity and how all these impact on our consciousness, if indeed they do.

Every day at least 4 million of us catch a plane, while every year 600 million of us touch down somewhere in the world, causing just under half a million hotel rooms to be built annually. Even in the UK, we now travel, on average, 6 800 miles a year – five times further than our counterparts did in the 50s – spending on average two whole weeks a year in motion.

And yet – and this is a big yet – 50 per cent of the UK population still live within five miles of where they were born! Think of that! Now think of how we view global brands, globalism, refugees, innovative products, foods, ideas and brands with great suspicion, especially if our immediate experience is closed or limited.

## ▨ Network cascades and inflows of knowledge

This is one of the key and vital ways of flooding your network with ideas, insights, uniqueness and – yes – more future downloads. By listening, looking, recording, doing, absorbing, remembering, reporting and then learning and extrapolating.

Don't assume, however, that a shift against science, for instance, suggests a shift against learning or inquiry or a thirst for knowledge. People are incredibly prismatic, and as well as living in prisms (remember our life prisms rather than lifestyles) or compartments, we live and think them so a stance against science shouldn't be seen as a rise in Luddism or in fundamentalism or a shift back to basics – that's how the traditional marketer would view it. It is merely a point or issue or area that people are rightly asking questions about.

When they do this, they are making those people in these areas of endeavour take notice, and perhaps revisit things they themselves have failed to consider. One man or woman's line of criticism is another's potential feedback loop. But more, an attack on one area tells you a lot more about what people are thinking, how they are thinking and why they are

> **❝ This is one of the key and vital ways of flooding your network with ideas, insights, uniqueness. ❞**

thinking what they are thinking. This is why listening is the one thing networks must do 24Seven. And why you must listen to their outputs in the same way.

# Content culture –
## the rise and death of no-brow living

Listening is something few of us do. We are encouraged to speak up and speak out, to create brands with presence and personality, to state our case and nail our colours to the mast, and so on. The problem with doing this? We hear only our own noise and miss the signals of change that the culture and – if we have them – our networks are filtering back to us.

This was why the Marks & Spencer of old went wrong. The same can be said of brands such as Marconi, Carlton TV and British Airways, which famously ditched its flag at the very point in the culture when our edge dwellers – in this case Britpop artists and musicians such as Damien Hirst, Tracey Emin and Jarvis Cocker – were in fact reviving it, making it sexy, adding new cultural, cool values and meanings to it that shifted focus away from its right wing or nationalistic associations.

It was also the time when Bob Ayling, BA's then chief executive, bought into the dotcom culture (his walk through 'dress down Friday' Waterside offices), ushering in a luxe class style and a sense that business (as in business class) was best just when dotcom was about to peak in terms of its 'trend' moment, and business class travellers about to be overtaken by a new class of cabin baggage-only no-frills flyer, keen to experience new cities and take part in compression breaks and short-stay holidays rather than package tours.

Ayling wasn't just off trend, he was way off how people were thinking and why they were thinking what they were thinking – and the context in which they were thinking it. He wasn't – or rather his marketing department wasn't – plugged in. Not listening.

This happens all the time – it is happening now. Look at how publishers, brands, TV companies and fashion labels continue to invest and inform trash culture and 'no-brow' attitudes and outlooks when even the least plugged-in networks are indicating a swing back towards 'content culture', to edutainment or one or more proactive involvements – according to Shell's in-house Scenario planning team.

Even middle England and middle America – those dual bastions of 'no-brow' – are looking for more. More history, more documentary, more drama, more intelligence, as the UK's Channel 5 – famous for its soft porn and hard police programmes – is proving with a shift away from sex and crime fests to surprisingly well-researched documentaries and docudramas on war and the monarchy, nature specials and the history of ancient Britain.

## ▓ Brightening up

While the so-called marketers and audience research panels are talking dumbing down and reality TV, prosumers of the kind we were speaking to, or at least those that hack through the paths the rest of us travel on, are talking about brightening up, or at least a return to pan-brow – programming with intelligence at its heart.

Even Radio 1, seen as the flagship of lads and sassy ladettes everywhere and a model of its kind for those looking to take the pulse of the culture, is reporting a drop-off in listeners – 500 000 or so. Lads mags like *Loaded*, *FHM* and *Maxim* are reporting a similar fall-off in sales as men, perhaps a little wiser to the ways of the world and womanhood, are beginning to demand substance to their reading material other than the kind you can shove up your nose. Sales of *National Geographic* and *Scientific American* are also up, as are those of magazines like *Prospect*, *New Scientist* and *Vanity Fair*, of non-fiction books and even subscriptions to CNN, the Discovery Channel, HBO, and listenerships to Radio 4 and Radio 2 as more of us brain up, or at least refuse to bland out.

If we're stupid, how come more books are being published now than ever before? UK publishers alone now issue 110 000 new books a year – books like *Stalingrad*, Norman Davis's *History of Europe*, Anthony Beevor's *Berlin: the downfall,* to quirky histories or social essays on everything from salt, to chocolate, from concrete to *Longitude* or Fukuyama's *Our Post-Human Future*. Subjects and areas once regarded as the domain of cultural study writers or obscure and arcane thesis lovers determined to make the ordinary obscure and the everyday impenetrable are now being discussed in book clubs up and down the land by thousands of men and women determined not just to learn, but to make a contribution to learning in the form of their own views and comments.

## ▨ Change comes slowly, but it comes

We are a different nation to the one so celebrated and loved in Ealing comedies, the poems of Betjeman, the soft mellow tones of Radio 4 announcers or the equally soft, quivering sensibilities of authors like Anita Brookner where all, including the tea things, teeter on the edge of some great revelation but never quite see it.

We have moved on, moved to the city, moved up, have gotten richer quicker. We are smugger and, in many ways, better off and more naffed off as a consequence than our parents or their parents before them.

Four times a year we call on our network to paint a portrait of modern Britain, and four times a year we are surprised by the changes that have taken place since the last time we looked.

As a nation we are money-rich (household wealth now stands at £200bn) and time-poor, leading harassed and ever busier lives – a 47.7 hour week. And technology makes more and more demands, not just on our time – the average worker now spends 90 minutes per day answering e-mails- but also how we use it.

> **❝We are a different nation to the one so celebrated and loved in Ealing comedies.❞**

Mobiles, faxes, WAP, e-mail, the internet and handhelds have made us more accessible, flexible and flattened in the approach to how we divide our social, private and public selves – or has it?

Our networkers from the hard edge of Compressed Living would say not! The very flexibility that technology offers us means that we are contactable 24Seven – at home, in the field, in the bar.

Time deficit disorder syndrome (TDDS) is now both a term and a trend that has entered the culture – along with deferral living which means using your mobile to reshuffle meetings, reschedule schedules, postpone or defer them while you are actually on the way to them! To buy more time or reprioritize, but ultimately to cram more in so that more tasks get left undone.

Thus we are time-poor, suffering from 'time famines', attempting to negotiate 'swing time' (using mobiles to switch between social and professional networks via the call-holding option), working in compressed time, even using watches with millisecond displays, as if this will extend or prolong time, but to what end?

## ▨ Zoning Out and switching off to tune in

According to our own networkers, such shifts and cultural changes are creating a new spate of microtrends. Trends such as Zoning Out (using all our hard earned cash to buy us out of 'the culture' for a few precious hours so we are invisible or unreachable) and experiencing the Limelight Syndrome (being pampered and preened like a celebrity). The latter of course being the reason why retailers are now introducing personal shoppers, offering us free makeovers. Why too there has been a noticeable increase in the hiring of white stretchlimos, or of airlines (even discount ones) offering a fast track service to customers, including the use of an executive lounge so they can feel a little more pampered and special!

All this has revitalized the once moribund hotel sector. Our demand for luxury, exclusivity, stylized leisure and moments and moods of glamour like those hitherto enjoyed only by celebrities seen in the pages of *Hello* or *OK!* All this has given birth to the boutique hotel phenomenon.

The Hudson, the Delano, the Costes, the Sanderson – swaddling-in-luxury urban retreats where the theatrical is made flash; mind and body soothed in a bath and battery of lotions, potions, fragrant candles and fantastically gorgeous front-of-house staff straight out of *Vogue* or a Robert Palmer video; lipstick and Donna Karan no-nonsense suits included.

This is the Ny-Lon of sushi and sloughing creams, tri-yoga and try anything twice, a world of Starck chairs and stark contrasts, of hotels that are urbane in all the right ways. There for those who live in cities, as much as those who travel to and from them.

They have, likewise, kick-started a trend for urban spas and wellness retreats, for corridor parties, where friends book a string of rooms, sharing the cost, and use them and the corridors between to party till dawn and beyond, topping up from mini bars or the hotel's main bar when thirst or manners require. A variant of this for the overwrought, overrun city dweller is the SmartSex weekend – a trend spearheaded by executive class thirty-somethings in London, Paris, New York, LA and Milan. They book in at their favourite hotel and call on their favourite drug dealer to supply them with something called a smart bag – a pouch containing just the right amounts of cocaine, ecstasy, valium, acid, viagra, cannabis and jellies or tamazepan to ensure that sex is high and hard, fast and furious, dizzy and dirty. By Sunday afternoon, the valium and jellies dropped and the last dregs of champagne and chardonnay drunk, everybody comes down in readiness for another week at the screens. Hetrohedonism yes, but between soft cotton Conran sheets rather than those in some poorly lit bedsit or grim council block with anti-crook bars on the window.

## ▓ Retrenching and going back to go forward

Perhaps because of this rush to embrace the hedonistic, the desire to be part of the VH1 or MTV awards moment, our networkers say we are witnessing the rise of a countertrend. One we've called 'retrenching', the buying of products – like KitchenClassics blenders, Aga or Viking stoves, Carlight caravans, HP sauce and Heinz baked beans, and Hershey chocolate bars – that suggest comfort, cocooning or plain old nostalgia.

We are also set to see a revival of the 'stay at home, saturated colour 50s and 70s moments'. Instead of travelling abroad, baby boomers and, more recently, US men and women in their mid-thirties, yearning perhaps for simpler and less harried times, are relearning the skills of backwoods camping and walking, of Coney Island

and the Catskills, the joys of cabins by the lake or ranches in the wilds of the midwest if they are children of the Kennedy and Camelot years.

The British are yearning for caravans and beach huts, Windermere and Whitstable, walking holidays and biking expeditions along West Country lanes, John Hinde postcard blue seas and wattle hedges in the middle distance. Yes, the England of Tennyson and Wordsworth, of British Rail 'bracing in Skegness' posters, but also a reappraisal and revival of suburban villa living, of mowed lawns and the kind of flower borders and gardens once quaintly described as rockeries.

> **❝ And that's why networks should never be turned off, ignored or used to put things on hold. ❞**

The B & B is back, products and games that reassure – Marmite, salad cream, skittles and rounders on the beach, with Jamie Oliver style friends and meat-rich barbecues.

In this world, the camcorder has been abandoned for the Lomo camera, the cheesiness of Super-8 colours and Snappy Snap moments.

As one of our networkers put it, this is not a trend for those in their twenties, but those in their late thirties and early forties – those who had it all and now want substance instead of surface back.

You see what happens when you let your network get on with it? A rush of ideas and possibilities, -isms and lifestyle gambits.

But there's more, always more, and that's why networks should never be turned off, ignored or used to put things on hold. Things we hear from our clients regularly include, 'But we've just had a trend briefing from you!' 'What, more trends?' 'Can't we just concentrate on this lot?' – as in there's meetings to be had, strategies to be worked out, plans to be laid, mission statements to be written up, research to be done, a committee to be set up to look into the viability of this, the implications of that . . .

Fine, but even if you're sleeping or slipping, the world and your competition isn't. Life goes on, and so too do trends and networks.

Remember this – once you turn your networks on, you need to keep them on and keep that knowledge and insight flowing through them. We live in a connected world. Just because you want to disconnect doesn't mean others want to.

# Connected hives –
## the new netocracies and how to surf them

'Connectivity' and 'blur' are among the most important trends our network members are reporting back on. The way technology connects but also the way it blurs – makes time fluid; public and private spaces malleable – and, as a consequence, your brand, your family and the way you live more transparent, accessible and vulnerable to outside attack. Attack from hackers, prosumer rights groups, your competition or, if you are a child of the blur generation, to marketers, brands or consumer profilers who can download your life, loves, likes or dislikes from a plethora of online and offline sources.

We are connected, but also spied on. Britain is one of the most watched and monitored nations in the world. We have more CCTV cameras trained on our streets than any nation in the world with even more coming online, as in the US post-September 11th. Also, as a consequence of legislation in Europe and the UK, we can now have our e-mails read at work, our mobile phone records checked, the websites we visit monitored, and details of our loyalty cards, bank statements, credit ratings, tax returns and even DNA records read by a growing number of government bodies, state organizations and ancillary interest groups.

> **❝ Yes they want things to get more personal, but no they don't want technology to get more invasive. ❞**

With technology enabling us to personalize things more than ever – Amazon's *BookMatcher* service can find books for us based on our previous preferences, or on those others have chosen after clicking on the same book – we are beginning to see a backlash and hear people express contradictory but very understandable views.

Yes they want things to get more personal, but no they don't want technology to get more invasive. Nor indeed do they want it to be used to store more data about them, unless they themselves approve. Even then, most of the people our networkers spoke to say that they are worried or very worried about how much big business knows about them. Neither are they happy that such information is shared around, even if it makes their profile with a particular company more intimate and personal.

And do they believe that all the information supplied to you is confidential? What do you think? And when they tick that box to say they have no wish to receive junk mail, do they really believe that this will happen? Again, no. They don't trust you. Nor do they believe that you, as a company or brand, are helping them to make better and more specific choices by keeping data on them.

More of them are becoming more litigious about the process and the way that brands and organizations target them unnecessarily. So in future, if you are selling pensions, holidays or simply a more personalized form of online shopping, you could find yourself in court countering charges of personal rights infringement from a growing number of trade unions, civil rights groups, consumer organizations and individuals all determined to re-establish clear and effective lines dividing their public and private selves.

## ◼ Self-interest groups give way to mutually active ones

Our own network has already predicted this – that consumer rights groups, NGOs, work councils, trade union movements will themselves challenge not just outside organizations but their employers over their new found 'right' to delve into personal e-mail. This is understandable. As we work longer and harder and allow our jobs to extend into our leisure time – those with most access to online technology work as much as a 14-hour day – we will demand, and have it written into our employment contracts, that our right to use e-mail, mobiles and phones for personal purposes during work hours is respected, in the way that we respect the fact that businesses can and do invade our own dwindling personal space.

Punitive measures will be taken if this doesn't happen. Brands and errant employers will be targeted in the way that environmental and animal rights groups have targeted brands. We are seeing this with fast-food giants like McDonald's who are being challenged by consumers for selling food thought to be injurious to health without stating so on the packaging. Swiss banks have been successfully sued by the families of holocaust victims for $1.25bn in respect of gold and other valuables lodged in their vaults during and after the war which they made no effort to return. South African civil rights organizations are now suing Barclays, NatWest, BP, IBM, Vickers and ICL for allegedly propping up a crooked South African government during the worst years of apartheid.

This is but the start. The legal profession sees consumer ethics as an increasingly lucrative area of business; human and civil rights lawyers, judges and tribunals make ever more favourable rulings for consumers; consumers themselves resort to the law more frequently as government sides more and more with big business. Areas such as our personal rights, or private spaces and the way we work these spaces, will become the new battlegrounds for prosumers and social rights groups determined to claw back control which is increasingly being taken by brands and business.

They will not only demand that privacy is respected and that confidentiality agreements be adhered to, but that all personal details kept on record can be inspected – online and free of charge – and have it amended if it is incorrect – again free of charge – or destroyed if they decide that the information is of no use to the company holding it.

They may even want you to destroy everything – what we call data snaffling. If you don't, as some companies are finding, edge group consumer organizations are now establishing infotech insurgency arms whose sole purpose is to launch snaffling software that seeks out and destroys information relating to named consumers online. Is there a caveat? The bugs, snaffler viruses, also splay other programs in ways that disable, or seriously taint, corrupt or 'put beyond corporate use' all information stored on consumers. Guess what – when we asked what people thought of this, many wanted to know where they could buy the programme!

Likewise, prosumers and ethicists plugged into our network are demanding that senders of unsolicited junk mail and e-mails be prosecuted for personal rights infringements. Moby Monkey, a UK e-marketing brand, has already been fined £50 000 for sending unsuspecting mobile users e-mails which, when opened, encouraged you to call a number under the pretext of winning a prize, only to charge you £1.25 a minute for doing so. Other demands are that public spaces, or spaces claimed for public use (parks, beaches, motorways, pavements, the streets we live on, the houses we live in) be maintained as advertisement-free zones, or that high premiums be charged to advertisers wanting to use these high visibility zones, and that a proportion of the profits be put into community coffers as opposed to swelling those of the signboard owners.

Some agencies are already working with local councils or neighbour rights groups in Canada, America and Germany on space-for-funds projects, but these are by agreement only and not because they have to do it. In the future, advertising – ALL advertising – will be subject to stringent position and presence codes as more and more consumers object to images, hoardings, on-air blips, stings trailers, jingles and computer downloads that demand their attention but offer little or nothing in return.

## ▦ Share of mind? Then pay for it

As we put ever more value on our time and employers demand more of that time, people in return will ask that brands, organizations or commercial culture pay for their attention and headspace if they want it.

Not permission marketing, but payment marketing. Brands are selling products, but more and more people are just waking up to the fact that to do this the brand needs to buy their time, and charge they will – in cash maybe but they might also do it on trust if they think that what you have on offer is genuinely beneficial or likely to simplify or better their lifestyle.

> **They want people to understand them better, treat them as individuals and not as faceless statistics.**

The dilemma here is balancing out what people want with how you treat what they give you. Yes, they want you to be more personal, more intimate, more in tune with their thoughts, needs and desires, but no, they don't necessarily want you to bombard them with personalized e-mails, text messages, letters or 'just for you' ads, on their BT Openworld broadband service.

On the other hand, when they shop, go to restaurants, speak to their bank or enter 'zones of stress' where the personal becomes reassuring and sought after (for example, flying, staying in hospital, undergoing a divorce), they want people to understand them better, treat them as individuals and not as faceless statistics.

But beware! Reading their name on their cheque card and using it to engender familiarity isn't quite what they are after. Nor is a personal mortgage tailored to their segment type needs, or a personal banking service that still requires them to key in their personal six-digit security number.

Mass customization, as our network indicates, isn't the way forward and consumers are rumbling this. Worse, they are no longer willing to pay extra for having your brand do what the corner shop or their local pub does for nothing – calling them by name, remembering their order.

Understanding that this kind of treatment requires more information, and more personal information at that, consumers will be happy to allow you into their lives to ensure that these relationships are seamless, smooth and ongoing if they trust you – and seriously believe that the information they give you is a bond between you and them (which they don't).

Technologies such as collaborative filtering or voice recognition software (when you speak, the faceless one at the other end of the line knows who you are and whether or not you are angry) offer up this illusion, but face-to-face, voice-to-voice, the personal touch businesses where bank managers, supermarket managers and sales assistants are familiar faces at front-of-house (like restaurant Maître Ds and pub landlords) are more likely than ever to succeed in a world where personalization technology ironically makes us less intimate.

Even our hypermobile elite, our cosmocrats shuttling from time zone to time zone, do so for one thing only – to meet their customers, look them in the eye and know that the deal they are brokering is trustable, and then use the only human technology interface device worth using more of, the personal handshake.

# Copyleft –
## the battle of open think freeware

Our Lifesigns Network also tells us that if we are entering a more intimate, tactile and emotional cycle of the culture, we are also entering one where old rules and laws no longer apply – even laws we want, or rules we ourselves intend to continue following.

Copyleft and open source economies, brands and organizations are areas that our network and others continue to pick up on, and yet most companies we deal with – especially those involved in the areas of design, medicine, music, film making and distribution – refuse to see these as legitimate areas of concern and debate, or indeed serious options for their futures. By this we can only assume they mean their profits and not their futures since one isn't always the same as the other, or indeed tied into the other.

This is why it is worth stating again – your network needs to be real, vital and plugged into the culture as it is, as it is also shaping up. It should not be kitted out with industry cronies, or indeed top heavy with cronies from your tangential businesses telling you what you want to hear or how to shield yourself from the outside.

Your network should tell you things as they are – make you look at things as you have never looked at them before; cast light on subject areas you know nothing about; tap you into people who can tap you into radical thoughts, contrary actions, open up new pathways and take you down deviant streets.

So if you are a music brand like Sony or EMI, you should have your network populated with counterfeiters, hackers, software pirates and customers who object to the amount you charge for CDs and DVDs that cost cents to make.

If you are a city business with software security problems, you should also find warchalkers like Matt Jones in your network – open plan hackers who leave hobo style chalk marks on city pavements and corporate headquarters, symbols recognizable to hackers telling them where they can find unprotected wireless networks they can firewire into free of charge.

Likewise, if you are a film maker, distributor or studio, you should have in your network the names behind websites like MusicCity.com that use Morpheus file sharing software, or Grokster LTD and Consumer Empowerment BV – in other words people who are enabling web users to download pirate copies of the latest Hollywood films. This is true network etiquette – the best way to do your market research. Deviance, then, is anything that is contrary to how you think about things, or indeed how you and your brand or company fit into the market. Just because you play this way doesn't mean that everybody else does, or will continue to do so.

> **❝ Just because you play this way doesn't mean that everybody else does, or will continue to do so. ❞**

Take Napster, or the hackers who learned how to turn Microsoft's Xbox games console into the hardware tool of choice for upmarket games, music and films counterfeiters and copiers. The Xbox allows you to log on to the web and play games in a virtual arena, or with other Xbox owners online. Tweaking the system's software, and with the help of a £45 chip available from most hacker sites online, you can convert the Xbox into a high resolution capturing machine that enables the swopping and sharing of software, and also the downloading of films, CDs and DVDs from legal and illegal content sites.

## ▉ Customers like pirates but hate excessive profiteers

Yes, this kind of activity is illegal and, yes, it might cost the movie business £2bn in lost revenues annually, but pirating as a trend is not something consumers are necessarily all that bothered about, especially when more and more of them – thanks to the connectivity the net offers – realize how little a CD or DVD can be produced for.

More to the point, they saw attempts to close Napster and similar sites as contrary to the spirit of the net and, worse, as open sourcing becomes a philosophy as much as a way of doing things, the notion of copyright itself has come under widespread scrutiny and criticism. Men like Lawrence Lessing, a Harvard professor who helped mount the case against Microsoft in the US Supreme Court, believes that the internet functions as an electronic commons and should be viewed as such – a means of free speech and free association. So much so that copyright (as in protecting an idea, area or development from being used by others) is, in effect, limiting creativity and runs against the spirit of the net.

Most online edge dwellers and early settlers agree and are now taking these ideas – of open sourcing, copyleft, collaborative practices and of intellectual tagging – offline and into the real world. Lessing sees it this way – the vast majority of current intellectual property used to be in the public domain (books, paintings, songs, poems, ideas) but now, as with many of the ideas expressed in this book, one has to seek permission to use them or one has to pay for them.

Lessing uses Walt Disney as an example to show how the Disney brand has killed the future. US constitutional law – thanks to lobbying from organizations like Disney – now states that copyright which automatically lapsed 14 years after its creator's death should be extended to 70 years, as it now is.

This, says Lessing, means that one of Disney's first cartoons, *Steam Boat Willie* – a clip of which he shows to demonstrate his point – effectively remains out of the public domain indefinitely as subsequent renewals of the copyright are sought by the company. As a historic document landmarking a key moment in the visual culture when sound animation came into its own, it cannot be shown or otherwise used without the express permisison of the owners – nor can a remake be made.

Fair dues some people may say but, as Lessing points out, if Disney were confronted with this law from its inception where would it be today? *Snow White and the Seven Dwarfs, Sleeping Beauty, The Hunchback of Notre Dame, Pinocchio* – how much, as he wryly puts it, have the Brothers Grimm had from the brothers Disney? His specific point illustrates a bigger problem with copyright and the ever greater emphasis that big businesses and corporations place on intellectual property and copyright ownership.

What happens if you are a billionaire and buy a painting by Van Gogh (you own the painting and, as a consequence, rights to its copyright). Then, as you are dying you demand (as one Japanese billionaire demanded) that the painting be placed on your funeral pyre!

Or think how biotech companies are patenting our genes – yes, our genes! Imagine then you have cancer, a liver complaint or need an organ transplant or medication to cure Parkinson's disease. Imagine that these have been biogenetically produced (which is happening). You will have to pay for the transplant, or the medicine without a doubt, but you may also have to pay a royalty for use of the genes involved – even if they are genes found in the human body, your body. Why? Because biotech companies are already registering them and slapping patents on them. Even worse, they are controlling and licensing out their use!

So cancer researchers, in addition to having to find funds for their research, may soon be expected to find funds to rent the copywritten genes so they can continue their valuable work. Now that creativity and intellectual property values outstrip the combined profits made from cars, chemicals, steel and the clothing industry in the US, brands and businesses are becoming even more litigious about protecting what they own.

Wrong says Lessing – this will kill creativity and hamper future research. And more and more people are agreeing with him. Netizens agree with him. To them copyright is a way of limiting creativity and controlling how ideas are used and developed. Biotech companies have also found this to be the case. Unless they own the rights to a particular gene, they now have to pay a royalty or usage fee to the companies – usually competitors – that decoded them in the first place. Many are finding this problematic and admit that it is slowing down research into areas such as cancer and heart disease.

## ■ Collaborative and open source infringement agreements are the way forward

Out of these deviations from the norm (or the accepted) our network is seeing two trends that all plugged-in networks should be picking up on – trends which we believe are set to cause huge social, ethical and commercial problems for brands and corporations of the future:

■ the shift away from companies going it alone in product development towards a more open source, federated approach;

■ the growth of copyleft patents, and pro- or positive infringement agreements where products, services or brand categories are created with a view to being continuously worked on, added to, improved or copied, in the way the original Linux software was created and grown.

**❝ Where a scatter of smaller, more federally structured companies can carry the cost of the research and development process. ❞**

Biotech brands are already seeing the wisdom of this. While pharmaceutical companies – crippled on one side by escalating costs and on the other by dents in their profits from the proliferation of generic medicines (an anti-patents trend in its own right and one we thoroughly applaud) – are choosing to work within open source style communities where a scatter of smaller, more federally structured companies can carry the cost of the research and development process and in return benefit from a share of the profits in the form of communal royalties when the product goes to market.

Certainly, as developing world economies run to catch up with their First World sisters, copyleft will perversely become one of the few ways in which a company can protect its ideas, medicines, clothing designs, products and brands in a market where generic medicines and product cloning are not only an accepted part of the development process, but deemed necessary since so many of the original products are way beyond the price range of even the most affluent of developing world wage earners. According to *BusinessWeek*, two-thirds of the global population now make £1000 or less annually.

Already brands like Philips, Unilever, Procter & Gamble and Motorola have taken a leaf from E.F. Schumacher's *Small is Beautiful* philosophy and produced miniaturized or 'one use' versions of their top selling products including shampoos, deodorants, mascaras, reading glasses and margarine sachets in an attempt to tackle this problem. Consequently, Unilever alone has netted a substantial £30bn from miniaturized product sales.

But this will not stop the cloning from happening – especially if, as developing world consumers do, people want more rather than less. And if these can be produced cheaply – as is happening in India, China, Brazil and South East Asia – by copying and with the tacit approval of governments, then the only way forward is to share the costs of R&D investment, manufacturing, distribution, sales and marketing across many companies, and by involving many (including the counterfeiters and cloners) ensuring that all have a collective interest in keeping cloning and counterfeiting to a minimum. It is worth pointing out here that regardless of what you think of cloning or counterfeiting, the consumer does not share your concerns. As our own researches show, they see counterfeiters as latter day Robin Hoods robbing the rich to aid the poor. Most have no reservations about buying copies and few are inclined to report the culprits – especially since digital technology has ensured that the clones are every bit as professionally produced as the original, but a lot cheaper.

Aside from cloning, current obsessions with cheapness and the lack of creativity among most mainstream manufacturers have given rise to what our Lifesigns Network terms 'copycat culture' or 'lookalike products'. This is a trick whereby brands bereft of ideas, clinging to old ways of reading or monitoring consumer shifts, simply wait for a competitor's product to be launched, see how it does and if it works simply swamp the market with a cheaper, not always shoddier, version.

Good for the consumer maybe, but for R & D or brands genuinely concerned about innovation, originality is a costly trend indeed. Procter & Gamble thought its £30 a pop *Swiffer WetJet* mop would clean up, and it did until a raft of copycat versions forced the firm to halve its price in seven months. Kyocera Corps QCP 6035 Smartphone likewise looked like a winner – a PDA and web-friendly package that came in at £300 was a guaranteed seller to cosmocrats and hypermobile workers alike, until Samsung launched a similar PDA package with a colour screen, forcing Kyocera to drop its price to £100.

Again excellent for the consumer, in the short term at least, but long term, what you are seeing is a growing reluctance by mainstream companies and brands to invest in the one area that insulates them against long term malaise – research and development, innovation, the sheer pleasure of coming up with something new. This is why our network believes copyleft and open source arrangements have yet to come into their own – as a way of sharing costs and keeping markets agile, but also as an emergent system of manufacturing that can keep cloning at bay. But only if the customer shares the same network and is granted the same access to that network as the companies working to provide products for them.

> **❝ Open source and copyleft are just what they suggest – radically different ways of satisfying tomorrow's market needs. ❞**

## ■ The future is about negotiated trust

Open source and copyleft are just what they suggest – radically different ways of satisfying tomorrow's market needs. As Max Nathan of the Work Foundation (one of the UK's most advanced think-tanks dealing with networks, social change and the way it impacts on our social and business landscapes) puts it, 'Networks are social capital engines: they run on trust and loyalty, just as much as technology' and this is something more and more companies, brands and organizations are having to come to terms with. The future isn't just about collaboration, it's about negotiated trust and about allowing the many rather than the few to own intellectual patents, ideas and copyleft agreements.

# Network people:
## and how to use them

# Anatomy of a network –
## working from the bottom up

All that from a few deviants! And, hopefully, between the lines you got a sense of how networks should be used and the kind of people you should be plugging into them. If you didn't, here's the simple, no frills version – the key to any network's success are the people you invite to join it. Your deviants. But so too is choosing the kind of deviants who think in the way E. O. Wilson believes we should think – consiliently – if we are to advance our store of knowledge and insight across disciplines.

William Whewell, in his 1840 synthesis *The Philosophy of the Inductive Science*, explains consilience as a 'jumping together' of knowledge, links, facts, ideas, theories and insights from a variety of disciplines to form a new theory, or common ground, that serves to throw light, not just on the areas examined but to illuminate new ones and in the process, perhaps, provide us with a more uniform or universal insight into bigger issues.

His belief, like that of Wilson and many of the economists, sociobiologists, market analysts and evolutionary biologists now studying complexity theory and emergent or agent-based systems, is that there are similar laws which affect all areas and that looking to one field will teach you about another. This will also allow you to observe parallel or similar social, scientific or cultural shifts and better understand how and why they work.

This is an idea bussed in from the Enlightenment – that period of scientific, social, cultural and critical revolution when a man with many disciplines and many understandings of seemingly disparate areas of life, was more of a thinker or player than one who saw himself as a narrowcast specialist, or that worst and boorish of all types of men, an expert.

Then you had one of the best and most famous of networks – the men of the Lunar Society, dilettantes, gentlemen farmers, doctors, eagle-eyed adherents to the many changes being noted by like-minded souls in France, Prussia and Scotland. All known to each other, all amateur scientists, all keen on self-improvement. Their names were Matthew Boulton and Josiah Wedgewood, the self-made industrialists. Then there was Erasmus Darwin, James Watt and Joseph Priestley – all luminaries whose exploits are writ large in the annals of scientific achievement, and also in lesser fields such as carriage design, steam, minerals, clocks, cylinders, the boiling of copal, the making and use of lenses, colours for enamels, alkalis and canals; even, as the historian Jenny Uglow puts it, 'the boil on Watt's nose.'

> **❝ The trouble with experts when it comes to networks is that they are myopic in outlook and singular in the understanding of the bigger picture. ❞**

Not experts, but intellectual extroverts. Open plan, open source idealists with open plan, open source minds that defied the lone and narrow. The trouble with experts when it comes to networks is that they are myopic in outlook and singular in the understanding of the bigger picture.

Indeed, rarely do they see the bigger picture – like in the Indian folk tale about the old elephant and the six blind men – more times than not viewing things via their little fragment of the universe. So the choice of networker is particularly critical. A deviant yes, but also a connector, a doer and engager; somebody that brailles the culture along consilient lines; someone who listens, observes, records and interprets but across a number of key interlocking social, cultural, environmental, economic and scientific areas.

As described earlier, by 'brailling' we mean reading, scanning, or engaging with the world around them in a tactile and hands-on way – in bars, clubs, offices, the university campus, along the street, in a house, in conversation, in the lab, in the city.

By 'record' we mean in descriptive diary format with a digital camera (easy to capture images and send them back to the office) or video – or if music is the issue, on tape or minidisc.

By 'contextualize' we mean putting their observations into the bigger micro- or macro-picture. The micro pictue is from the area the phenomenon was observed – in design perhaps there is a shift towards emotional, softer surfaces; in advertising a more emotional and poetic way of selling financial services. In the macroworld, or in our bigger picture, it is a mood that is about US rather than ME.

## ■ Feedback and reporting

This is how a trend report begins – a shift in the visual, social or scientific culture around us is noted. From a single, seemingly inconsequential observation like the one made by Liz Hancock, one of our network members (who writes on architecture, the environment, design, beauty, fashion and technology), beauty editor of the UK fashion, music and lifestyle indie, *ID* magazine.

In one of her conversations she had commented how beauty products – as in the ingredients they contained – seemed to be getting more edible, as she put it. She didn't mean you could eat them, only that they seemed to have the kind of aroma and ingredients that made them more tantalizing or appealing in terms of how they played on the senses. Tactile, in other words, emotional, things that were about the senses or the soul.

Another network member, Lakshmi Bhaskaran (who also writes on design, interiors, ethnography, fashion, culture, street tribes, graphics and architecture) agreed that she knew what she meant, well almost. She had been interviewing designer Marc Newson for *Viewpoint* magazine and had made a similar comment to him about his design style and a car project he was working on for Ford.

She said it reminded her of a 'Noddy car, something cheerful, tactile – the kind of car that made you want to give it a name and regard it as a friend.' In another interview she had done with Apple's Jonathan Ives, the man who gave us the

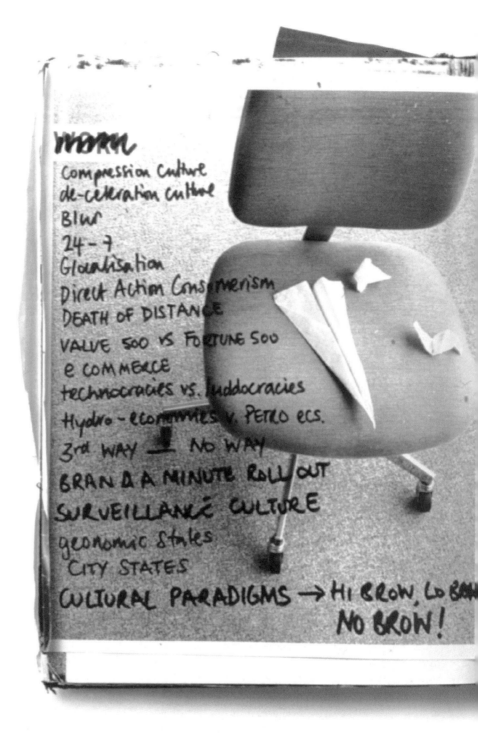

WORK
Compression Culture
de-celeration culture
Blur
24-7
Globalisation
Direct Action Conservenism
DEATH OF DISTANCE
VALUE 500 VS FORTUNE 500
e COMMERCE
technocracies vs. luddocracies
Hydro-economies v. PETRO ecs.
3rd WAY ⊥ NO WAY
BRAND A MINUTE ROLL OUT
SURVEILLANCE CULTURE
geonomic States
CITY STATES
CULTURAL PARADIGMS → HI BROW, LO BROW
    NO BROW!

Lifesigns Network notebooks are assembled by researchers in association with gatekeepers and key 'edge' or deviant groups. In this case, 'new economy' executives who are trying to identify what constituted 'work' or notions of work in the latter years of the 90s.

# BUZZWORDS du jour

NEW HEDONISM

TASTE-OCRATS

GATED LIFESTYLES

STATUS ZONES

THERAPY TRAVEL

COSMOCRATS

GRIT GIRLS

SINDIES

LIMELIGHT PEOPLE

PROSUMERS

NUPPIES

ZONING OUT

OPEN SOURCING

KNOWLEDGE

INFORMATION

IMAGINEERING

SIGNIFICANCE

ENERGIZE

?? BACKGROUNDING

CREATICITY

IMAGINARIUM

KNOWLEDGE CONSUL

FACILITATOR

SLINGSHOT

MARKETING

?COSERIATRICS

ROBODRUGS

P2P

SINGULARITY

SCRIBBLE THEREFORE I AM

jellybean iMac and the titanium G4 notebook, the product that has become the cosmocratic tool of hypermobile types everywhere, she recalled a phrase he used about the iMac. Talking about the design of the housing for the product, how much of the cabling and bits that normally stick out and clutter desks had been incorporated in such a way that the end product appeared 'self-contained, and I think that makes it feel vital and a little bit cheeky.' 'Vital' and 'cheeky' were the words that struck Lakshmi – words usually used to describe people or characters, not objects.

Another network member who had just returned from one of those brainstorming sessions at Philips Design in Eindhoven suggested that we should check out some of the work they're doing there on the shape, texture and 'personality' of the products for tomorrow.

We did and were duly impressed, not just with the products themselves, which were tactile, emotional, touchy-feely shapes and surfaces, in tactile, emotional, touchy-feely colours, but also with where it was leading us. Or what it was suggesting.

So we put some questions out to our network – all our networkers can log on to the Future Laboratory's extranet – and started trawling through the week's reports in case there were any images, bulletins or rants. Occasionally networkers simply stream down their thoughts as 'bloggs' or web logs as and when things are happening, so the results, although fresh, vital and energetic, can also read like a bit of Irvine Welsh without the benefit of full stops or paragraph spaces!

The replies, usually within 24 hours – which is what makes the network so useful – gave us more than enough of what we were looking for from the week's diaries, e-mails and jpeg downloads. There was a note about a new club-class chair designed by Tangerine – a soft rounded, tactile unit that interlocked in a love seat S-shape making the area, and sense of area it enclosed, snug and emotionally inclusive.

Somebody else had sent us images of jet interiors by Marc Newson, which looked vaguely, and for our purposes reassuringly, like the ones just executed for BA by Tangerine. There was short piece on a kettle from a company called Softroom and a chair by Ross Lovegrove. From a networker at the Milan Furniture Fair – our networkers have digital cameras which attach to their laptops to e-mail photographs to our London studios – a piece about LuxLab (a group of French designers) and their attempts to create products and spaces that were 'about the physical and spiritual sensuality of the elements . . . a naive seduction . . . a generous innocence. Emotions are brought closer to pure sensations, leading to the rediscovery of a tactile, visual, olfactory serenity that does not depend on one's cultural references . . .'

Okay they were French, but you get the point – their work was about tactile surfaces, malleable materials, gardens that grew into the house! When this happens, when you see things cropping up in one discipline that are similar to ideas, shapes or material usage in other disciplines, then you know you're onto something.

The objects and images we were looking at were soft, malleable, almost edible. The designs were curved, human, tactile and, in many cases, finished in colours that were bright, or at least funny and uplifting – tangy oranges, yellows, blues, dancing greens and sharp reds. Not rectilinear, not hard, not about minimal surfaces and slick metallic or concrete finishes.

But we also noted something else. Some networkers had scanned in and jpeged images of offices they had visited during the course of their work. Some showed us images of people on microscooters hurtling along parquet floors (one was from Palo Alto, the other Seattle). Others featured offices with grass lawns, playground swings, desks with beds under them, garden furniture and golf buggies being used *Prisoner*-style (the cult 60s TV series) to transport people up and down corridors. There were images of people chilling, having fun, being happy and emotional, but also images of people in the very places these emotions are not normally allowed to flourish in. So we contacted our networkers in the city, those working in the area of sociology, and asked them to ask the CEOs, or researchers they were in touch with, if these shifts had been noticed there.

One of our people at KPMG came back with details about areas they were now looking at – 'emotional intelligence' and a phrase they kept hearing, 'irrational exuberance'. Another networker put us in touch with the early research work of Bruno Frey and Alois Stutzer who were to eventually publish their *Happiness and Economics* to much acclaim – a study of how the economy and institutions affect human well-being – and also Andrew J. Oswald, whose *Happiness Index* has now become something of a cult measuring, as it does, the things, moods, emotions and financial incentives that make us happy across Europe.

We also heard from Rob Clarke, CEO of Leo Burnett, Sydney, whose office featured in two of the images. He told us, 'We wanted an open plan environment which would promote creativity, interaction and communication among our staff because the most important aspect of our business is our people. Leo Burnett is an open, energetic, innovative company and our building not only fosters this culture, but helps promote this image.'

All the companies we contacted – including Tellme.com; Deckchair.com; Thomas Cook's call centre in Falkirk with a stream running through it, real palm trees and a sensorama with tropical sounds and smells; the KI building in Tokyo with its air conditioning designed to simulate real breezes; the Amsterdam offices of advertising agency KesselsKramer, with wooden towers, garden sheds and astroturf floors – offered similar responses. Their buildings were about fun, humour, emotions, making people feel they belonged or connected more positively with their environments. All this seems a long time ago now.

When we checked the network responses to our queries about whether or not members had noticed similar patterns internationally, we were, as usual, amused and surprised by the results.

Check out the work of Ron Arad – accompanying images showed us soft curve, anamorphic shapes and products. Look at this by IDEO, this by Sony, Dell, Zenith, Samsung – a single product rather than a range, a one-off, a statistical blip, a post-modern anomaly but across ranges and cultures, communities and disciplines. We were getting images from architects like Zaha Hadid, Daniel Liebeskind and Frank Gehry that spoke of ecstatic buildings – buildings for the emotions rather than the mind.

Key words then, along with key images and asides, were coming thick and fast – vitality, humour, emotion, tactility, colour, engagement, soft, edible, inviting, fun. Words and phrases that connected, words and phrases and images that seemed to be suggesting a similar sensibility, ethos or outlook.

> **The great advantage of running a network that works federally is the feedback that starts coming in.**

The great advantage of running a network that works federally – as in each hub talking directly to the others, as well as to the Future Laboratory in London – is the feedback that starts coming in at the same time. A flow of details about books, papers, journals, people, magazines, TV programmes, websites all containing similar references.

## ■ Network cascades

This is what we call a 'network cascade' – it suddenly goes live with the kinds of things that flood our computers with jpegs, e-mails, PDFs and video streams; our website with a backlog of e-mails to sift through; our faxes with photographs, photocopied articles; our mail with books, CDs, magazines, microzines and rants.

At this time the main Future Laboratory team meets to discuss what the trend means, or what it suggests. 'Mean' and 'suggest' being two completely different things. One is about the evidence as presented. The other is about the possibilities or insights the evidence throws up. The present versus the future.

In this stage it should be noted that the network is gathering and collating ideas, images and snags of information – it isn't interpreting or making assumptions about its findings.

It is important to keep these activities separate. Too many wrong questions at the beginning of a braille or a cultural dig (as some networks call this process) can skew the quality and diversity of the information (as opposed to knowledge) being collected. In this stage we are still dealing in the realms of information. The next step is about turning this into knowledge.

# Network procedures –
## etiquette and communication

It is important that all your networkers agree what it is you are looking at and talking about. This is a common big failure of networks – talking differently about the same thing or, worse, talking the same about different things!

From the outset, ensure that everybody understands what it is that is under discussion – especially if your network includes members from different countries or different geographic regions, which it should. This is easily done by posting an abstract of the issue under discussion on the network's bulletin board.

But keep it short, and keep it open. Make sure it is a statement that defines the task under review but not one that constrains investigation. A common fault we find with many companies using this method – they pin their networks down. Don't! Networks need to be open, to reach out, especially at the brailling stage of the research exercise.

Remember, what we've been looking at so far came from a single, some would argue throw-away, comment by one of our network members about cosmetics and beauty products being edible. This is the starting point from which all our discussions and considerations begin. So do not say things such as, 'We are only concerned about edibility and the food sector,' or 'Edibility and what it means to designers or to a brand's intangible assets'. Just define at this stage what your network has identified so far as 'edible' or 'edibility' and then allow the network to start exploring the potential of this word – to work out and away from the original statement.

But towards what? Well not just edible cosmetics, but edible everything – or at least designed products, offices, ideas and buildings that seem to come with the same in-built characteristics.

We do, however, attempt to kick-start things with the in-house Future Laboratory team. This is made up of an ethnographer, our creative directors, a design anthropologist, a psychologist, a videomaker, an artist and our network futurologists. They will discuss this and attempt to come up with a term that encapsulates the key characteristics of the areas, activities, shapes and sensibilities we're picking up on.

Emotion was key; likewise technology. Many of the shapes were curved, malleable, textured, deformed and could only have been created like this via CAD and by using extruding moulds and techniques that allow the creation of shapes not easily achievable with traditional assembly techniques.

After some debate, the term 'em tech' was coined – em for emotion and tech for technology. Emotional technology because these were the key words and characteristics we were picking up on in the design of the objects themselves.

'But what about the offices?' our anthropologist asked, 'or phrases like irrational exuberance?' They're about emotion yes, but they're also about fun, engagement and play.

There were other points he picked up on. Someone had contacted another networker about a book they were working on that was intending to look at how creativity could be released in the office and in the boardroom. They had described the book not in numbing number-crunching terms, but in terms of emotion and soul. Could this relate in any way to the issue in hand?

Okay, soul wasn't necessarily fun but it was emotion, and didn't somebody – the guy from Leo Burnett's – mention spirit or spirituality? There was also Daniel Goleman's 'emotional intelligence' our anthropologist said, not new but it certainly had a key point to make on the subject. So maybe there was something else happening – we hadn't quite rumbled irrational economics yet, or that *irrational exuberance* was actually the title of Rob Shiller's book; one that would, as *Fast Company* magazine put it, turn him into 'the E. F. Hutton of the new economy'.

But we knew one thing – it wasn't just about em tech. The trend or mood we had hit on was the tip of a much bigger shift that we wanted to know more about. Another networker sent through a note, someone who worked at Bloomsbury Publishing in fact. They'd had a manuscript in – one about spiritual intelligence – and it might be worth checking out. Something about how we need to reconnect with the world around us on a more intuitive level. This always happens when you're chasing up a new trend or cultural shift – you stumble on one thing and get led into another.

Which is why teasing issues out at this stage is vitally important. Our em tech trend, as we dubbed it, was and is about surface, and the way surface has changed from hard to soft, linear to curved, minimal in colour to colours that warm and amuse. (It is now going back to lines, to luxe, to lacquered surfaces and rich, expensive colours and finishes – but neutral, calm, quiet symbols and symptoms of stealth wealth and whispering below-the-radar luxury.)

> **❝ This always happens when you're chasing up a new trend or cultural shift – you stumble on one thing and get led into another. ❞**

This new current or strand we were picking up on was about the spirit, the soul and exuberance and, as we were beginning to see, irrationality and chaos. Our anthropologist and ethnographer wanted to know if it wasn't two sides of the same coin. Or – since we have a habit of thinking of trends as viruses, or surface symptoms of an inner malaise, illness, spiritual shift or yearning – an eternal manifestation of an inner mood or movement.

Both were about emotions after all, or sensibilities that were doing similar things – playing on notions of spirit, poetry, tactility and engagement, childish exuberance. One showing up as a paradigm shift in how we design and sculpt things, the other as a paradigm shift in how we think about work and the places we work in. Also how the economy should be read or regarded – not as a rational and linear system, but as a rollercoaster with dip and plunge, playful and childlike perhaps, irrational and mischievous. This would make sense. Particularly to another network member who spends most of her time – between baking sourdough loaves and walking dogs on Normandy beaches – trawling obscure websites, ancient PhD theses and learned journals for ideas that slip though the culture.

She drew our attention to a publication called *The Elliot Wave Theorist*, a monthly journal based on the works of Ralph N. Elliot, a Los Angeles accountant who, jobless and in poor health during the Great Depression years, spent his time investigating stock market figures and trying to work out why the markets lost 90 per cent of their value over a three-year period.

He experienced one of those great leaps we've already discussed. He noted that markets worked to cycles, but also that these cycles didn't originate within the markets themselves but within society, that they were driven by human, and therefore very volatile, needs. 'Human emotions are rhythmical: they move in waves,' he said, 'of a definite number and direction. The phenomenon occurs in all human activities, be it business, politics or the pursuit of pleasure.' He also noted that these waves were made up of two waves, where each was either an upward impulse or a downward corrective movement.

Further investigation told him however that these waves were in fact far from straight or curved, but were subdivided into smaller waves. An impulse wave might contain five smaller waves, and a corrective wave might be divided into three down-up-down waves. An Elliot wave then, far from being a wave, was something of an updownupdownupdownupdown affair, but one he was able to use to predict quite accurately that the worst bits of the market's fall in the 40s were in fact the worst bits and that an impulse market was on its way – one that would last for quite a few decades.

There was, said our networker, something emotional and irrational in how Elliot read the markets and how his wave system worked – a system also used by the financial gurus to second guess the markets during the 80s.

But there was more. In a piece in the *New Scientist*, she noted that the Elliot wave, or rather the fractional ups and downs of the wave and its sequences, were all too similar to the series of numbers 1, 1, 2, 3, 5, 8, 13, 21, that had been identified as a Fibonacci sequence, the underlying pattern found in fractal generation, or the sequence that led people to look at the much bigger issue of chaos and chaos theory. Something for us to think about?

The chaotic play of markets – or rather markets played to a chaotic rhythm?

Something to think about indeed. Already it had taken us quite some distance from our starting point 'edibility'. Which told us we were on to something – or as Holmes would say, 'The game is afoot, Watson.'

# Freeform thinking –
## keeping it fluid

So we put the network on it once more – this time telling them to ignore the visual world and look at the corporate, the scientific, the cultural. What were the themes people were picking up on here? Wellspring buzz words? Moods? Anything that seemed contradictory to current business practice?

Needless to say, this being towards the end of the 90s, there were themes beginning to bubble up. Everybody was talking about engaging with the customer, about being excessive, emphatic and fresh, about dressing down, having fun or breaking out – and also about how 'irrationality was becoming the new rationale' as Robert Shiller puts it.

Everybody we looked at seemed to be doing it – Ernst & Young, IBM, Merrill Lynch – soul, sensitivity, having fun and letting go, but also looking at how the chaos these things could cause wasn't necessarily bad, but part of a bigger system or shift. The dotcom thing was in full swing then, and the markets were going ballistic, 'an irrational, self-propelled, self-inflated bubble' wrote Shiller.

There were even economists at Stanford, LSE and the Sante Fe Institute talking of the emotional qualities of a market – how markets were as irrational as people and perhaps should be measured with this in mind.

Somewhere in the office there was an old copy of a then little-known magazine called *Fast Company* dating back to 1997. Emblazoned on its cover were the words 'The New Rules of Business' and other firebrand statements such as 'work is personal', 'knowledge is power' and, better still, that all readers should 'break the rules'.

So this newness, or new sensitivity, wasn't fresh off the press as a trend, merely new to the areas we were plugging into – the mainstream, or as our anthropologist kept calling it, the old economy. Em tech might be part of this move, he argued, but was probably a product of it, or simply the same shift happening in a different area of the culture – E.O. Wilson's consilience theory – a dressing down of products, if you like, in the way that old company models and methods were dressing down.

## ■ A more soulful bottom line

Like products themselves, their makers were becoming more soulful, more concerned about emotions, about the net worth of the bottom line in terms of people rather than profits. Internally and externally. They were also putting customers first – a response Wilson thought to the whole Palo Alto latte and chinos thing – he was and is a wag as well as a keen cultural observer.

Nerds may be nerdy, our anthropologist told us, but they've come up with things that people can't ignore – and 'I don't mean the plug and play office, but the way it seems less threatening to staff and customers, especially the latter.'

He was thinking here of Google, Hotmail, wi-fi, bootlegging, open sourcing, Linux, MP3, Napster. Of names like Shawn Fanning, David Filo and Jerry Yang, Larry Page and Sergy Brin. Oh yes and Bill Gates, Steve Job and Tim Berners Lee – all nerds plugged into networks of one kind or another and all dedicated to the idea that connectivity (okay, maybe Gates no longer wants to play in the sandpit), free association and idea sharing were a good way to kick-start new ideas and outlooks. And the latte? Well he had this idea that good coffee and this kind of approach to work went hand in hand.

And irrational exuberance? Was this part of the same thing? Is it just about fun?

This we couldn't decide on, but one thing you learn to do quickly as a networker, or as part of a network team, is to chase things up, doing one of those random, wide ranging cultural trawls that clients do when they visit the office, soon leaving with a look of despair on their face or, if they're the right kind of clients, pulling their sleeves up and tucking in – which is what good cultural brailling is all about, wading in and setting to.

So by now, having identified one trend we were happy with, our em tech trend, and having sent researchers off to produce the required visual, emotional and reference-based reports on this (some of which appear as part of our trend briefing sessions, others as issues of *Viewpoint* magazine – on personalization, fun, connectivity, blur, networks, sonic branding, regendering, etc.), we were working on the premise that the fun office bit might or might not be part of it, might in fact be part of a shift towards a new kind of workspace or place to hang out in. A 'transpace' or a transgressional space where home, office and socializing met. So could this be the new office? The new way of working for all those portfolio careerists the transient economy was throwing up? We thought it might, so we hived it off and looked at new economy work patterns, at the federal office, at 'transpace' work politics, and produced a number of keenly read reports, from the design of these spaces to how people worked and negotiated them.

But there was still this thing on irrational exuberance – talk of complex systems; of irrational expectation models; of papers being written by W. Brian Arthur and Matthew Rubin about systems that behaved irrationally and emotionally, from biology to economics; of work being pioneered in places like the Sante Fe Institute that was attempting to map out the rules and by-laws of complex adaptive systems; of other investigations being carried out into social structures and people management systems by Robert Axelrod (now Professor of Political Science and Public Policy at the University of Michigan) and Michael D. Cohen (Professor of Information and Public Policy at the same university) that looked at how complex systems could be observed to better understand how people work together.

Or why regions in northern Italy prospered because of how they interconnected, worked along emergent lines with node and hub mechanisms that held them together, pumped wealth, ideas and knowledge through them in the way power curve networks do. And why those in the south remained poor because of few network connections, fewer loose-tie associations, less variety and, dare we say it, the social deviancy built into their social structures (the church, family, the Mafia) to keep them vibrant and alive!

> **Prospered because of how they interconnected, worked along emergent lines with node and hub mechanisms that held them together.**

Their book *Harnessing Complexity* is a model of its kind. It lays out for those who want to know more what complexity means to organizations and how it can be harnessed to kick-start creative drives, mine new markets and offer keen insights into how and why consumers think, act and behave in the way they do.

## ■ Be led by your network – don't lead it

From their work, and the names mentioned with them, we began to explore complexity as a trend, as a science, but also as keen way of understanding networks better, and how they might be developed to read the future. All that from a throwaway comment by one of our networkers on how she thought cosmetics were becoming edible!

Which is the beauty of networks arranged along the lines we've been discussing. They put out far more than any one individual can put in, but because all are connected, all speaking to each other – and to the team back in the office – the information gathered is shared and also converted in the process to knowledge and from that, when things are teased out, juxtaposed and blurred together in a particular way, a thing called insight.

Insight comes after knowledge, and knowledge after information and data. Insight is the thing that will help you see where you need to go; knowledge is the fuel that ignites insight; information and data are the stepping stones that enable you to walk towards knowledge.

It is important then that you understand this sequence and observe this process. Your network collects and assembles as much information and data as it can concerning the areas or trends under review. You then attempt to distil knowledge from them, and it is equally important that you tap into all the knowledge nodes that the gathering and processing throw up before you attempt to negotiate the next stage – the one that illuminates opportunity and future possibility.

# Enchanted looms –
## using networks to gain insight

This ability to hold things together, to think or work over a number of areas, or 'see' things all at once is what networkers call 'burning'. It is analogous to what radar operators in the US navy refer to as 'having the bubble' – a synchronous, almost spiritual moment when all that appears on the radar screens in front of them becomes a shifting, ever readable orrery of vectors, paths, planes, topographies and height-to-ground ratios and wind speeds that they can visualize in all dimensions, in real-time and with seemingly preternatural abilities to understand and then read them with insight.

These abilities allow the radar operators to read and manage all or individual elements of the scene as it is now, and as it will become in the future. They can use these moments of absolute lucidity to guide pilots through the most complex procedures; to soar high above an immediate event and look far ahead, guiding that pilot, missile, ship or convoy away from danger or towards its objective long before either of them has any idea that there is danger involved or even an objective to be achieved.

It is a 'cognitive leap' that allows them to integrate such diverse inputs as combat status, information flows from sensors and remote observation, and the real-time status and performance of the various weapons and systems into a single seamless picture of a plane's overall situation and operational status.

The great British neurobiologist Charles Sherrington saw the brain in similar terms. He described it as an enchanted loom, an elegant apparatus that could weave together a very insightful and beautiful picture of the external world, where it is, where it will be.

Good forecasters work and think like this, and when they hit the 'burn' this is when most of what they are looking at makes eloquent and profitable sense.

It is difficult to articulate but we all know that moment when it happens. For composer Aaron Copeland it was like eating or sleeping; for Wagner, like a cow producing milk; for Saint-Saëns, an apple tree producing apples. The reason says Howard Garner, author of *Frames of Mind: The Theory of Multiple Intelligence*, is that many kept notebooks with them to capture themes, ideas and snatches of musical notation that seemed to come to them 'as a gift from heaven, much like automatic writing.'

The best networkers think and operate like this. They store their knowledge, melding facts, ideas and fragments together in a way that outputs them as insights which sometimes seem quite distant from the initial facts as presented to them by outsiders. Our own networkers keep notebooks, visual, textual (and in some cases video, photographic and sound snatches) of moods, moments, trends, ideas, surveys, people, places, things and half-formed, still to be articulated, shifts they may be picking up on.

The notebooks on pages 22, 23, 96, 97, 110 and 111 are samples of this process. In many cases they are rostrum shot directly from life and used in client presentations to illustrate what it is that is being articulated. See these things as you see bar charts, pie charts, the hum of the Powerpoint display or the linear clarity of the Excel spreadsheet. In many cases they tell you as much, if not more, of what you need to know, the world in the round and real but also in the way the customer sees it – not as numerical peaks or troughs, or synthetic wedges shaded out of a perfect circle, but with the raw inconsistencies that makes this customer or that trend stand out from the rest. Once we asked customers to provide us with a shopping notebook of their trip to Sainsbury's, and expected back images of fruits, vegetables and the occasional shopping trolley.

What we got was a volume of missed opportunity – of crowded checkouts, trolley jams, poorly labelled aisles, fears about GM food and CJD, doubts that claims on the packaging were true and just, doubts too that processed foods were healthy, that things like chicken nuggets, fish fingers and beef burgers actually contained chicken or fish or beef.

Single mums, students and young couples felt victimized, or put out by the shop's obvious bias towards affluent, well-to-do families. They hated its Jamie Oliver displays and 'mockney' or mockcockney pretensions. Some had even gone to the trouble of explaining what they were doing to fellow shoppers and asked them to scribble in their books, so what started as a set of notebooks handed over to a diverse but representative group of shoppers became a spontaneous, engaging, and collaborative sortie showing how people shopped and what they thought when they were shopping.

## ▓ Consumer networks allow things to spread out and up

Those others who were asked to annotate the books by the shoppers we had chosen became very much a part of this process. Some even demanded (and were given) notebooks of their own because it looked fun, pleasurable, worthy of their time and energy. More importantly, it allowed for free range association and the

MONDAY

do notes on A CONSUMER MAP OF
TOMORROW

* Despite Naomi Klein rumours of Consumerism
DEATH — these are GREATLY EXAGGERATED!

REMEMBER - while only 20% of pop.
Think it's important to
wear designer clothes,
40% of 18-24's Say
* IT'S A MUST *

MS/ 8.05 pm
Naomi Klein
from Canada
Called -VAN.

* only 1 in 20 under 20's say they WOULDN'T buy
products from a multi-national That has done wrong

* 50% of young people Think it's important to
STAND OUT — brands They Say are just
one way to JUST DO IT!

* full book W @ Euro RSCG re both

Network notebooks – part of a series of notebooks created by city brokers and financial analysts in a workshop designed to illustrate how data and information can be used more dramatically when your insight network also contains artists, photographers, designers and visual analysts.

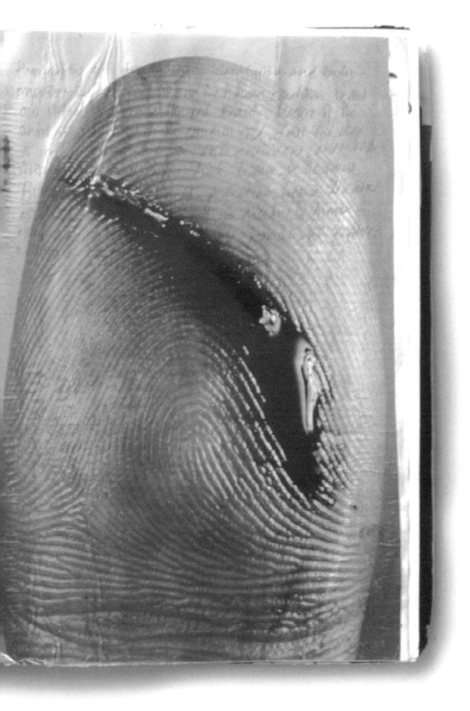

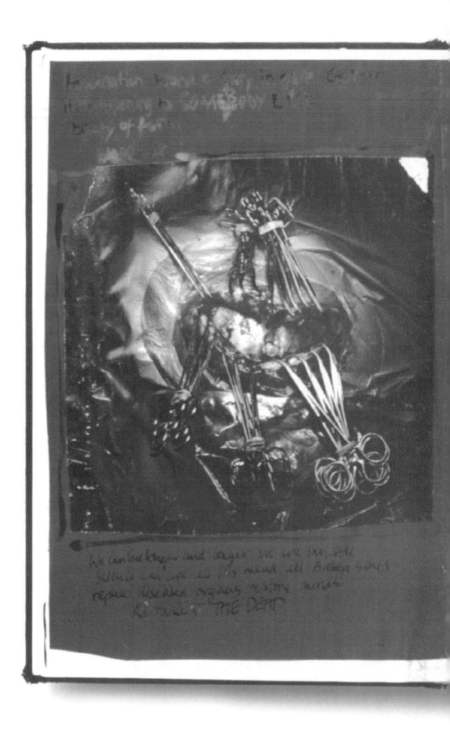

The cut and paste mechanisms and image juxtapositions we normally associate with the art student or more traditional fashion or lifestyle forecaster can and should be used to add emotion, drama and a sense of impetus to statements which in themselves may seem to be obvious.

TH

# IS THIS A CONSUMERIST CHARTER?!

CHANGING NATURE OF CONSUMER BUYING PATTERNS

RAISING SHOPPER EXPECTATIONS
RAISING THE BRAND EXPECTATIONS/NEEDS
RAISES RETAIL VALUE REMIT
REWRITES SHOPPING ACT AS:

> INFORMED
> INVOLVED
> INTERACTIVE
> INTERROGATIVE EXCHANGE OF
> MONEY FOR HOLISTIC EXPERIENCE

✓ MAKES ACT OF SHOPPING POLITICALLY/SOCIALLY
ENHANCING

✓ I SHOP THEREFORE I PARTICIPATE

"The status generation" replaces baby
boomers, Xer's as new core market
influencer

REDRAWS CLASS/SOCIETY LINES ALONG PATTERNS OF
CONSUMPTION

← getting to the
HEAD of the !
matter...

creativity for them, if we must put it bluntly, to design a marketing survey (for in essence this is what it was) to their specifications and not to ours nor Sainsbury's (who, by the way, didn't commission this). As a consequence it was something that they had a vested interest in doing to the best of their abilities.

Many, it has to be said, hated handing back the notebooks – they had become cherished items, minor works of art (although most were too modest to use such phrases). Oddly, and mainly, they had become that thing we took so much pleasure in doing as children – creating scrapbooks, private diaries, notebooks, memento moris of a journey or event. In this case, it was something familiar and banal, and in many cases time consuming – but done this way, and visited with intention, purpose and a sense that even in small things, bigger moments or ideas can be articulated, valued and thus become pleasurable and enabling acts.

## ■ Empowering customers empowers their responses

Who doesn't dream of going to the bank, the supermarket or the pub and having things their way? Who doesn't, when faced with a problem such as a queue, a jobsworth assistant or bar person, or poor service fantasize a way through this minefield of service sector indifference? People are good at working things out, so why not let them do it, and use it accordingly.

> **❝Who doesn't dream of going to the bank, the supermarket or the pub and having things their way?❞**

Many, it has to be said, do it in their notebooks. Some not so politely – indeed a few can resemble the jottings of Nirvana's Kurt Cobain, or those of a demented serial killer with bic biro in hand, but again this only reminds us of how angry most consumers are with the way brands and organizations treat them. Most, however, do it in ways that provide easy, ready and innovative solutions. For example, in our supermarket work, a fast track convenience aisle was suggested – one that contained only essential items so that time-pressed shoppers could slip in and out without cruising the aisles for household and fridgehold basics ('having a one-basket aisle' rather than a one-basket checkout as one shopper put it). Another suggested a section where customers were encouraged to take samples of their favourite items, best buys, healthiest, most indulgent foods and leave them in a customers' selections area so that others could benefit from their tips, make their own suggestions and generally build up a food and produce area of customers' favourites.

A place that was theirs, but a place too that provided a good way for the store to see shopping as their customers saw it. This would, as the notebooks put it, allow customers to talk and interact with staff and other customers, but also to allow them to feel that this experience was as much about them as it was about the store and staff – who only ever seemed to be doing anything when you approached them with a question!

Notebooks and networks allow you to do this – to encourage and grow and ride with spontaneity because there are few hierarchies, and even fewer rules that prohibit outward growth and development. You can literally let the network go with the flow and do what it needs to do.

Federal networks, because they interconnect the way the brain interconnects, aid this influx of stimulation tenfold. They offer up greater levels of insight, better possibilities for feedback, forward momentum and a more rounded view of how and what the consumer or market is thinking.

They also offer better structures within which to articulate and live out long view planning scenarios of the kind used by our network and network forecasters like SenseWorldwide, the Contemporary Trends Institute, the Global Business Network, Worth Global Style Network, Demos, the Tomorrow Project, Sociovision, CaptainCrikey.Com and Sputnik, all of which field a network of experts, or edge dwellers, into which each network proprietor delves or digs to braille the culture at that particular moment in time.

Networks of this nature tend to contain a small number of fairly select thinkers, radicals or cultural outriders. This can be as small as 150 – the number of people in our tribe or social milieu who we see daily, speak with face-to-face, and with whom we develop the kind of intellectual relationship that allows us to trust what they say, but also to develop short cuts in the way we communicate and work with them.

It is a kind of social telepathy that comes about because we develop a working understanding of their habits and thought processes, and the way they make intellectual leaps that others outside the group may find difficult to follow – and in the process slow down the capacity of the group to make the kind of collective jumps, or great leaps that good forecasting requires.

Historically it is a process whereby men or women as a tribe, group or new social order developed utilitarian or higher activity skill sets to a point where the 'intermingling' of key skills leads, as Steven Mithen (an archaeologist who has focused his work in this area) puts it, to a seemingly sudden and higher level of consciousness, or intellectual or spiritual 'jumping together' of the real or tangible world. In groups of 150 or so, this intermingling, these seemingly intuitive jumps or leaps, can be maximized to good effect.

Again, not necessarily by design or management, but by more radical and compelling evolutionary processes, according to Paul Brett (Professor of Organizational Behaviour at the Harvard Business School) and his colleague Professor Nitin Nohria (of the School's Organizational Behaviour Unit). They believe that man's nature is driven by four very different characteristics.

These characteristics are:

- the drive to acquire – why so many of us want to be rich;
- the drive to bond – why we see social, sexual and business bonding or networking as being so important;
- the drive to defend – why we are territorial about everything, from the houses we live in to the organizations or social groups we work in or belong to;
- the drive to learn – the one we see as the most important and the most far reaching when it comes to why networks are formed and how we can get them to work more insightfully.

This is why the small, discrete network can be most effective in making large, far-into-the-future predictions. Pooling ideas and resources, and their own higher intellectual 'takes' on a particular subject or area, they can and do create a new level platform or playing field from which to make even higher and more insightful leaps into the future.

This is why networkers tend to start with what they know and, like enthusiastic and curious children (curiosity being one of the great underlying factors in our drive to learn), start filling in the dots, or creating a communal or common pool of knowledge from existing information gaps and known facts or conjectures that they can then work from towards a higher, mutually stimulating goal.

When they reach points in this process which have ideas or information missing, then discussions take place, questions are asked, intellectual pylons are driven into the banks of existing knowledge. Then a significant minority – about 20 per cent of the network (remember the 80/20 rule?) – build bridges to facilitate that leap to the next stage of the puzzle they are grappling with.

The psychologist George Loewenstein, in his 1994 paper *The Psychology of Curiosity*, explains this as an attempt by the group or network to close or bridge what he calls the information gap, also named the ingenuity gap by Thomas Homer-Dixon, the environmentalist and political scientist in his book of the same name. These gaps are seen as good rather than bad. Challenges or puzzles that add to the pleasure of learning, because they remind the network that there are things to be learned after all, and that solving them will not only increase the total store of knowledge the network possesses, but also its sense of value and self-esteem.

The gap also 'Motivates the group, or individuals within it,' say Lawrence and Nohria, 'to seek an insight that reconciles the new observation by re-ordering their previous knowledge in a way that accommodates the new observation . . . Faced with inconsistency, the brain generates or imagines a set of possible resolutions (variety) until it finds one that restores consistency (selection), which is then preserved in long term memory (retention). This is how Darwin saw man as a species developing – via his V/S/R algorithm.'

It is also how Richard Dawkins describes the progress of the 'meme' gene through our culture and consciousness. Networks, we know, work very much like this – an idea colonizes a few select hubs and these hubs in turn pump it through the network, but only after they've boosted and amplified its strength or resonance.

Once this new level of knowledge has been attained, or a new bridge into the future built, the network will use it as a base line to operate from until a new 'information gap' challenges the supremacy of the old or accepted one.

> **❝ Once this new level of knowledge has been attained, the network will use it as a base line to operate from. ❞**

This is how something like 'edible cosmetics' becomes a trend called em tech design, which in turn leads to insight about fun, about new work practices, about third space work politics – and then on to higher concepts such as irrational exuberance and, finally, complex adaptive systems and emergent networks.

The connections may not be all that obvious to those outside the network, but to those within sometimes they don't even have to be articulated, in the way old Vaudevillians worked through their material when they met in one of the many bars they frequented around Times Square.

Instead of telling jokes, they would call out numbers, '2, 7, 28' and each in their turn would shrug and start laughing. People watching them thought they were mad, until it was explained that they knew the book of jokes they used so well that they only had to call out page numbers!

Again, this is why the most successful networks consist of the best, most adventurous, intellectually, spiritually or artistically acute people you can sign up. On the GBN roster you'll find Laurie Anderson, Napier Collyns, Brian Eno, William Gibson, Kevin Kelly, Manuel Castells, Douglas Coupland, W. Brian Arthur, Francis Fukuyama, the neurobiologist William Calvin, the head of Nissan UK, Ian Gibson – job title isn't important but the ability to work across disciplines, to broker new ideas and strategies from existing ones, is.

And to do it with flair, élan and an almost operatic imagination. Average has no use or place in this process whatsoever – networks need to raise the bar, not create one, and average does nothing but this.

Which is why discrete networks like those established and operated by collectives such as Sputnik or SenseWorldwide have taken so long to catch on in corporate UK and America. Operating outside the loop – beyond business, beyond marketing, beyond the arcane quantitative research methods used by agencies and brand managers – both work their network of DJs, web developers, film makers, electronic musicians, artists, club promoters, concept engineers, architects, designers and sonic brand specialists alongside their in-house team of forecasters to create portals or corridors through which the future can be glimpsed.

## ◼ Tactile browsers

This is about the network as a tactile browser, about tapping into the organic nature of the street as described by Jane Jacobs in *The Death and Life of Great American Cities*, and using its sometimes chaotic and informal networking structures to locate and identify edge players, dwellers and emergent Mindtrends, as Sputnik refers to its trend breakdowns.

SenseWorldwide runs its networks on an 'age is, as age talks' basis. It recruits through friends in key and below-the-radar places in order to keep researchers and in-house teams in the same mind-set as the subgroups and tribes they are talking to.

The network identifies the new look or cultural shift and then researchers are sent to interview key individuals in the identified group. This adds flesh, substance, philosophy and insight to the general trend previously identified.

This, stresses cofounder Jeremy Browne, is not about focus group research or consumer identification in the strictest sense – interviewees or network members are not prompted about product or brand type (nor is this the issue that is being teased out in any of the many field interviews they carry out) – it is about the experiences of the people being spoken to.

It is also about identifying conflicts – and social, spiritual or political contradictions or inconsistencies – rather than attempting to homogenize, or explain things away. Anomalies and the identification of such blips are key to understanding how and why their network functions so successfully. Likewise listening – rather than assuming – and of course, using the 'pattern match' – what things link other things and thoughts and actions together.

Unlike the Global Business Network model (which is in many cases pitched towards the grand plan scenario), SenseWorldwide, Sputnik and the Future Labora-tory itself come very much from the cultural underbelly and are in effect what we call feral networks – concerned with the tactile, the sensuous, the emotional, the spiritual, the sonorous and the visual, as well as the intellectual.

Because of this cultural fecundity and determination to work from the street from the bottom up, it uncovers, more times than not, cultural insights that are missed by even the most sophisticated business metric mechanisms.

As far back as 1997, when many were still coming to terms with dotcom and the rise of the casual or dress down economy, Sputnik networkers were already talking about the arrival of 'I' culture, technoshamanism, the rise of personalization, positive anarchy, the coming of the organic food movement, the advent of the geek, irony as cultural codifier, the passing of GenX and the arrival of Gen.Why? (or GenwwwY as we like to call them) and yes, you've guessed it, no focus groups here, no arcane telephone polling or clipboard visits to malls in New Jersey to find out what real people want, but a quiet probing of people with ideas, and alternative cult tendencies.

# Open source networks –
## extranets and online creativity

Ernest Rutherford, the man who split the atom, once said, 'We don't have much money so what we have to do is think.' This is what networks of the kind we've just described are there to do – make you think, create insights, but also to save you money. Networks, you see, aren't just any marketing tool, they are the only marketing tool you will ever need if you use them well.

Even better, if your network is configured properly and deployed carefully in and outside the company, online and offline, it becomes a reservoir that all depart-ments can dip into – from design to marketing, from PR to sales, from consumer intelligence to management, manufacturing and distribution.

Because these departments are hubs in their own right and all potential members of the network, they can use their position not just to listen to and monitor network activity, but to use network feedback to influence product design, brand realization and brand possibility. Instead of debating things internally and being encumbered by the internal politics, restrictions, prejudices and internecine conflicts that departmentalization inevitably causes, assembling your network online or in the flesh can create a federal moment, or a flattened corporation, even inside the most hierarchical and constrained structures.

We call this kind of online network system an extranet. It is an intranet system that opens out to include not just your select band of deviants, but also consumers with a vested interest in telling you what they think, especially if they are current users of your products.

As multinationals like Procter & Gamble are discovering, assembling vested interest groups this way is not only four times cheaper than putting a focus group together through 'consumer recruitment specialists' – the average focus group now comes in at £20 000 when all cost are added up – but more likely to offer up insights of the kind that take you beyond the product into the current and upcoming obsessions of the market.

On pg.com for instance, Procter & Gamble have teamed up with software specialists Recipio to create insight extranets with links like 'Try and Buy New Products' or 'Help US Create New Products' where you can log on into a virtual focus group that lets consumers try, test and comment on new concepts or ideas our network members may be coming up with.

Interactive session-application software also permits members of P&G to join in, or to use the live site to garner instant feedback on any area they may be interested in.

As Mark Schar, P&G's vice president for iVentures and consumer knowledge says, 'You can see literally as a consumer goes through a concept and get instantaneous feedback about what they liked, what they didn't like in ways you could never do in a paper-based environment.'

**❝ Or to use the live site to garner instant feedback on any area they may be interested in. ❞**

Other companies have started going along the same route. General Motors uses this kind of software and approach to get customer feedback on all its brands and new lines. NBC uses it to feedback into the programme-making process, while household names like Whirlpool are using it to test the critical threshold credentials of new products before they take them to market.

Even financial service providers are beginning to cotton on to the potential of network systems that allow you to speak directly to the consumer about their needs and how financial packages or 'lifestage bundles' can be created to accommodate their current and future circumstances.

These kinds of networks, however, haven't yet been allowed to realize their potential. Brands still insist on having network 'monitors' or moderators, still insist on asking questions (rather than brailling thought streams as they flow through it) or attempt to channel activities along one route, or towards one end.

Apart from the obvious problems this causes – you get answers to questions you think are important but miss out on what the consumer thinks is important – you are attempting to run what is, in reality, a complex adaptive system, or an emergent one, in a way that not only dampens what you are seeing running through it, but is likely to throw up problems elsewhere as the network, sensing your attempt to channel it, will simply create new protocols to work around what it sees as an unwanted incursion.

A decentralized or federal network is far more democratic than a central one and tends to encourage creativity, innovation and deviancy in the way brands and organizations need to work if they are to plug into the new and emerging consumer mindsets. The best kind of decentralized networks are also consilient ones.

## ■ Emergent lives

Networks, remember, are live in more ways than one – on a conscious level but also subconsciously. This is why the best networks are allowed to free flow, and to regulate themselves.

Everything2 is an online people's encyclopedia that works very close to these principles. The site employs neural net type programming to allow you to interact with its content in a way that permits you to post topics that you are keenest on writing about, but also to peer access and tag existing or ongoing site editions, so the encyclopedia grows organically and regulates itself.

In this way, new additions to the site are monitored collectively and verified. Each person who verifies a piece leaves a tag, so they in turn become responsible for the item's provenance and integrity. Since everyone wants to be a verifier who can be trusted, or a peer monitor who is to be sought out, you have, unofficially, formed a group which ensures that all work posted is challenged, assessed, improved or questioned on an ongoing basis until all are satisfied that it is the best the piece or posting can be.

Networks that follow this process are taking us closer to the idea of open source creativity. Jumping this term beyond its 'nerds online' association to a more open plan, inclusive way of working. One that will take us a step closer to copyleft agreements, shared objective design or 'brand pools' where companies (because of cost, resources or the need to involve more and more outside voices or brains in their projects) will not invoke copyright agreements or patents because they will be seen in much the same way as we see moderators – as limiting the potential of the work being undertaken.

The added advantage of open source networks of this kind is that much of the grading work involved in trend analysis is done by the network itself. As ideas are voiced and concepts articulated, the site – let's say it is a site devoted to future narratives – asks network members to don the hat of the forecaster and blogg out their version of tomorrow. You can then use the network to grade these snapshots of the future in accordance with how they themselves see the likelihood of all or any of them coming through.

Networks sometimes do this organically, especially if this has been one of the reasons for convening the network in the first place. Once networks know what is required – realistic scenarios of tomorrow's world today – they will, collectively or otherwise, start grouping certain ideas together. We call this a topobiological grouping or a topobiological neighbourhood.

The process was first identified by the biologist Gerald Edelman who noticed that cells, being singular but genetically gregarious entities, read what other cells around them were doing or picking up on and then picked up on these things themselves. Other cells then 'huddled' until you found that many cells in the organism were engaged in the same task – a bit like the activities of our slime mould.

In the network sense, you have to view this as individual networkers picking up on an idea and then grouping or housing (also called hubbing) this idea and similar others in the same place (topos is the Greek word for place). This happens not because they are from the same area but because they more or less articulate the same idea or pattern happening in other areas.

This is not about defining a trend, as yet, but about grouping a category, or suggesting a broad church box into which a concept, or association of similar words, activities or cultural shifts can be housed. Again, some open networks, because they are open and inclusive, allow you to create such houses or categories without, at that stage, asking why, or what such emergent patterns or anomalies mean.

## ■ Chatrooms as metric monitors

But you could, if you wish, use this activity as a simple measure of importance, or as a means of establishing a ratings system. Counting the number of hits a site gets, or monitoring the level of activity within a site chatroom, is a very simple way of gauging the popularity, or otherwise, of a trend or subject. And this, as simple as it seems, is one of the best ways of pacing the culture. Many forecasters use this approach, establishing online 'entrapment' areas where they open chatrooms on a series of subjects or emerging trends that their own networkers may be picking up on. They then monitor these sites and note the most popular – the ones generating the kind of debate that suggests an upsurge of interest in a particular topic. This in itself becomes a good way of answering that question we asked at the beginning of the book – what's new?

Or, braving your critics – and many companies avoid the extranet route because it only encourages online blogging, negative at that – you could do what ntl, the troubled cable company did when it was alerted to the nthellworld.com website where disgruntled customers were venting their spleen about ntl's shoddy treatment of them.

Rather than close the site, as most companies would do, or take up a law suit against the site provider, as more are trying to do (note that only 200 lawsuits have ever been effective against the thousands of sites that have appeared since 1999), its new director of corporate communications suggested that they buy the site, use it as a way of tapping into customer concerns and to improve their own customer services record.

This could be one way round the growing number of rant sites appearing daily online. A survey of 600 chief executives in the US by Hill and Knowlton says that they are more concerned than ever about the damage these sites are doing to their stocks and brand value – but only half had strategies in place to deal with managing internet communications, despite the fact that the Ross *Report on Cybermedia* says that 60 per cent of journalists will go to print with an online rumour if they have just one other confirmation.

> **❝ You have nothing to lose but your fear of the truth, of hearing the kind of ideas your customers are keen on. ❞**

Buying the sites out might help, but establishing freeform extranets where customers, brand managers, CEOs, designers, sales people, creatives and PRs can talk online freely, clearly and honestly might save you a hell of a lot of money, and also provide you with a ready-made prosumer testing group and ideas generation network.

You have nothing to lose but your fear of the truth, of hearing the kind of ideas your customers are keen on or what they think about the ideas you might be working on. There are other ways, however, of using your network – as well as listening into the culture, they can take what they find there and use it as a way of envisioning the future. Or future mapping or scenario planning.

# Futurescapes:
scenario plannning and
futureproof narratives

# Storytelling your futures –
## scenario planning and our many tomorrows

Online or offline, networks are exceptional at doing two things – microtrend identification and macrotrend analysis (future or scenario planning).

In micro terms, networks can be used to listen, accrue and identify new or emerging consumer types. The Lone Wolf, the Grit Girl and the Sunshine Teen for example, were all categories sensed by our own Lifesigns Network. Lone Wolf is a new male prototype with very independent views; Grit Girl his female doppleganger; Sunshine Teen a motivated, optimistic, and politically aware 16–19 year old.

In macro terms, networks can take those types, or a particular scenario involving those types, and envision how the scenario is likely to pan out, or impact on the culture, if the network deems the trend to be a macro type.

By macro we mean those networks that have long term, national or global possibilities or ramifications – biogenetics, nanotechnology, stem cell research, environmental pollution, fuel cell systems, declining birth rates in the west, the growth of megacities, corporate governance, copyleft, health and well-being as a new economy in its own right.

It can also be about 'what if' scenarios. What if the internet became conscious (likely)? What if we made genetic screening at birth compulsory (highly likely)? What if water becomes the new gold and hydro-economics a reality (very likely)? What if non-GM foodstuffs are seen as tainted or suspect (a given)? What if we could grow our own bioplastic buildings (already being worked on)? What if we could have products 'faxed' directly to our houses (already being prototyped)? What if machines developed not just their own intelligence (likely) but their own spirituality? What if, as man and machine converge, and each becomes not just connected to, but interconnected with the other, his intelligence becomes a singularity (very likely)?

## ■ Narrative pathways

What a network is doing here is taking the platform that has been established – i.e. the micro- or macrotrends it has identified – and using its collective knowledge to make a cognitive leap into the future, but in a way that tries to establish a 'narrative pathway' that is, in effect, brailling the future as it will be – projecting oneself forward, but not haphazardly so. This kind of macrotrend analysis must be done carefully, collectively and in an informed and insightful way if it is to work properly.

There are many closed network groups already doing this – from think-tanks like Demos, BrainReserve, the Centre for Policy Studies, The New Economics Foundation, the Work Foundation and The Future Foundation, to larger global concerns like Forethought, The Rand Corporation, GBN and The Foundation For Economic Trends, Shell's powerful Global Business Environmental network.

> **This kind of macrotrend analysis must be done carefully, collectively and in an informed and insightful way if it is to work properly.**

The model used more or less conforms to those created by military planners during the Second World War, and refined by men like Herman Kahn, Pierre Wack and Peter Schwartz, who went on to found the Global Business Network. Military men have always understood scenario planning as a process – they call it strategy, while artists and writers call it narrative flow or compositional structure.

Whatever its name, the end goal is fairly similar – a format or frame to work within where certain ideas, scenes, scenarios or 'what if' possibilities can be played out in a structured and meaningful way. It is also a good way to use the knowledge our network has garnered from the present to construct versions of the future that may or may not come to pass.

The US airforce was very good at this sort of thing, and in the 60s Herman Kahn, a key player in their scenarios machine, took the processes he learned there and applied them to business, eventually heading up the influential Hudson Institute and becoming, according to Stanley Kubrick, a futurist of a different kind – his inspiration for the character of Dr. Strangelove.

Kahn, it was said, 'would and could think the unthinkable' – a rule he himself believed was central to any kind of scenario planning, and a rule that should also be central to your network philosophy. Inevitabilities, remember, never are – or at least never are on the terms those who insist on them would like, or want. Human irascibility sees to that! As a consequence, Khan became America's top futurologist, predicting the boom economy, 60s promiscuity and the rise of feminism.

Pierre Wack was a deviant in the best kind of way – a French mystic, he practised meditation, was a confirmed Cartesian, a student of Gurdjieff, a seer keen on the arcane philosophies of Sufism who studied garden design in Japan – all of which he claimed made him a better envisager. In the 70s he went to work at Shell where he took this process even further, bringing experts together in a department called Group Planning – a concept then unheard of. They were asked to look into the future, not just by collecting data or information but by getting experts in key areas to use their knowledge and intuitions (about markets as they were) to look at markets as they were most likely to become if, say, OPEC raised its prices at a time when the US was beginning to worry about its oil reserves running out.

A similar exercise was under way with a group called the Club of Rome. This was a panel of academics, scientists, thinkers and economists working out of the Sloan School of Management (at MIT). They were attempting to pitch their wits against World3, a supercomputer of sorts trying to make the same predictions. The computer, fed with 120 variables, came up with the answer, not disputed by our experts, that the world's oil reserves would run out within 20 years – by 1990 in other words.

Wack, however, applying the illogicality of the human condition to the situation, asked the unaskable – if oil was running low, why wouldn't the Arab states increase its cost? Against this he placed what he called his 'tendances lourdes' – the bigger picture things that are not likely to change and therefore impact on the smaller scenarios being played out between or around them.

Wack maintained that if the situation was reversed, the west would have no qualms about doing the same thing – jacking prices up. With 1975 being the year designated for oil prices to be renegotiated, why not do it then? Especially if you knew the opposition was worried about their own resources drying up. But what if something bigger precipitated things even quicker? As it turned out, the Yom Kippur War kick-started a lurking crisis more quickly than expected – but at least a company like Shell was prepared as they had scanned these 'what if' possibilities. Under Wack's supervision, and because of his team's foresight, they held the discussions needed and, even if they did nothing, at least they weren't so numbed by the shock of rocketing prices that they couldn't act.

They did act, and from being one of the weaker oil lords of that time they became one of the most prominent and profitable.

Wack believed that some elements of the future were preordained in that they would be the consequential outcomes of events that had already happened. If there is a heavy downpour upstream, there will be a swelling of the waters, possibly flooding downstream. So in some ways, aspects of the future can be determined with a high degree of certainty simply by looking at the world as it is now and using the detail accrued to create a level of knowledge that allows you to project forward.

Wack, although he wasn't aware of complex adaptive systems and their effects on the culture in the way that we are now, did understand how 'critical uncertainties' could affect the future in ways that may not be all that apparent. This is why and how he insisted that imagination could be used in conjunction with analysis to overcome this, and this, of course, is how we create emergent modelling systems, or how good networks operate. They use the sum total of their collective input to create elaborate and rich future narratives or stories – to make that great leap we wrote about earlier.

## ■ Gentle art of reperceiving

Wack also coined a word that is key to how futurologists still work – reperceiving. In his now seminal work *The Gentle Art of Reperceiving*, he explains the concept as a way of challenging or revisiting accepted notions of how we see the world. In other words seeing it through eyes that shun and deny prejudice – not to see it as you see it, but to see it from the other person's point of view (in your case the customer). Still a problem for brands now, but back then in the 70s such an idea came as divine revelation.

GBN founder Peter Schwartz is perhaps the best known of the three. Using their methods and building on them, he is the one who has done more to move the processes of prediction on from the realms of 'what if' to the more measurable and useful area of 'what then'. For the future, as Wack indicated in *The Gentle Art of Reperceiving*, is about measuring the consequences of change as much as it is about anticipating change itself. Schwartz was at Stanford when people like Abraham Maslow were working towards the VALS system of measuring consumer need against consumer fulfilment, and when Willis Harman, the futurologist, was setting up the school's futures group. Schwartz used what he learned from these men, from Kahn and from his own time at Shell to develop a more strategic system of scenario planning.

> **Is about measuring the consequences of change as much as it is about anticipating change itself.**

A system which is divided into easy and logical steps that we have, in the spirit of true copyleft agreements, since refined and built on to incorporate recent research into complex adaptive systems and narrative plays – all of which are noteworthy because they offer a fairly good framework for how the future can be insured against at a very basic level. This is how it works.

# Scenario planning –
## the lowdown

To start with, Schwartz suggests that you work from the inside out (we do the opposite, but more of that later) and look at the decisions that have to be made which are likely to have a long term influence on the fortunes of your brand or company.

We have expanded this procedure into a 16-step path of action that allows you to plan scenarios in a more comprehensive and insightful manner. Each step requires you to ask a series of questions and to input specific pieces of information. You are then required to build on these in ways that convert the information gathered into knowledge, and then to turn this knowledge into valuable insights about your market, your consumers and how hitherto unseen trends or cultural shifts may or may not impact on them. It is important that each step is adhered to and that each instruction is followed to the letter – too little information and poor research at the beginning will lead to weak insights and even weaker outcomes at the end.

Imagine then you are a burger brand. Your network has noted a shift away from red meat towards fish or lean meat, away from 'Americana' and towards Mediterranean and fusion, even towards rampant vegetarianism. This is what we call the trend direction or trend path. The vibe says your network is towards health, leanness and simplicity, but also because of food scares – CJD, BSE, the increased use of hormones in our livestock and the rise of foot and mouth – people are no longer convinced about the safety of farmed red meat.

## ■ Step one: the initiation stage

Imagine you are McDonald's or a supermarket chain with a lot of products selling into this category. What happens now? What happens next? How is this shift likely to impact on your brand or market share? How do you continue to sell your products? Do you continue to sell them? What can you do to make them more appealing to consumers? Here you are looking at how this trend shift might impact on your business affairs, but also on the perception of your brand. This is step one, the initiation stage.

## ■ Step two: know the culture of your internal and external marketplace

This requires you to look at what your customers, competitors and staff are up to. Not as simple as it seems – it involves painting a fairly in-depth and exhaustive picture of your internal marketplace (what we call a cultural profile) as well as the external one you are trading in.

This is where either the extranet works or a network that includes customers comes in. There is a tendency to role play customer needs and ideas at this stage. Don't! Always ask the customer, always have the customer plugged in at all stages of the scenario plan. We differ from Schwartz – experts are as experts do – and in this case the only expert that knows the customer is the customer! Not the market analyst, not the consultant who claims to know the customer. In your cultural profile stage, always involve as many outsiders as you can when gathering information about your brand or company and how people see it.

## ■ Step three: establish your narrative drivers

Here you need to list the key social, environmental, political and technical forces likely to impact on the brand or idea you are worried about. These will become the driving forces of your scenario – your 'tendances lourdes'. Schwartz also recommends that you look at the forces behind these – What's influencing them? Why are they behaving the way they are behaving? This, he says, is the most research-active section of the exercise.

We suggest that research should cover markets, new technology, political factors and economic forces. This is where the real worth of your network comes into its own – for listening, divining, digging out and up the things you need to make your scenario comprehensive, all encompassing.

Again, the ideal organic network does this as standard, this is where they are at after all. If not, then I'd expect to see copies of the following publications being read by all scenarists and network members – *Nature, New Scientist, Scientific American, The British Medical Journal, National Geographic, Geo, Adbusters, Vogue, Vanity Fair, The Economist, Newsweek, Time, Fortune, Brills Content, The Baffler, The New York Times, The Washington Post, Le Monde, Libération, Harvard Business Review, BusinessWeek, Ergo, Prospect, The Guardian, The Vegetarian, Wired, Surface, Metropolis, Nest, Design Week, ID, Frame, Art Flash, Blueprint, Byte, Fast Company, The Art*

*Newspaper, Tank, Vice, Citizen K, Salon.com, Slashdot*; along with executive summaries of relevant consumer or lifestyle reports from McKinsey, Roper Starch Worldwide, Mintel, Datamonitor, Retail Intelligence, Nielson Sofres, Mori, BrainReserve and the trades relevant to the areas under review.

What you are looking for here are the big picture trends and the glitches likely to skew these in a particular way. As Schwartz says, 'Novelty is difficult to anticipate.'

## ■ Step four: rank your research or 'narrative drivers'

When your research has been done you should rank it on two criteria (again we use our network members to do this) – the degree of importance for the success of the focal issue or decision identified in stage one; and the degree of uncertainty surrounding those factors and trends.

'The point,' as Schwartz says, 'is to identify the two or three factors or trends that are most important and most uncertain. By doing this you are establishing the axis along which the eventual scenarios will differ.' You are also establishing, as storytellers or narrative planners like Gerard Fairtlough will tell you, a framework within which the narrative can flow. Its spine or backbone if you will. 'Using narratives like this is a useful way of bringing up difficult issues.'

## ■ Step five: agree your scenario or narrative pathways

Determining these axes are the most important steps in the scenario-generating process. The goal is to end up with just a few scenarios – three, perhaps four – too many scenarios and the process becomes vague and uncertain. In each scenario, however, the trick is to identify the key areas of crucial uncertainty, and to make scenarios as rich in useful, logical and hidden detail as possible.

> **￼ Determining these axes are the most important steps in the scenario-generating process. ￼**

What we mean by this is ensuring that the narratives, or structures, you've built for your respective scenarios are as rich in 'local colour' and factual and emotional texture as possible. We call this narrative texture – remember our journey from the word 'edible' to the world of the exuberant and the irrational?

## ■ Step six: define your narrative textures

Narrative texture can be had from networkers themselves, or like IBM's Cynefin Centre for Organizational Complexity, can be harvested from knowledge pools or banks of areas of culture relevant to the company's progress in the market.

These can be online databases of the personal or pooled experiences of existing employees, outside experts, retired employees, or even competitors. Dave Snowden, the centre's director, sees it as a good way of getting everybody to see a new or emerging market from the same point of view, but with each adding their own depth and insight – as we all do when we tell and retell a story.

## ▨ Step seven: clarify your scenario or narrative pathways

The truth isn't always in the tale but in the retelling of it. Each time you talk a possible scenario through, you will bring new insights and new levels of meaning to it. This is what happens when you read and reread a book, or watch a film for the second or third time – each time you see something new; each reading or viewing allows you to move deeper into the plot.

This is what we mean by 'talking the tale'. That you should tell each scenario to your network group or team two or three times so that all hear and understand the tale being told – but also bring new insights to it as a consequence of listening to the telling of it again and again. It is like weaving, reworking the threads of your narrative. By doing so, your brain becomes the 'enchanted loom' that Sherrington spoke about – a magical, almost mystical engine that shuttles back and forth creating the kind of sparks or insights that lift you and your team to greater levels. This isn't the same as worrying a problem but of using the narrative framework to add value and useful layers to each step of the scenario-planning stage.

## ▨ Step eight: keep your narrative paths and plots distinctive

Always ensure that the three or four plots or scenarios you choose are sufficiently different and distinctive. Too many planners create possible plots or scenarios that make it difficult for their networkers to create a clear and intelligible picture of how the future might map out. This can impact badly on the kind of insights they are attempting to gain.

Here's a good example. Our network was asked to do some work for a well-known vacuum cleaner manufacturer. This manufacturer produced suction-style vacuum cleaners and wanted to look at how products would shape up in the future (the 'what if' question).

> ❝ What is known cannot always be articulated, so we often recommend that research is done 'live', in the home. ❞

In scenario one, the network suggested that technology would stay more or less the same, but that the 'housing' or surface styling would change. A good bet, but how? They then had to research all design shifts, trends, tastes, colour and styling details that consumers were talking about.

In scenario two, they decided that carpets, being unhygienic and unfashionable, would become a thing of the past or something for minority tastes only. Everybody would opt for wood, laminate or tile floors, so the company would need to develop a suction and brush system that worked on smooth surfaces. They even looked at how or why carpets would become outdated. They considered the rise of the affluent, design-conscious twenty-somethings who associated carpets with fusty, class-conscious suburbanites; a desire for lighter, more minimal living spaces; carpets being seen as parental, olde-worlde, vulgar, environmentally suspect, ethically questionable (many carpets are produced by children expected to work in appalling conditions) etc.

Again, listing these things is never as good as having those people there who believe those things – so get the customers to tell their story or involvement with the vacuum cleaner! What is known cannot always be articulated, so we often recommend that research is done 'live', in the home, where the product is used, so that the texture of the story can be felt.

In scenario three, the network considered the idea that competitors would come up with a new, improved suction system and, with good product design, produce a cleaner that worked on both carpets and floors to make the competition look a tad old-school in the process.

They thought they were working along what seemed to be the most likely scenario – the new and improved system – so how would the competition improve it? Better suction valves? More efficient internal motors? Maybe, as some networkers suggested, the solution was a combined one – an improved suction mechanism, slick housing and a shape that suggested a designed artefact, created to appeal to a consumer demographic that rates design first and function second in its key purchasing decisions. Especially if the product they are being sold is seen to be generic, a household staple.

## ▨ Step nine: the rogue scenario

In scenario four – the least likely according to the manufacturer – a competitor abandons suction for cyclonic action improving the cleaner's lifting ability by 300 per cent. They design it as a translucent, iconoclastic piece of kit that makes it a 'classic' overnight. This will appeal to the faddist, the functionalist and a new group of design-aware, brand-acquisitive consumers your team has identified as Lone Nesters – single, brand conscious, urban twenty-somethings who invest in lofts and living rather than family and savings. Improbable said the manufacturers, but not impossible said the networkers.

## ▨ Step ten: always think the unthinkable

In each case, what goes in will obviously influence what comes out. But what goes in should be accurate, plausible and possible. In the case of scenario four, it may seem implausible to the manufacturer (and these things always do – if we haven't thought of it then it isn't possible!) but to the outsider, to the networker with the grasp of the bigger picture (as unlikely as this scenario seems), the more one fleshes it out, the more likely the unlikely scenario will become.

## ▨ Step eleven: always look for the anomalous!

Look at the facts, no new breakthrough has happened in this sector of the market for years (established from your initial researches). This simply means that there is an increased chance that something will.

Design and lifestyle are both hot topics at the moment, and maybe your products are not exactly cutting edge, nor talking points. One of the great influencers of people making a purchasing decision based on design over function, or design with function as we shall see, is our so-called D factor – does it have a story, a talking point later? There is also the feeling among consumers that the big boys have had their day – now it's the turn of the maverick, the deviant . . . the anomalous! A good network will pick up on these things, build them into the equation and see some pretty interesting things taking place.

## ■ Step twelve: always assume that there is a factor X

This stage is about piecing together driving forces – micro- and macroevents, the notional factors behind these events; and the colour, texture and shade of the events themselves – into a structure that holds all these together in a way that makes the scenario still plausible and probable.

It is important at this stage to look once more at people as key influencers as well as trends, or societal shifts. If we're looking at the issue of the vacuum cleaner, all things being equal, scenario three would seem to be the best one to opt for, unless you thought of someone called Dyson, or at least a man somewhere tinkering with an alternative way for lifting dust. This is why the outside network, the extranet, is a better way of envisioning the future. It will consider the unthinkable, since the unthinkable is usually something you don't consider. Not because it isn't possible, but because you are locked into a culture, a mission statement and a product-to-profit cycle that place too many constraints on your ability to cast your mind forward.

Even Shell, the brand that developed scenario planning, fell into this trap. In 1992, it looked at globalization and saw it to be good for the world, and also for Shell. Its scenario planners, all Shell people, did their homework and came up with quite a few erudite observations – about how globalism would change markets, the world, how we traded and how people viewed culture.

## ■ Step thirteen: every scenario has a hidden counterpoint – always search for it

The counterpoint, the anomaly, that globalism would be seen as bad, damaging, and dangerous to the environment wasn't explored as well as it could and should have been. Shell, after all, was involved in the very process of damaging the environment, or rather liberating oil from some rather inclement areas and climates.

Then came Brent Spar. The world saw TV pictures of Greenpeace protesters being hosed down with high pressure hoses while they were doing something most of the viewers wished they themselves were doing – trying to contribute, to save something globalism was fast reminding us we were losing, our soul, our individuality, our differences, our past and our planet.

Then came Ken Saro-Wiwa, an Ogani tribesman and leader, attempting to save his people and land from oil explorers and government-backed forces desecrating it for the sake of oil and global commerce.

Shell, rightly, became an enemy of the people. Even if people needed their oil, they did not need or like Shell. Their goodwill and emotional stock plummeted, until Shell did the unthinkable. It began to speak and listen to its critics, to work with them. It began to help finance their needs, their aims and, under a process of sustainable exploration, cut costs by £2.5bn per year. It began to invest £0.7bn in seeking out alternative energy sources, and spent millions annually to aid causes and incentives hitherto judged to be against their better interests.

> ❝ It is doubly important to keep your network open to dissenters, but also to keep it open to the unthinkable. ❞

## ■ Step fourteen: even the right solution creates negative offshoots – know what these are

Yes, there are those that argue Shell was simply buying its way out of bad press. To some extent this is true – but it is also engaging, listening and becoming a tactile company or brand in the positive sense. For their part, environmentalists working with them are learning better ways of dealing with errant corporations, and to admit that they too can get it wrong. In retrospect, the dumping of Brent Spar was more environmentally acceptable – not to say useful in creating a new marine ecology or sanctuary – than the cost and environmental damage of breaking the rig up on land. So it is doubly important to keep your network open to dissenters, but also to keep it open to the unthinkable.

At this stage, all scenarios considered and all looked into thoroughly with the right measure of facts mixed in with the right amounts of imagination, it is time to look at the implications – what if a man called Dyson comes up with the cyclonic cleaner?

## ■ Step fifteen: consider implications but do not set parameters on them

Here you look at the implications of each scenario outcome on the original question or proposition you were trying to test.

- What does it mean to you?
- Can you respond to each scenario outcome?
- If not, why not?
- What do you need?
- How quickly can you move?
- What happens if you don't?
- Can you put plans, procedures and protocols in place to help you deal with all scenarios, with most, or with only one?
- If the last, are there are other serious issues to be considered?
- How flexible are your response times?
- What if you can only react to one change in the market at a time?

## ■ Step sixteen: remember that scenarios are only 'what if' possibilities

Remember that scenarios are neither accurate nor final models of how the future will look. They are hypothetical strategies that make the future easier to contend with and allow you to prepare resources now for things that may come to pass tomorrow. Use them and work with them, but always keep them flexible and open because people change, attitudes change and society changes and these changes will always have an impact on the way your scenario pans out. So do not be rigid, do not be inflexible. Allow ongoing monitoring, ongoing vigilance. Always have feedback systems in place and when change is noted be prepared to splice it into your model.

Although network scenario planning isn't quite the same as game theory in the way that it is practised in business, in our view it is far more accurate. Scenario planning, like complexity theory, allows you to factor in all aspects of a situation, and in most cases makes no distinctions between irrational or compulsive behaviours and those deemed to be smooth, or rational and accepted. Likewise, it encourages the plot twist, or the factor X which could, and usually does, turn minor inconveniences into major catastrophes!

## ■ Game theory and why you should avoid it

Game theory, by its nature, forbids this approach. Fixed players work to fixed rules along plot lines or variable narratives that are seen as possible, but more or less smooth or acceptable narratives. The underlying assumption being that nobody is going to play the game outside the bounds of credibility or acceptable taste – however this is initially defined. As we've seen, human nature doesn't work like this. Nor, as more and more game theorists are finding, does it pay off to assume that it does.

Trevor Newton, Chief Executive of Yorkshire Water, discovered this to his cost in the 90s. While preparing for a regulatory review that would send prices down from 1995 to 2000, he used game theory to work out how his company would be treated by the regulator. The result? Very well indeed – a good company, with a good track record and an impressive brand presence.

The regulator had different ideas. As it happened they set tougher price controls than Newton and his players anticipated – the rogue scenario – but it also opened up an inquiry into Yorkshire Water's operating performance – the impossible scenario!

None of Newton's game theory scenarios had even tinkered with this possibility. But worse was to come. The following year a freak drought caused unforeseen regional water shortages (our factor X) and the company's brand, and standing with its customers, plummeted. Newton, again not anticipating this, resigned – the end game or doom scenario as narrative planners call this one.

Numerous reported incidents such as this have led to what amounts to a backlash against the use of game theory as a way of forecasting the future – and certainly as an effective way of anticipating competitor activity or customer needs and desires. Scott Armstrong, a marketing professor at Wharton Business School at the University of Pennsylvania, thinks it has more or less had its day.

After conducting exhaustive reviews of the literature, he says that he is 'unable to find any evidence to directly support the belief that game theory would aid predictive ability.' He's not alone in this belief. Work by Kesten Green adds further fuel to the debate. Green, a researcher at the Victoria University at Wellington, New Zealand, believes that game theory is useless when it comes to predicting outcomes in complex situations.

Game theory enthusiasts were asked to predict the outcome of a set of typical bargaining situations. The scenarios were actually theoretical versions of real life situations so Green already knew their outcome. One involved a conflict between artists and government over financial support; another a conflict between sports team owners and players over broadcast revenue rights; a third a conflict between a pharmaceuticals company and consumers over one of its drugs.

As well as setting his game theory scenarists to work on the problem, he also roped in a number of his students and asked them to predict possible outcomes using only 'unaided judgement', in other words common sense.

The result? The game theorists proved no better at predicting the outcomes than his untrained students. In some cases, where students were asked to role play the situations out, Simon London reported in the *Financial Times* that 'they were the most accurate of the lot.'

This is why narrative planning is more appropriate. It combines intuition with analysis, expertise and imagination, but also with behavioural techniques that are far more feral and enriching in terms of what they can bring to network knowledge and insight.

# Part 8

# Consumer hides:
## in bed with Mr and Mrs Deviant

# Tactile marketing –
## living with the enemy

The kinds of network scenarios, or narrative maps, we've been discussing allow you to weave pictures of what the future will look like and the kind of consumers that may live there.

But identifying the consumer – even talking to them online – isn't the same as knowing them. Nor does it give you the kind of in-depth knowledge needed to read them in tandem with the trends they may be part of – or, if they are edge dwellers, have a hand in creating.

To read them you need to see, hear, watch and observe them in the field. To do this effectively it is necessary to make your network tactile – one that uses the tools and techniques of the artist and photographer, the video maker and field researcher, the ethnographer and anthropologist, the behavioural scientist; even the techniques of the contemporary archaeologist, or garbologist as they are more commonly called!

As Dorothy Leonard and Jeffrey Rayport put in the *Harvard Business Review*, 'A set of techniques we call emphatic design . . . at its foundation is observation – watching consumers use products or services. But unlike focus groups, usability laboratories and other contexts of traditional market research, such observation is conducted in the customer's own environment – in the course of normal everyday routines.'

## ■ At home with the Jones

Behavioural researcher and Housecalls founder Bill Abrams, whose clients include Johnson & Johnson, Colgate–Palmolive and Kraft Foods agrees. Abrams, a one-time creative director of Ted Bates and Kenyon and Eckhardt, pioneered the use of ethnographic research tools like this in a commercial environment when he noticed that much of what passed over his agency desk in the form of marketing information, or consumer segmentation and profiling, was nothing of the sort.

Rather, it was merely data without consequence – things to be read that offered little or no insights about brand, product or how people actually related to or lived with the commercial world in their home.

Abrams wrote, 'The greatest single value of observational research is that it provides you with the kind of knowledge you need to secure a relationship with your consumer; an intimate knowledge of the way your consumer actually lives with your product – not in the abstract, not by the numbers, but up close and personal.'

It is also done, like our organic and open network approach, to record the abnormal and not so everyday. As well as teaching us how to improve existing products or create new brand possibilities by allowing observers to identify information or ingenuity gaps in a consumer's or group's narrative of how they live, as Abrams suggests, it is by far the most useful way of observing new social groups like Lone Wolves, Grit Girls, New Essentialist Shoppers and Rainbow Youth as they crystallize and happen.

Not a portrait of numbers or neat statistics, not a study of averages or average lives, but the probing, unpacking and decoding of an individual or a group of individuals with a view to extracting insights that better aid our understanding of the future scenarios our network may have drawn up. It also allows a better understanding of them – what motivates their needs, their desires, their reasons for needing brands; or not.

For in the how (in what people do and how they do it) is embedded the why – key to understanding the consumer's deepest needs and desires. This is nothing new. The Greeks understood it when they wrote their plays, and Shakespeare when he wrote his. We are as we act and, more appropriately for the consumer profiler, we are as we live and act things out.

Writers like Flaubert and Proust and painters like Holbein and Gainsborough also saw the truth in this. The description of Emma Bovary's dressing table is as much a description of her inner longing and yearnings as they are of her possessions. Holbein's Ambassadors, flanked by their globes, furs, books and instruments of science and astronomy, is as much a painting of their sense of self in the world – their emotional and intellectual prowess and standing as a coded display of wealth and position.

> **These things, fixed in the now but coming from a person's internal world, tell much about what they are thinking.**

This is what we call the 'visual map' or symptoms created or exhibited by people when they are externalizing a trend or lifestyle gambit as detected by our networkers. These things, fixed in the now but coming from a person's internal world, tell much about what they are thinking and who they are, but also where they may be going.

## ■ Residual lives

In John Steinbeck's *Travels With Charlie*, the writer alludes to the way we leave the residue of our inner lives and yearnings on the things we come into contact with. 'An animal resting or passing by leaves crushed grass, footprints and perhaps droppings, but a human occupying a room for one night prints his character, his biography, his recent history and sometimes his future plans and hopes. I further believe that personality seeps into walls and is slowly released.'

Forensic investigators and criminal profilers are of very much the same opinion – that we leave behind us physical and psychological clues or trace elements of our personalities, our narrative maps, the stories that shape and motivate us. Likewise, behavioural psychologists who, more and more, are coming around to the idea that you really should judge a book by its cover, or a person by the car they drive or the house they live in.

Certainly the houses we live in, according to psychologist Edward Sadella, who asked 12 upper-middle-class couples to create comprehensive and in-depth profiles of themselves using a 36-point checklist that covered intellectual as well as physical and aspirational attributes. He and his colleagues then photographed the living rooms and the exteriors of the houses they lived in and asked 99 students to profile the inhabitants of each house using the same 36-point checklist without seeing the people who lived there.

Their assessments were staggeringly accurate in terms of personality traits, and also – and this surprised Sadella and his team – in terms of how accurate they were in assessing their intellectual, cultural and political leanings. They could even say – from examining interior objects and comparing them to exterior ones – how 'private' or 'public' the owners were likely to be and how these things would impact on their sense of self or self-aspiration.

## ◼ Worlds in a handful of dust

In a more recent study of how bedrooms and work spaces reflect the character of the people who work and live in them, INSEAD and some University of Texas researchers were able to show that even untrained observers, working independently of each other, could create a character profile of the inhabitants of these spaces that was very much in keeping with how they saw themselves and their characters.

A visit to the Francis Bacon studio at the Hugh Lane Gallery in Dublin provides convincing proof of this. Here, the entire contents of Bacon's Reece Mews studio (South Kensington, London) have been reconstructed with meticulous archaeological precision. The photographer, Perry Ogden, captured the studio in precise detail on film, in close up, in long shot, in sequential images that pinned down the studio in all its chaotic, poetic and freefall dynamism.

With the aid of archaeologists and Ogden's photographic record, the studio and its contents were then shipped to Dublin and reassembled in a way that makes it possible for the visitor to stand inside Bacon's 'head' and view the chaotic world he lived in first hand.

Two things strike you when you do this. The fact that there is no sense that you are not in his studio at Reece Mews – so perfect is the reconstruction, so accurate the placing of papers, paint cans, bottles, brushes, newspapers and even paint dust. The second is the sudden realization that in this room, with its 'thousands of papers, books and photos; the rotted curtains, the moth-eaten bedspread, the brushes and paints, the discarded canvasses' is a three dimensional map of Bacon's life, his loves, inner yearnings and outer tastes.

If you didn't know the man, you could know of him here – that he was a painter; that he drank whiskey and vintage champagnes (there are Krug bottles, cases of Le Mesnil, Tattinger boxes); that he was gay (magazines, newspapers and torn out pages all contain male nudes, Spanish bullfighters, body builders and images of his lovers George Dyer and Peter Lacey). We can assume too that he had a morbid interest in pathology, skin disorders, surgery and other medical matters and conditions from the number of books and torn pages with images of skin and facial diseases scattered about the studio floor. He adored Spanish painters, especially Velázquez, the French painter Georges Seurat, the work of Lucian Freud, the Swiss sculptor Alberto Giacometti and the photographs of John Deakin.

We can also tell that movement fascinated him. He was intrigued by the body in motion – there are pages resting on a drawer and paint splattered radiator that come from Eadweard Muybridge's *The Human Figure in Motion*, and others of wrestlers caught fighting on camera.

From the doors and walls he cleaned his brushes or tested his colours on, we can tell that he liked blood reds, greens, bruised purples. Cutting in close to shelves containing paint pots, rags and old socks, we can even see something of the foods he favoured – Batchelor's broad beans, Noel's capers, Libby's orange juice, Chiver's Old English marmalade, Elswood's sweet and sour cucumbers.

Beans figure prominently – indeed one could say that when it came to beans, Bacon was a man obsessed. Butter beans, broad beans, green beans, baked beans – tins of these are everywhere, adding sudden and more revealing glimpses of the man within perhaps, than the screes of newspapers, magazines and books that litter the floor, or ride up and over half buried cupboards like Wonderland tea terraces sprouting step after step of brushes, paint tubes, rags, pink, paint encrusted towels and discarded tins of plum tomatoes.

If you didn't know Bacon the artist, you'd certainly know Bacon the slob, the bean eater; Bacon the lover of men, good wines and low rent Soho roughs. It is a profile that could never be assembled from speaking to him alone, never garnered just from his work or his few public pronouncements. But by stepping through that door and delving into his drawers and cupboards; seeing that tin of Bachelor's butter beans next to jars of paint marked up as Alizarin Crimson, beans and blood, beans and the colour used to taint and make great his screaming Popes, laid out like that on the same shelf say it all.

> 66 **We choke them with numbers, kill them with statistics, murder them with mindless segmentation.** 99

What the Bacon studio tells us is just how much we can learn from the visual world. We suggest looking at the works of Michael Landy, Sophie Calle. Also at realist photographers and photographic artists like Mischa Haller, Nan Goldin, Alastair McLellan, Ewan Spencer, William Eggleston, Martin Parr and Richard Billingham. But how little of the visual world is apparent in the kinds of reports that brands or companies commission to better understand the trends of emerging markets?

We choke them with numbers, kill them with statistics, murder them with mindless segmentation, and in the choking and killing and murdering, lose the very thing that matters most – the essence of the person; the soul.

# The unlearning of data –
## when seeing is believing

Business ignores the visual world, say behavioural researchers and design ethnographers Genevieve Bell, Ken Anderson and Tony Salavdor, because of its perceived lack of relevance in a corporate system where all research must be backed up by statistics, numbers and quantities. 'It challenges the twin operating perspectives of business and production.'

Business – because it challenges accepted ways of measuring and collating detail about a consumer's likes and dislikes – and production – because behavioural research of the kind we and they use (and the kind more and more future-faced companies are turning to) – require a collaborative approach to reading the market. Also to how creative, marketing, design, sales and manufacturing teams need to work in a more consilient way rather than in the fragmented manner most work, and are happy to work in at the moment.

## ■ Hands on design

IDEO (Greek for idea) is one such consultancy. An Anglo-American design house, it has revolutionized the design business from the inside out, and also from the bottom up. The brainchild of Bill Moggeridge, Mike Nuttall and David Kelly, it is a practice that realizes many of the processes and technologies that tactile corporations are now just beginning to look at and explore.

Kelly dreamt about the first computer mouse and made it happen for Apple. Moggeridge produced a design for the world's first portable GRiD computer with folding screen that has since become an industry standard.

So successful has the practice been that the ABC news network devoted a 30-minute Nightline documentary to IDEO and its then idiosyncratic approach to designing products or creating brands. According to Kelly, good companies should employ people who don't always listen to the boss – deviants in other words. They should be about 'who comes up with the best ideas, not where they are in the corporate pecking order. We encourage craziness because it sometimes leads to the right ideas.'

## ■ People-friendly designs

He could have said 'always'. IDEO brands, products and the distinctive IDEO style – those soft ergonomic shapes, humanist proportions, optimistic colour schemes and user-friendly interfaces that suggest tactility, playfulness and a sense of personality – are everywhere and have spawned many imitations.

But the products themselves are instantly recognizable – for their shape, their tactility and, above all, how easy they are to use and engage with. As a consequence, many have become best sellers and design classics in their own right. Because of this they have unusually low critical threshold ratings – Polaroid's Izone disposable camera, the Palm V, the Leap Chair, the Insulin Pen and the Flashcast Sp2000 spin reel fishing rod.

> **" As a consequence, many have become best sellers and design classics in their own right. "**

True to its principle of being a tactile brand, there are no official job titles at IDEO and no particular departments which employees work in. As a company it has avoided such workplace traditions to ensure that ideas flow freely and that knowledge and insights are exchanged federally. This means there are few power bases, fewer managerial fiefdoms, and hardly any of the management hierarchies found in competitors' design studios.

They wanted products to be 'experience products' – artefacts that did not distinguish between design, engineering, function and end-user use. Function was the form, they argued, and attempted to instil this rule in their teams, products and the brands they worked for – Nike, Amtrak, NEC, Samsung, Canon and Nissan.

Design then isn't just about design of product but a process that begins much further upstream, with the consumer but also with how the company is structured internally. As a cell, or rather a group of cells (think Nagasaki's slime mould) that functions independently but comes together for larger projects or to pool creativity and insights during the course of one project that may help other cells better understand new projects they may be working on.

Each cell at IDEO consists of 25 people and is run on a collective basis. Team structures are flat, inclusive, multidisciplinary and most decisions are made without referring to other cells although, as with all networks, ideas and decisions are circulated to all rather than passed up the line for approval. In this way, the collective knowledge of all company cells in London, San Francisco and Japan can be used to test, regulate or add to an idea.

Each cell is allowed to sell itself independently, to compete with another or to sell skills collectively. Even letterheads can be adopted without checking with the company founders that they are local, personal and, like all IDEO offices, highly individual and reflective of local cultures, rather than having a look that communicates a global presence of a unified corporate brand.

Anarchy and argument are encouraged but, to ensure that knowledge is exchanged and insights passed on, regular round table discussions are held to keep, as Kelly puts it, all cells connected and plugged in.

Each cell has two seats at the table – a creative person and an operations person. This prevents technology, design, creativity and execution from being seen as individual specialisms.

Running through this, and holding the network together, is the company philosophy which is about understanding, observing, visualizing, evaluating and implementing – the five cardinal points of the tactile brand's compass you might say. The things that give insight and make even the most proactive organization a future-faced, connected one.

It is a process similar to that we ourselves use to determine a design, or a brand's critical threshold rating.

## ■ To understand is to see

'Understanding' is about brailling the culture in the way we've spoken of – where it is at, where it is going, what consumers are thinking, doing, saying. This can be done by the team involved, or by plugging into networks like those convened online or in the flesh by SenseWorldwide (one of the network companies IDEO works closely with) to scan key cultural or consumer groups for insights that help 'make real' the kind of product being discussed.

Sometimes it can be a brief relating to a specific product, or it can be a client looking to extend a brand or to improve brand impact, visibility and leverage by creating a new category or product that connects with a new mood, or can ride an upcoming trend. 'Understanding' is about context, about mining the bigger picture.

It is also about brainstorming, about jotting down initial insights, noting competitor activity, consumer needs, what products in other categories – especially unrelated ones – they are showing an interest in. Also how and why this new product is different from what is already there – in other words, is it needed?

The 'observe' stage is where the fun and fieldwork begin. This is about getting all those involved in creating the product – from designers to engineers, to the commissioning clients – out of the studio or marketing department and into the field.

Here designers work with consumers, ethnographers, anthropologists and behavioural researchers to watch, look, listen and engage with how the product might be used. This is where we find out how people do certain tasks or perform key social functions that offer further insights into how the product could look, what key functions it should have, what people are expecting from it and how it enhances and improves, or makes easier or more pleasurable what they now have or are now doing. Says Kelly, 'This enables designers to build empathy with users on site and start thinking creatively about how they can improve things.'

It is, as his brother Tom Kelly, IDEO general manager, tells it, 'about non-interventional research, about watching, recording and then acting on the insights gained.'

This approach is essential. Male users, for instance, will not admit to problems with new technology when you interview them. Nor will, as behavioural researcher Paco Underhill points out, male shoppers articulate the problems they have when shopping because (as hunter gatherers) to admit things like this is to admit failure. Easier then to say you 'don't like shopping'. Yet when they were observed in the shopping process, it wasn't to do with not liking it, as Underhill discovered, but to do with the fact that most shops were emotionally, physically and ethnographically mapped out or designed for women.

Men like to see to the back of the shop when shopping (it makes them feel in control – there are no assistants waiting to pounce, no traps). They like to know where the dressing rooms are (a bolt hole, a place to get to when things get tough). They like information, leaflets, points in the shop that provide them with knowledge and a sense of product because they don't like asking questions – nor indeed do they like to admit ignorance on certain issues.

Faced with a lack of knowledge, or knowing and pushy shop assistants, they will retreat rather than confront. After observing this process, Underhill was able to work better with designers, retailers and hardware manufacturers to be create more male-friendly spaces. IDEO do the same with their product and design work. The consumer is the focus – the way they work through processes and tasks being the key to understanding them.

> **The stories may be narratives about the problems faced by consumers when using existing versions of a particular product.**

In the 'visualization' stage, stories of how, why and where people might use the product are created. These are used by designers to put together product prototypes.

The stories may be narratives about the problems faced by consumers when using existing versions of a particular product, or they may be stories about a journey – negotiating supermarket aisles, say, with a trolley that seems to have a mind of its own.

In the process of describing this journey, they outline what it is that troubles them. For example, the trolley design – difficult to manoeuvre, not compartmentalized enough, dangerous metal corners, uncomfortable child seat, nowhere to hang a shopping bag from, nowhere to put your shopping list so your hands are free.

There may be other external factors the designer may have to take into consideration. The narrowness of the aisle, the fact that there are no turning circles or places to pull into so that other trolley pushers can pass. And when you get to the bottom of the aisle, all that confusion! That crossflow of trolleys, the people at the cheese and meat counters stopping trolleys in their tracks. Why are they there? The people, the cheese counters? Why isn't there more space? Why are all the reduced offers and about to expire sell-by-dated foods loaded on shelves at the end of the aisles where they are likely to cause more trolley jams as people consider if they want to buy them or not?

Why, why, why? All these things we call the internals of design (the form, function and values of the product or brand) and the externals (the environmental factors that impact on its success) have to be considered. This is just the same for a brand or an organization, by the way – design isn't object specific, merely customer specific.

Initially these are sketched up and discussed. When the design team has agreed on a shortlist, the best are mocked up or turned into three dimensional working prototypes for the client to look at – and also for consumers to engage with, once more being studied using the product in the social context or cultural environment they have been designed for.

In Jeremy Myerson's book *IDEO: Masters of Innovation*, which looks at IDEO's approach to work in depth, this process is known as 'faking the future' or as an exploration of a future with a number of possible outcomes or pathways.

This is very much in keeping with how we determine the way the future will shape up, but very much against how most organizations operate. Here the future is fluid, malleable, rich with possibility. By going back to the client at this stage, or by connecting with the consumer once more, it is possible to hone this process further.

Prototypes and ongoing fieldwork can be used to check your assumptions about what a product should or shouldn't look like against what the consumer thinks.

There is the assumption, for instance, that we all use keyboards or the keypads on mobile telephones in much the same way and that this is true across cultures and ages. It isn't.

Research shows that teenagers use mobile keypads differently to adults. They are not just faster and more dextrous, they carry out most of their tasks on it with their thumb rather than their index finger. In Japan, where some of the fastest text messages in the world are written, this has given rise to what researchers have named *oya yubi sedai* or 'thumb tribes', teenagers who use their thumbs not just to text, but to point, ring doorbells, even greet each other in the street. The thumb has become the primary digit and, already, keyboard designers are having to take this into account as more and more teenagers go down this route.

Questioning teenagers about how they work a keyboard or send a text message wouldn't necessarily have offered these insights up – nor for that matter the more revealing insight that the musculature of the thumb and its flexibility are also changing as evolution adapts it to new technological circumstances. In contrast, Japanese designers and ethnographers have, from studying Japan's ageing but affluent population, come up with a design philosophy called *Raku Raku* – easy easy – which puts customer usage, observation and ways and means of interacting or engaging with a product at the heart of the design and manufacturing process. In doing so they came up with one of NTT's DoCoMo's most successful mobile phones, a design that sold 200 000 units in the first two months of operation.

Why? Because observation told them that elderly users needed larger keypads, brighter displays, bigger hand units in loud colours (arthritis, failing eyesight) and even louder ring tones. So successful was the project that 18 Japanese firms have banded together to form a network for universal design, which looks to consumers first and then designers before creating market-driven products.

As Housecall's Bill Abrams says, 'These are the kinds of things behavioural research is best at throwing up, the unexpected, or better still new insights on the ordinary and everyday.'

In his own work for clients, he has seen products pulled back from the brink because prototypes were observed to be causing problems for consumers – for example, when they were trying to take a cap off some container or other, or a product 'fail' in the eyes of the consumer because a product did not make surfaces shiny when it cleaned them. In the consumer's eyes, shine was about cleanliness and hygiene. Smell, as he once noted, didn't just tell consumers that a product was wholesome, healthy or good, but also safe.

Abrams writes, 'One study of bathroom cleaners revealed that consumers reacted negatively to a product that was clearly superior in its category. On the early videotapes, they were seen to wrinkle their noses when they were asked to open the bottle and use the cleanser.' Asked why, consumers said that the harsh acidic smell made them think the product was unsafe to use in areas where children were likely to play.

## ▨ Evaluation is about listening, then learning and doing

In the 'evaluation' stage, prototypes are refined – in this case the harsh smell was removed – and then the consumer was consulted once more. Here observational tools are used alongside more traditional market research ones. Consumers are asked their opinions on the product, in groups or alone (but on camera), to describe how they feel about the product, or to suggest any improvements that could or should be made to it.

This process, Kelly believes, is among the most important – listening and then prototyping up, then going back to the consumer and watching how they interface with it once more, listening again and asking their opinion for a second time. Here other insights may be gained about the consumer's lifestyle that have a direct impact on the hidden technologies of the product.

When an insulin pen was being designed, issues of profitability came up. Likewise size, aesthetics – it shouldn't look like a needle – but also the fact that it should make the diabetic's lifestyle easier, less constricting. Which is just what the final pen did, allowing users to carry insulin for up to 28 days without having to refrigerate it.

This is always the crucial question to ask – how does it makes things easier? How does it simplify a customer's experience? In other words, how can I make my product invisible, as in how can I make it *essential*? Invisible products are the ones we need most – the bank we never think about because it always does what we want it to do; the corner shop that's always open when we want it; the train that is never late; the laptop that never falters; the car that always starts.

Invisibility is about seamless acts, about things that do what they say they do on the tin. This is what all products and brands should aim for – not presence in the showy, look-at-me sense, but presence in the sense of dependability, reliance and longevity. Think of wristwatches, umbrellas, plates, cups, your favourite bar – only noticeable when it goes missing, closes or breaks.

But consider these things again. They are like this because they have evolved according to need, been cultivated according to minor refinements made over the years. Each generation, each customer, each user leaving a tiny residue of themselves behind – a comment to the potter that his mugs need to be bigger, easier to hold; chats with the watchmaker about the annoyance of having to keep pulling a fob from one's pocket rather than being able to consult it at a glance. The colours, tones and textures of your favourite corner shop or bar – open late because many customers over the years expressed a preference for this, said they liked that kind of fruit, that kind of beer, lights that were low, no music, snug chairs or a cheese counter! You see, we have always done market

> ❝ **They are like this because they have evolved according to need, been cultivated according to minor refinements made over the years.** ❞

research like this, and yet we puzzle over why some companies spend so much time looking into these things.

As we have just said, this is the way it has always been – it is just the white heat of technology that has blinded us from seeing and doing the obvious. Especially with objects that we think are beyond refinement – the office chair for example – chairs, we know, are for sitting in. But are they? When IDEO were asked to design one, they decided to go out and see how and in what ways we were now using office chairs.

When we get bored, office chairs are used like go-karts – people use feet to propel themselves back and forth across the studio floor. Other people use them to swing and loll about, pivot to get to filing stations, as a rocker, to menace Jasper the office dog, to huddle in corners at impromptu meetings, and occasionally, when they have nothing better to do, to sit on as they work their keypads, or sit at their desks. But each desk is a different height so the chairs are constantly adjusted, people are forever pumping themselves up and down – and this becomes a game and distraction in itself and, doubtless, another point for a chair designer to consider. Then there are back problems, curvature problems, keyboard strain, rockability, ergonomics of shape, of location, of momentum . . . All of which has to be tackled and solved.

The IDEO *Leap Chair* is perhaps one of the best examples of this process of asking questions and attempting to refine a product that most people would think has been refined to the limit. Studies were carried out on how people worked in an office environment – how they sat; the many ways they leant forward, sat back, slumped; how they used their chair to wheel themselves over to a colleague. Spinal curves were studied along with how people hunched when on the phone. Then IDEO designed the chair along 'anthropometrical lines' – what IDEO call the human factors that affect how we relate to the products we use, the cars we drive or the houses we live in. In other words, products that are designed to accommodate our physical limitations, as in how far we can reach, stretch, extend our arms, open our legs or flex our bodies. Yes, they even looked at the chair as go-kart and made it appropriately robust.

At the 'implementation' stage, all these things are brought together so the final product is an innovative, beautifully designed artefact that has the consumer and their needs at its heart. And their success rate? As Myerson, who also heads up the Helen Hamlyn Centre for Innovation at the Royal College of Art puts it, 'phenomenal'.

David Kelly's mouse for Microsoft sold more than 7 million units in a year. The Neat Squeeze toothpaste dispensers for Procter & Gamble captured 5 per cent of the $1bn market in the first year following its launch. A redesign of Ford's own brand audio equipment caused the numbers of Ford customers choosing to keep the equipment shoot from 13 per cent to 97 per cent. An ergonomically designed keyboard that made it easier for users to tilt and use sold $40m worth of keyboards for its commissioners in the first year of trading.

In other words, ethnographic observation, and behavioural research isn't just about making products look, feel and function better, it's about making them pay.

part

9

# Human factor interfaces:
## envisioning products and brands that stick

# Invisible branding –
## factors that affect a product's take-up

Using IDEO's five point process will help you build the kind of future-faced products that are user-friendly, but unless you regulate a product or a brand's critical threshold, measure its ability to delight consumers – the D-factor – and plug into key consumer trends, you are failing to maximize its true value, or trend worth.

By critical threshold we mean the factors – design, social, ethical, environmental and ethnographic – that make a product or brand more or less visible or appealing to the consumer's critical eye, and thus raise or lower the brand's ability to ride a trend or fit more readily into a trend path or cultural shift.

By the D-factor we mean the intangible, or sometimes tangible, aspects of a brand or product that delight us or make us smile in a way that encourages us to talk about the product to others – a key feature, its ethos, colour or the emotions it causes inside us.

Marketers and brand strategists talk of critical thresholds and D-factors in terms of making a product 'sticky' but few, when we question them, truly know what this means. In essence, 'stickiness' is the product or brand's ability to go viral – as in being at the right point in the culture, and having the desired look to it. Or carrying the kind of intangibles that make it appealing to a core but important group of consumers – the ones we have described as deviants or the power curve 20. With these things built into them, they become like the flu. This is how you should see your brand or product – as a virus.

### ◼ Making your brand or product futureproof and trend perfect

Talking about this is hardly enough. We need to know what these critical threshold factors are and how to build the D-factor into our brands, products or organizations.

These things are essential if a product, brand or organization is to make itself futureproof and trend perfect. Many of us buy into products, ideas or brands because they are convenient, or because they have been recommended (90 per cent of the brands we use and products we buy come to us via this route). These things only happen because the brand or product itself has a low critical threshold, a high D-factor and is plugged into the right kind of trends, or trend groups, that can impress on us why these things are needed now.

If we are talking about a venereal disease, the 'buy in rate' can be very high, if both parties have no knowledge of the fact that one of them may be infected, since sex as an activity has a low critical threshold – many of us want it, take it when it's on offer and often do so when intoxicated or in situations where we are less than rational about the act we are about to engage in.

If it is a new product – the Blackberry 5810, the Handspring Treo or the pocket PC from T-mobile – the idea itself may seem 'good' but the end user may have significant problems with the product. The technology may be too complex, the handwriting recognition software too quixotic, the design too awkward – so the critical threshold level becomes high, causing a high resistance to take-up.

> **We need to know what these critical threshold factors are and how to build the D-factor into our brands.**

Trends and future ideas invariably have critical thresholds that are high initially because most, by their nature, are unfamiliar and tend to run against existing communal or cultural experiences – think mobile phones here and how early surveys showed that as few as one in ten people believed they would ever need a mobile; now nine in ten say they can't do without them!

## ■ The tipping point

This is what Geoffrey Moore meant about 'crossing the chasm' or, to a lesser degree, Malcolm Gladwell's 'tipping point', a phrase originally coined by sociologists in the 50s to describe white people moving out of US suburbs when black people moved in, attracting more in their wake. The critical threshold in this instance was very low – the areas were affordable, the houses spacious and most were located close to where people could get jobs.

Once a critical threshold has been reached, then it is possible for a trend or idea to go viral or 'follow the curve', as viral marketers put it. This threshold can involve the design of a product, the number of functions it has, or the tasks it is meant to perform against how it actually performs them. But it can also involve an off-the-shelf product, or a boy band. This is perhaps a better way of showing how critical thresholds can be refined and reduced in such a way as to make things not only palatable but bland, homogenous and

> **Once a critical threshold has been reached, then it is possible for a trend or idea to go viral.**

entirely non-threatening – as many products become as they sink from good idea to good copy, to fair copy, to poor copy, to lookalike, to not quite like, to bland, to boring, to suburban, to instantly forgetable, to just-might-sell in Milton Keynes.

This is the 'product trajectory' or curve of most boy bands – Take That, East 17, Backstreet Boys, Boyzone, Westlife, 911 – to the neutered, non-threatening tones of boy band pop and their pap idol follow-ons.

What you get here is what you get in every product cycle – the innovator followed by the subsequent models that sandpaper off, or smooth out, anything that might have made the previous version resistible in some way or other (they weren't sexy enough, were too sexy, had an ugly band member). This is now known in the music business as the Gary Barlow syndrome – too gay, not gay enough, too anarchic, too whatever.

So each version is refined in a way that lowers the critical threshold, and thus improves the product's stickiness, take-up rate, or speed at which it travels along our curve. This is why Hollywood is so fond of testing films on target audiences and why theatre producers do try-outs; why restaurant owners and hoteliers have things called soft openings; why designers build prototypes; why publishers like Condé Nast mock-up newsstands and put dummy covers on them to test which face works, what cover lines attract, which typefaces or colours sell. But what are the key points that affect our critical threshold model?

# Your critical threshold checklist –
## key adjectives and indicators

The critical threshold model is simple, it's one we use all the time when gauging the likelihood of a trend or brand going viral, or the trend fit of a new product – does it slot into an existing trend corridor or is it part of an incoming one?

It works like this. Marks out of ten are given to the answers of each of the following questions – or as we call them Post-it queries (we usually put the trend, product or brand on a wall or table and work it over with Post-it notes).

- Is it original? New, a one-off, the first of its kind? If so, does it need explaining?
- Is it innovative? Something doesn't have to be original to shift the nature and performance of existing products in some way. The Dyson, for example, wasn't the world's first cleaner but it certainly revolutionized the market in terms of how it cleaned carpets! Likewise the Segway HT or the Palm V.
- Does it innovate? A product can be innovative in terms of design but familiar in terms of function. Philippe Starck's lemon squeezer, Rem Koolhaus's new Prada shop in New York, the Oki-ni stores in London and Paris are all examples of new carapaces for the existing objects.
- Is it intuitive? Can it be understood and used, or its functions deduced without an instruction manual? Simple products sell if they connect with our intuitive processes. This is why most of us still can't programme video recorders – they are not intuitive. A simple rule of thumb for this one? If I lost the instruction book, could I work out all the functions? If the answer is yes, I've got a viral product in my hands; if it's no, it might be a case of someone having designed and manufactured another also-ran. Think of the Palm V, the Segway HT, the Easy brand franchise – all simple to work out and appreciate.
- Is it tactile? Designwise do you want to handle it, touch it? If so does it feel good or awkward? 'Tactile' is a word used by design critics to describe the work of designers such as Marc Newson, Jonathan Ives, Ross Lovegrove, the Eames brothers, Robin Day, Arnie Jacobson and Eileen Gray. It is also used to describe

the graphic style of Paul Rand and Saul Bass, the clothes produced by Marc Jacobs for Hermès, or Tom Ford for Gucci and Yves St Laurent. In essence, it means products that have visual properties which compel you to touch or stroke them. And as field studies by behavioural researcher Paco Underhill have shown, products that do this increase their sales potential by 30 per cent. In the retail trade it is called a product or garment's 'petability'!

> 66 Is it ethically, environmentally and socially accountable? A citizen brand? If not could you make it one? 99

- Is it 'on trend'? Can you see where it fits into the culture in terms of its target audience, or in terms of the key cultural shifts that have led you to create this product in the first place? Does it have a raison d'être? Does it connect with people via the trend they are buying into? In the way boutique hotels, for instance, plugged into trends for Gated Luxury, Limelight Living, Zoning Out (see Part 12), wellness breaks, a shift from the minimal to the maximal.

- Is it authentic? Has every effort been made to ensure that it functions well and will stay the course, with an authority, integrity and honesty in how it fits together and performs?

- Has it lineage? Is there a brand DNA it can plug into? A history or tradition that it comes from likely to further inform the consumer about the product's provenance and credentials? BMW cars and bikes, Sony's entertainment hardware, Barbour jackets, Viking stoves, Canon office equipment, *Vogue* magazine, Ducati motorcycles, grand marque champagnes and Havana cigars all come with this guarantee and provenance implicit.

- Is it a firestarter? A brand, product or organization likely to kick-start a new trend or cultural shift? Think *Big Brother*, for instance, and how it spawned a hundred UK, US and European mainland lookalikes.

- Does it have a 'values' proposition? Is it ethically, environmentally and socially accountable? A citizen brand? If not could you make it one?

- Is it essential? Is it something the consumer or market really needs? This is a difficult one to answer since much of what is produced is hardly ever needed, so the contrarian in us will ask why you are bothering. Or rather have you identified what makes this product unique – its manufacture, design, value or unique values proposition? Whatever it is, you should identify it and then test it against all critical threshold indicators in its own right.

- Is it easy to replicate? Perversely, the easier a product is replicate the more likely it is to become viral, plug into a trend or, indeed, firestart one. Coco Chanel, the French fashion designer, knew this better than most. Instead of objecting to US manufacturers sending sketch artists along to her shows to copy her work, she dispatched dresses to them to make sure they got the designs right. Without knowing, she was working very close to Barabási's rule of preferential attachments – the more Chanel dresses people saw, the more they would want to wear one and the more she would profit from this process, especially since those who could afford her creations were unlikely to buy copies, but instead opt for the original.

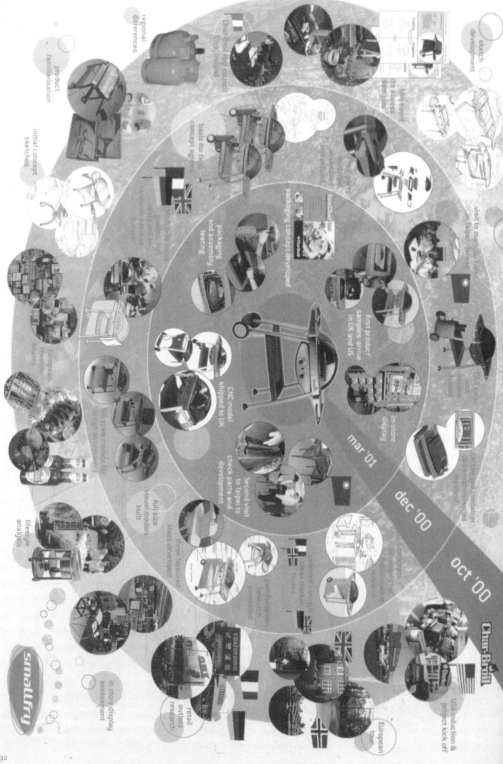

sketch development

take present to assess samples

visit to manufacturer to inspect samples

product familiarisation

regional differences

initial concept sketches

basis for final concept agreed

packaging & concept developed

packaging and assembly finally tested

first product samples arrive in UK and US

in-store display

CNC model shipped to UK

Second visit to Taipei to check parts and development

full size visual models built

three favoured ideas developed

European lifestyle boards

lifestyle analysis

in store display assessment

retail outlets research

European tour

USA induction & project kick off

mar '01

dec '00

oct '00

smallfry

Char-Broil

92

■ How does it compare pricewise to other models? Cheaper but does less? Expensive but does more? Cheaper but does the same? Expensive but does less? Cheaper but does more?

■ Is price the only consideration for buying this thing or wanting this brand? Yes? No?

All of these questions are important and the answers must be rated, not only by your own people but by consilient teams, thinkers and networks made up of people from R&D, designers, consumers, manufacturers, PR marketers, managers, sales executives and even competitors. Some of the questions, as we shall see, are more important than others, especially those concerned with originality, innovation, tactility, its values proposition and how, if at all, the product slots into a particular trend corridor.

Yes, value or 'cheapness' is important but not when it comes to deciding if something is on trend or likely to go viral. In itself, a low cost brand or product can increase profits in the short term, but making a product cheap – especially if that is the only reason for doing it – does not necessarily make it viral but it can, and usually does, give it a high critical threshold level because cheap products are invariably sourced in areas and under conditions that breach most ethical, social and environmental guidelines.

## ■ Critical threshold ratings

Our team or network tends to work through these questions one by one, asking each team member to say what they think and give their reasons for thinking that way. We do this in a fairly obvious and visual way – with good old Post-its. We use blue for low critical threshold scores or positive attributes – in other words, if a product gets a score of five or less, it has a high customer appeal – and pink for those with higher scores, in which case they have low customer appeal.

> **❝ The one thing you won't find out from your network, however, is the one thing that will make or break any brand. ❞**

Each Post-it has a comment scribbled on it with a number – for example, 'not intuitive, requires an instruction book and diagram to assemble it, 8'. When all critical threshold points have been assigned and the blue and pink Post-its allocated, the final assembly is then discussed, debated and further refined.

This process is followed for each question, each network member ranking it in accordance with how it is seen until all have been answered. The one thing you won't find out from your network, however, is the one thing that will make or

◄ Smallfry's cartographic or 'narrative map' of product usage and how external factors impact on the design of something as ordinary and everyday as a patio barbecue. Working clockwise, from the outside in, it is possible to follow the journey of the product from the external factors of the culture that impact on it, to those caused more by design constraints and aesthetic considerations. This system, used by Smallfry on all of its designs, is a very effective one for identifying a product's critical threshold.

break any brand or product – what we call the G-(Gioconda) factor, what product researchers and academics call the D-(delight) factor. This is key to the success of a product or a brand, and it is one of the many aspects of research, as we shall see, that has to be done in the field.

# The D-factor –
## making products sticky or viral in the true sense

The D-factor is something all customers recognize. A taste, smell, shape or even an intangible quality embedded in a product's design that makes a customer smile, sigh or think yes, that's for me. Some call it the Gioconda factor (after the da Vinci painting) and brands or products that have it are sure winners because the D- or G-factor is the very thing that makes us talk about a product and thus connect it to other people. In other words make it sticky.

Think of Jonathan Ive's work for Apple – his jellybean iMacs. Ross Lovegrove's Ty Nant water bottles that look like a twist of water frozen and immobilized in time. How about Bilt Hildrebrand's Mini Cooper for BMW – a tough-looking cookie of a car that preserves the quirky personality traits of the original mini. And Jones Garrard's Eurostar nose – that gallic protuberance of aerodynamic zest that has become not just the symbol of Eurostar but the thing that reminds us of the grand old days of luxury travel, and holidays in the hard and fast lane. Likewise Gehry's Bilboa or Norman Foster's 'Gherkin' in London. All D-factors we are keen to talk about, pass on and wonder and murmur about.

Consumer murmur, as researchers at Cranfield University see it, is one of the key attributes of the D-factor and how to embed it into your product. By 'murmur' they mean the things that customers talk about or identify with when they first encounter a product or brand experience. Murmur is what they are thinking or saying without being asked – in other words, a spontaneous and unprompted comment about what they are looking at or buying into.

As Andrew Burns (one of the researchers in Cranfield's ongoing work into empathic design mechanisms and what makes customers buy) puts it, 'Capturing the authentic murmur of the customer allows you to gauge reaction to concept ideas, identify concerns to be addressed in product improvement and to understand the evaluation behaviour of your customers during product and service encounters.'

Using hidden cameras, tape recorders, cameras and ethnographers, Cranfield researchers look at the following aspects of customer behaviour for clues as to where the D-factor of a brand or product lies.

- What initially arrests their attention? Is it the design of a product, its colour, the sound or smell it makes, its location, a prompt, comment from somebody else? What's being sought here are the attributes of first contact.
- Frequency and duration of behaviour? Sure they're looking – but for how long and where?
- The nature of the gaze? Is it a favourable look or a negative one. One that suggests puzzlement, understanding, surprise or amusement?
- Tone of response? Is it overall negative, positive or both? More puzzlement than surprise? More surprise than amused pleasure? The timbre of the tone is important here, along with the duration and depth of the reaction.
- Reaction to response? When they respond, how is this communicated to others? Verbally and in a positive light? Visually with gestures, with expressions of pleasure, doubt, indifference? What is the reaction to this? Universal agreement or do some agree and others think differently?
- Duration of response? When do they respond, how long do they respond for?

## Isolating the D-factor

From this, a list of key indicators is established. For example, the customers talked about design, colour, shape, texture, comfort, safety and so on. Then the same exercise is carried out on similar products in the same

> **What influences a customer in one category will certainly influence them in another.**

catagory with other similar customer types to establish a pattern match, or to see if there are similar indicators that catch the eye, or elicit comment on competitor's designs.

As well as doing this across competitor categories, researchers recommend that you do it across other non-related categories. In other words, if you are looking for the D-factor in a car, you should look at what makes customers buy a particular vacuum cleaner, or electrical goods for the kitchen.

Design houses such as Porsche or BMW's Designworks have long used this trick to their advantage. For what influences a customer in one category will certainly influence them in another – especially if the D-factor relates to durability, longevity, authenticity, if the product breaks down in simple, easy to reassemble sections still maintaining (as the Dyson cleaner manages to do) its sense of uniformity and coherency as an artefact as well as a household product.

Once you have placed your customer across categories and across product types, you should then have a master list which can be translated into the kind of feedback mechanism, or customer diary, that allows you to more readily isolate and identify the visible and intangible attributes comprising the D-factor of your product.

This can be as simple as the product's colour scheme – identified from the scope, volume and type of comments on your feedback sheet referring to colour. Or it can relate to usability. Indeed many designers are now discovering that the D-factor can be nothing more than the fact that a product's design tells you how to use it. The Apple iPod is a key example of this kind of approach. The iPod's outer rim with its indicator arrows says it all; its pimple button at the centre of its circular control wheel invites you to push it down, while the display prompts on the iPod's screen with their associated arrows suggest what should be done next.

## ■ The D-factor might be an intangible asset

But each product and brand has its own D-factor. To identify them more accurately you need to actively engage customers with your list created from those initial, but all too general, observations. This list needs to be more specific – to ask questions, pin them down, ask them to identify and isolate the things that most delight them about the product in question. Function, novelty, surprise, emotion, simplicity, colour, shape, comfort, sense of luxury?

You should also ask them to photograph what the D-factor is – disposable cameras are good for this – and, more importantly, to photograph other people demonstrating the same principle. This should be done even if it is something as intangible as a brand, or a retail experience. In one project we were working on, a retail redesign, we asked customers to find the D-factor in a competitor's store. And they found it in the changing rooms. Initially the client didn't get it. The colour? The shape? The featured bench?

Sort of, but what five of our customers were focusing on was the changing room's width – the fact that they could get into it with friends. Also the fact that they could try on as many garments as they liked, with their friends helping them, without having to step outside into the main drag of the shop or, worse, be accused of shoplifting. This was the real D-factor we discovered when we probed further – they were teenagers and here was a shop that trusted them. Now that surprised them!

Once you've established what your D-factor is (or what your critical threshold indicators are), you can truly use your network or team to create a sense or prototype of what the brand or product should look like. During our assessment meetings (with anything from 7 to 15 people) it is surprising how consensus emerges (more on this later) from all this debate and discussion. Also how you end up with a run of points which allow you to plot fairly

> **Points which allow you to plot fairly accurately whether a product has a high or low critical threshold.**

accurately whether a product has a high or low critical threshold or entry point into the market – will it whizz along our trend curve or go slowly?

Within each set of answers you may find some variation – a few will give something 7, some 8 or 9 but, with rare exceptions, you tend to find that most people, consumers and networks tend to mark within similar bandings. Indeed, if there are noticeable anomalies or huge differences in terms of ratings you usually find that these are caused by so-called experts – those too familiar with a particular market – or seasoned hacks who have seen everything before, even the newest of products!

## ■ Avoid having specialists in your network

It is important then to weed these out of your team at the start, and also to avoid using professional consumers or jobbing focus group types who know the ropes. These are likely to skew the marks involving those questions key to knowing if a product has a low threshold rating or not – the ones relating to innovation, intuition, values, tactility and authenticity. To know what these things are, and how to use them, you have to leave your office and live, work and design in the field. It is here that you see people using brands, products and dreams as they really are being used, dreamed and deployed. Not hypothetically but ordinarily, realistically and, in many cases, solving problems you've not even considered – better still, showing product gaps that lead you towards the next little big idea, or brand.

# The insight game –
## when seeing is learning

Good behavioural research 'shows' rather than tells. This is why those who use it 'observe' rather than ask the kind of questions that might distract or disguise the lifestyle narratives people are living or creating for themselves on a daily basis.

This is also the case with introducing new products. Rather than 'telling' what a product does, our research has shown that the uptake is better when people see it in operation, or watch other people within their own network or social group using it – they are learning, in other words, from a fellow consumer's narrative, or from the story of the product. By doing things this way, you are not only lowering the critical threshold of the product but establishing the product's etiquette, or how smooth or easy it is to use.

Watch how people do this when they are confronted with new ways of eating – using chopsticks, say, or sampling a new cocktail or trying a new food type such as sushi, fusion or pacific rim. They watch, record and then engage usually with friends or in situations – at work, on holiday, with a new partner – when experience or experimentation is a way of creating group cohesion or demonstrating one's willingness to try something new, even if there is the possibility of failure attached.

> **❝ Experience or experimentation is a way of creating group cohesion or demonstrating one's willingness to try something new. ❞**

As long as others can fail, or others are engaged in the experiment, people will have a go. If the product is 'there' however, or being promoted as something new, the uptake is slow. There is no narrative path along which the consumer can proceed, no security net into which they can fall if they make a mistake or if they look foolish when trying out this new thing.

We've seen this in bars when new drinks are being promoted or new cocktails being tried out. If the environment is busy, loud and dynamic, our researchers noted that drinks with names that were easy to pronounce, or generic types of drink (such as beer, whisky, wine, brandy) were invariably asked for instead of more expensive, exotic or difficult-to-pronounce brands.

Likewise we discovered that all drinks asked for had a perceived and obvious characteristic – high in caffeine, contain a shot of pure alcohol, a drink with a story, 'have', as one consumer put it, 'the kind of facts about its origins you're happy to pass on, or can use as a chat up line or conversation starter'. Absinthe is one such drink – the choice of poets, artists and wayward boho types. It comes with a challenge, a story (madness, romance, abandon) but also a promise that by drinking it you too can adopt a character and a history to suggest that you aren't quite the bore you look wearing the suit or tie you've got on. Poteen is the same, certain Scotch whiskies, authentic Russian vodkas, wines, champagnes – all have their stories or D-factors. But look to modern products such as Archers, alcopops, Bacardi Breezers, Moscow Mules – what's the story or D-factor here?

Our researchers came up with the following – underage drinking, cheap nights out, grim sex, morning-after hangovers, bad, vomiting, feeling shite, sweet tasting, naff, good for a laugh, superclubs, loud bars, girlie, for slappers. Hardly products with the kind of story or history you'd want to pass on. In short, products launched for a moment, a mood, a knee-jerk reaction to falling profits or a perceived gap in the market – 'something for the ladies', a bit like the legendary Babycham but, alas, with none of glamour or faux ironic moments.

## ■ A product's narrative goes beyond the point of purchase

The connections customers made between these products and their experiences with them were pretty base and basic – the grimness of the morning after, the fact that they were cheap and that they 'hit the spot'. Good for the short term, but not if you are trying to establish a brand with a credible history or with a strong and positive narrative. In the case of brand names such as Archers and Bacardi Breezers, even those who drank them saw them for what they were. They even call them slapper cocktails, while Bacardi Breezers are referred to as 'Bacardi heavers' for reasons all too familiar to those who drink them. Not the kind of things that bode well for these brands in the long term – a product without a history, or a story, is no product worth considering.

Nobody out for the night wants to say things that are pointless or stupid – or indeed that these things make you throw up or make you 'mad for it' – especially if they are on the pull. On the other hand, as our researchers record again and again, everybody wants to be a knowledge carrier, an insider – this more than anything is what sparks interest in a new drink or way of drinking.

They can learn and then pass that learning on – become, in other words, a pathfinder, a connector. Not just a link in the hub, but the hub itself. But of course, people do want alcohol to do the things they want and expect it to do –

get them drunk, make them less inhibited, unwind – but these, as we've discovered, are residual facts, part of the residual nature of brand or product design and history. They are there without being stated and, rather like the 'Ratner' effect (after Gerald Ratner, one time millionaire jeweller, who famously described his own products as crap only to send the company's shares plummeting and customers scurrying), once you articulate them they can do long term damage to your brand. So beware!

## ■ Location, location, location

We also discovered that people were more likely to try new drinks and those with long and unusual names when they were seated and among friends rather than when they were at the bar or alone.

They were more likely to consume wine and spirits instead of beer and, if you added sofas, low tables and created 'nesting areas', were more likely to be female or mixed, as opposed to male only, especially if you made table service standard rather than an extra.

Table areas also acted as knowledge hubs for those standing or seated at other tables. They tended to watch what people were ordering and then, if they liked what they saw, ordered the same thing themselves.

Without knowing it then, bars with tables or seated areas in key positions were, in effect, creating the 'experience' or 'learning' hubs that customers needed to learn about new products and brands!

Observation cuts through what people think you want to hear to what they actually do. But it can also show up details of social habits or expose reasons for doing things that people may be unwilling to talk about.

A superclub owner we worked for noticed that there was a fall-off in bar sales between 3 am and 4 am when he was, as he put it, 'Expecting things to hot up.' We studied crowd patterns, bar configuration, consumer types and watched what his club customers were doing. At about 2.45 am many were still arriving but others, quite a significant number, were queuing to collect their coats. They were also queuing with their partners, or people they had just met. They had scored and were heading home. The average time spent in the queue ran to 30 minutes or more, and out on the street a similar scenario of waiting for cabs and night buses was unfolding. In all, of the couples we tracked, 20 spent an hour or more waiting or hanging about!

> **❝ Initially the club didn't see this as its problem – it was just how things were. ❞**

When a second group was tracked and subsequently questioned, we discovered that they were leaving the club partly because they had met somebody they wanted to go home with or, if they were with their partner, wanted to get back to do the 'deed', as one put it. But in the main they were leaving because experience had taught them just how difficult it was going to be to get back home.

Initially the club didn't see this as its problem – it was just how things were. We persuaded them to trial the idea of opening a cab list for regulars, where they could leave their details and then wait in a special shorts-and-shots lounge kitted with inscriber boards where their numbers were displayed along with appropriate saucy messages. The customers couldn't believe their good luck.

Knowing there was a cab on the way and that their coat would be waiting at the cab booth when their number was called, the couples tended to relax and drink more. Furthermore the shorts-and-shots bar became something of a cult destination for other couples who wanted to read the messages – some very frank indeed – that partners were posting to each other onscreen.

## ■ Observation improves a brand's leverage

Observational work like this can improve a brand's leverage, or indeed a brand owner's insight about how a brand is perceived. It can also point up a few home truths about how little consumers actually consider products despite our attempts to target them.

FutureBrand's managing director Christopher Nurko noted this when he established the FutureBrand House in West London, in response to arguments with brand managers about how consumers saw and used their brands.

Eight volunteers or housemates were selected. All were 30, very brand aware, early adapters and highly articulate on the issue of brands and the part they played in their lives. Imitating the *Big Brother* reality TV model, they were filmed over a 24-hour period living, eating and hanging out in a house rigged with static cameras, hidden mikes and broadcast cameras – all feeding details back to psychologists and clients who were observing the household activities via remote control.

The house itself came equipped with brands the housemates were familiar with and others they might or might not aspire to – from Tesco to NatWest, to Saab, to Nokia, to Gap and Peugeot.

Nurko says, 'Brand owners have this idea that the brand was somehow important to the consumer, in that they thought about it in the way brand owners think about the brand. You know its perceived benefits, its characteristics, what it can do for you. But for most people this isn't the case – and observing their daily rituals demonstrates this. Brands are really a means to an end, a way of getting what we want, not what brand owners say we want, and if a brand can become that stepping stone then we'll use it.' He continues, 'But we only think about it for a fraction of a second during any day of the week – a brand window if you will, or a brand clock when that name figures in your consciousness, but only when you open the cupboard or think, "Gosh it's time for breakfast!"

'Brands like to think they're in your head all the time. Why they talk of share of mind, as well as share of shelf. But our FutureBrand House disproved this entirely and, better still, brand managers could see the evidence for themselves – their brands being used or ignored, overlooked or criticized in the way they are every day in the average home.'

How one housemate reacted to Kellogg's Fruit and Fibre is a case in point. Keen on healthy eating and looking good, the housemate liked the idea of a healthy breakfast that contained fruit, yogurt and bananas. So why not Fruit and Fibre – one of the products lying about in the house's kitchen? When it was advertised, it was all about dieting, about helping you to slim. In other words, the kind of brand you'd expect to find in a fat person's house, rather than a healthy household. Since the housemate wasn't fat and didn't like that kind of association, it wasn't the kind of product to aspire to or the kind of product to leave out on the table!

Smirnoff Ice on the other hand, seen by consumers in other surveys as a bit tacky and common, came out tops with these housemates and for reasons already mentioned – convenience, brand smoothness, easy to say.

As one of the housemates put it, going to the bar for a vodka, lemonade and ice just seemed like too much trouble – and asking for a vodka and lemonade sounded a bit girlie. But Smirnoff Ice didn't have that kind of hassle attached. It sounded cool, a solid drink.

Observation is good, immersive research better still.

# Being there –
## gatekeepers and access culture

Sean Pillot de Chenecey, aka Captain Crikey – along with a growing number of field researchers and consumer ethnographers – takes this 'living with the enemy' process a step further and uses behavioural research along with friendship groups, or weak tie ethnography, to elicit insights that are useful as well as honest.

De Chenecey spent several years in Europe and the Middle East serving with the 5th Airborne Brigade and the UN Scout Car Squadron before working undercover with the army's Special Forces Unit. He uses the covert and overt surveillance skills learned there to better understand how consumers work and where they are going. 'Dividing up different levels of intelligence work and relating them to military operations isn't a million miles away from discovering why people prefer Labour to Tory or Pepsi to Coke,' he says.

He believes – like old school ethnographers such as Margaret Mead, Colin Turnbull, Clifford Geertz and Claude Lévi-Strauss – that it is important to engage with the community you are brailling if you are to truly understand them and if they, in return, are to trust you enough to tell you what you want to know.

'Passive observation as the army teaches you isn't worth a thing. Doing is seeing, and in the process of doing it is possible to ask questions and to elicit cogent and insightful answers in the field, or rather on the hoof and in context.' Questions should be open ended and framed to invite answers that are about stories or narratives ('. . . the tattoo you're wearing, I've noticed a few other people you've introduced me to with similar ones . . . ?') rather than questions that are closed and final (as in 'I see you're wearing a tattoo . . .') which if the respondent reads as a criticism may cause them to clam up entirely.

## ■ Gatekeepers and key actors

Contextualized questions are just as important – especially if you are working undercover – because it gives the researcher a frame within which to ask them. In this case, the replies will be open and, if the question itself is an open-ended one, leads on to other areas and pathways.

To establish yourself in a group, however, and to gain the trust of its members, it is important to identify who the gatekeeper is, or the hub through which all knowledge flows to and from the group. This can be the group's leader, the instigator of the new look or trend, or it can be what ethnographers refer to as 'key actors' – brokers or connectors who straddle two cultures and who are comfortable in both; the one the mainstream lives in and the one you are attempting to infiltrate.

These gatekeepers usually know who and what you are – and why you are doing what you are doing. Rarely do they work in ignorance of your true brief but sometimes, for their own reasons – usually to maintain credibility, power or indeed to ensure that there isn't too much animosity towards either your presence or reasons for observing the group – they may not tell the full story to the group being observed.

> **❝ If they are to negotiate access to a group's inner sanctum and allow you to observe its rituals. ❞**

It is important, however, that you tell them the full story. If they are to negotiate access to a group's inner sanctum and allow you to observe its rituals – anything from drinking to drug taking, to getting ready for a teen sleepover – or to take part in group activities, the gatekeeper needs to know that you can be trusted, and that they in turn can trust and depend on you. This is especially so if the group becomes unhappy with how you are monitoring or writing them up (which happens more times than not) and the gatekeeper is called on to get you out of a fix. Gatekeepers are more than mere brokers – they are your guide, pathfinder and the painter of the bigger picture. They put you in touch with the friendship groups and weak tie connections that make your observations truly insightful.

De Chenecey, one of the advertising industry's best known behavioural researchers, conducts ethnographic-based field research at music festivals and in bars and clubs, etc. – 'going to where young people hang out, rather than expecting them to come to me.'

He continues, 'I've often spent several weeks living within local communities, getting to know young people and their families in as "real" a way as possible. I was inspired to do this style of research by William Finnegan and his excellent book *Cold New World*. He staked out as his beat the disenfranchised – the sort of people most agencies have no contact with and couldn't care less about. He immersed himself in the world of the young and the lost, and having spent a decade working within the exciting but totally unrepresentative world of advertising, I often try and emulate some of his fine work – this is why finding your gatekeeper is key, the person who can plug you in – and no this isn't about "the professional focus group" member, but about finding a man or woman who can be your hub or pivot.'

'A recent and ongoing project has involved me,' de Chenecey continues, 'in the development of advertising activity in the US for anti-tobacco communications targeting young people. One of the agencies I've worked with is Maris, West and Baker based in Jackson, Mississippi. For this Mississippi anti-tobacco campaign I flew from London into Jackson airport in the dead of night. After hanging around for ages a cab pulled up driven by an old African–American guy. As we drove towards the Hilton I asked him about Mississippi. He told me he was called Purify Johnson and had lived in the state all his life. He'd driven for the Deluxe Cab Company for years.

'A 60-year-old man whose grandparents had grown up living on the plantations that their parents worked on as slaves, Johnson himself grew up during the beginning of the Civil Rights movement. He served in Vietnam with 82nd Airborne, only to return and find himself gaoled for taking part in anti-racist demonstrations. He later married and had children who eventually went to Jackson State University, the black university which was a hotbed of political activism in the 60s.

'Johnson's story and family,' as de Chenecey explains, 'perfectly encapsulated modern Mississippi. But no one in the mainstream advertising world typically wants to hang out with a poor black cab driver and his kids, even though what they have to say can be deeply interesting. In this instance, they gave me a really clear view of life for that group of people.

'During the next month, I conducted numerous focus groups throughout Mississippi, with kids and teens. I interviewed them using my preferred method-ology – friendship groups or weak tie networks. These involve recruiting a seed respondent, or gatekeeper – in this case Purify – and getting them in turn to recruit a bunch of relevant friends who are happy to be interviewed in their own home or place of choice. This has a great effect in gaining swift, deep and honest answers.'

De Chenecey concludes, 'Through Johnson and his contacts, I was able to hang out with a bunch of poor black and white kids in Mississippi, and their insights into the realities behind everyday life in Mississippi fed straight into the planning process for an award winning series of ads by the MWB Advertising titled *Question It*. This *Question It* campaign hit the airwaves a few months later, and utilized community-based guerrilla style activity and language and social indicators they would be familiar with – street awareness and street credibility. Like the bigger, national *Truth* campaign, *Question It* aims to change youth attitudes towards tobacco, an opportunity to expose the deceptive marketing tactics of the tobacco industry and provides teens with the tools to make informed decisions.'

## ■ Identify the motivators

To reach teens, Maris, West and Baker took a two-pronged approach – general, mass media advertising and local, community-based activity. Statistics tell us that 13% of all 12–17 year olds are 'open to smoking' whilst over 35% are 'sensation-seeking experimenters' who are not regular smokers. The psychographic profile of these sensation seekers suggests they have few moral anchors against wrong-doing and lying, that they're more likely to have materialistic and self-serving daydreams, whilst they're both daring and feel less positive about their lives and themselves than their contemporaries. Cigarettes satisfy various needs of sensation-seeking teens – their need to rebel, take risks, fit in, be independent, show self-expression and feel respected. A key research insight de Chenecey found indicated that tobacco is a tool of control: 'So if we wanted to take tobacco away, we had to replace it with something that fulfils those need states and provides control.'

> ❝ Teens use brands and brand narratives to communicate something about who they are. ❞

Therefore, the *Question It* (QI) strategy is to give teens the knowledge (the product), the motivation (a way to rebel and take risks) and the power (by putting control in their hands). The tactical way of doing this is to deconstruct the mythical narratives or stories these teenagers have created or bought into, lies and deceptions of tobacco – which could only be done with a campaign that knew where these kids were coming from, how they looked, where they hung out, what they thought and talked about.

To have absolute credibility, QI was positioned as an alternative brand, in terms of being an alternative to the bland brands that surround youth culture in the US – Old Navy, Pepsi, Adidas, etc. QI was treated as a brand for the obvious reason that teens use brands and brand narratives to communicate something about who they are. So QI – again just like the *Truth* campaign – had to become an aspirational symbol, a badge or narrative which stood for rebelling, taking risks, fitting in, being independent, self-expression and respect. Something perhaps that 'non-joiners', the teens at greatest risk for smoking, will adopt.

Thus, as de Chenecey pointed out, any attempt to target them directly – especially the white children – would be seen as a threat, the very thing they would rebel against. Weak ties had to be built between families first, between community groups, and then the information communicated along the organic networks that these in turn generated using gatekeepers to enhance and boost this process – to help create the textures, terminologies, contexts and ways of entering another person's world or culture on their level. The narrative, or story, they can now buy into. But also pass on.

## ■ Gatekeepers are cultural translators

Gatekeepers – as was the case with Johnson – also help put a group, or group situation, in perspective. It may not always be appropriate or indeed judicious to ask questions there and then. Worse, the stupidity of the question might in fact damage your cover, or the credibility you've worked hard at building up with a group. So gatekeepers can keep you from looking foolish or saying foolish things.

They also provide you with the keys needed to decode many of the words, phrases, and bonding rituals that hold groups together and act as a key to keeping them exclusive and distinct from the mainstream. This may be jeans worn in a particular way, a hierarchy of brands that only the group understands, or a set of phrases, colours or verbal bonding rituals each uses to signal belonging, as Tom Wolfe notes in his brilliantly observed, *The Pump House Gang*:

Somebody further down the stairs, one of the boys with the major hair and khaki shorts says, 'The black feet of the black panther.'

'Mee-dah,' says another kid. This happens to be a cry of a well underground society known as the Mac Meda Destruction Company.

'The pan-thuh.'

'The poon-thuh.'

All these kids, all seventeen of them, members of the Pump House crowd, are lollygagging around the stairs down to Windansea Beach, La Jolla, California, about 11 am, and they all look at the black feet, which are a woman's pair of black street shoes, out of which stick a pair of old veiny white ankles, which lead up like a senile cone to a fudge of tallowy, edematous flesh, her thighs, squeezing out of her bathing suit, with old faded yellow bruises on them, which she probably got from running eight feet to catch a bus or something. She is standing with her old work-a-hubby, who has on sandals; you know, a pair of navy blue anklet socks and these sandals with big, wide, new-smelling tan straps going this way and that, for keeps. Man, they look like orthopaedic sandals, if one can imagine that. Obviously, these people come from Tucson or Albuquerque or one of those hincty adobe towns. All these hincty, crumbling black feet come to La Jolla-by-the-Sea from the adobe towns for the weekend. They even drive in cars all full of thermos bottles and mayonnaisey sandwiches and some kind of latticework wooden-back support for the old crock who drives and Venetian blinds on the back window.

'The black panther.'

'Pon-thuh.'

'Poon-thuh.'

'Mee-dah.'

Here the rituals are plain, the rolling 'lollygagging' language and ranginess of the gang written into the report itself. The way he and they indicate otherness is implicit – their collective jibes about the panthers, or old people as they are, caught not just in the way he shows how the gang sees their clothes – the anklet socks, their sandals, but the way they use chanted references – 'pan-thuh', 'poonthuh', and coded asides, like 'Mee-dah,' to flag up their sense of belonging to the gang, the tribe.'

This is the true ethnographer at work – capturing, framing, showing and telling but not at this stage making value judgements or allowing the feeling for one group or the other come into play.

In many ways, good ethnography and good behavioural research reporting is reportage photography or journalism with none of the subjectivity, all of the facts and as much description and list making as time, and the project under review, permits. This process is important for if done correctly it brings to the video and photographic material collected the added dimension of the poetics, ironies and possibilities of what is being observed.

# Consumer narratives: capturing them and using them to build future-faced brands

# Consumer narratives –
## and the self-actualized shopper

Just as customers work against a grand narrative – a trend, a bigger cultural shift, an incoming mood that impacts on the way they feel about things – so too do they work to inner narratives and stories that govern their lives. Stories about the 'I self', the 'looking-glass self', and the 'extended self', stories or narratives that keep these consistent and in keeping with how the 'I self' wants the rest of our being to appear, behave and interact with the exterior world.

This is why the best products, brands and campaigns sell. Not as objects but, as Christopher Nurko discovered in his FutureBrand House experiment and de Chenecey identified in his anti-tobacco work, as ways of aiding our daily attempts to move from being mere consumers to prosumers or 'self-actualized' shoppers – people who use their wealth (as the father of motivational psychology Abraham Maslow saw it) to become less led and more self-determining – I shop therefore I am, but also I shop therefore I can effect change.

Our climb up Maslow's ladder or pyramid from base needs to self-actualization isn't as straight up, or indeed straightforward, as Maslow and his followers believed. Culture, upbringing, our sense of propriety, what is required and what is or isn't accepted in private and public circumstances all inform the many narratives we carry inside our heads. As a consequence they affect how trends are bought into or passed from edge to mainstream.

In other words, even if we want something – a look, a bigger car, a better house, cosmetic surgery, a better body – there are social and psychological choices, or critical thresholds of a different sort that keep these things in check. Usually it is our family, friends, colleagues, associates, neighbours; our class, income, levels of expectation; anything in fact except a real or tangible barrier.

Because of this we sometimes keep under wraps the dreams we have, the ideas of scampering above our station. Occasionally, away from our cultural and social fetters, we test and challenge – on holidays we take greater social and sexual risks, experiment more with food, the types of people we associate with and the activities we engage in.

Researchers say we do this with lovers – chemicals in the brain actually alter our behaviour. Psychologically we want to be seen as interesting, as individuals, as having a character or personality the other person wants to be with, so we feign funkiness, being original, well travelled, plugged in, cool, connected.

Likewise in our career awaydays, corporate game playing or, the latest craze among forty-something KPMG types, Lego lounging (using Lego bricks to create personalities, build strategies, encourage lateral thinking and notions of networks and connectivity) are all part of this breaking out process, of making us 'other'.

For the most part, however, we herd and conform, or at least keep our heads down and run with the pack until increased awareness, a growing self-knowledge or outside knowledge (via books, TV, cinema, newspapers and the internet, but mainly our peers and strong tie connections) and a broadening of our perspective and confidence levels (via income and education) increase our levels of

> **" For the most part, however, we herd and conform, or at least keep our heads down and run with the pack. "**

worth – of how we value ourselves and our social position. That's how Maslow read things way back in the high octane optimistic 70s. The more culturally confident we become, the more we say, do, feel and think what is really about us or our inner selves rather than about what we think people expect from and of us. This is because the inherited narratives we carry inside our heads – tacit narratives about family, about friends, about morality, about accepted modes of behaviour – become modified, or become narratives we can no longer live with as our life experiences and the opinions of new people, colleagues, a lover or a subgroup we join begin to colour the narratives we have failed to challenge. This is because human nature, at its most basic, demands that we be consistent, and oddly – despite purely western obsessions with individuality and non-conformity – blend in. Which is why for much of our work we spend time with and seeking out people who are, for one reason or another, challenging the day-to-day narratives or schema we carry about with us.

## ▨ Tacit narratives and the stories we live by

These can be things attributed to Jung's sense of the collective unconscious, things we know without knowing why we know them – 'blonds are better fun in bed', 'fat people are stupid', 'Russians drink lots of vodka'. Truth isn't the issue, it's just that we know we know!

As we develop, interact and grow our social and cultural networks, the archetypes or stereotypical narratives we carry about modify themselves and we begin to create narratives that are more personal, as in self-learned and in many ways self-determining. Rather like Peter Schwartz's long view narratives in microcosm, in that we use them to develop scenarios and stories we can live in or up to. The best brands, products or advertising campaigns do this, even if their creators have no idea that they are doing it. They act as ladders, as means to a self-actualized end.

Imagine a Martha Stewart moment? A Ralph Lauren one. Or the lifestyle possibilities conjured up by phrases like 'very Nantucket' or 'very Ivy League'.

Even if we have never experienced these lifestyle remits, we have a good idea of what they look like – clear-eyed, freckly skinned men and women in white shirts and no-nonsense perfect jersey knits, a dog perhaps, a chocolate Labrador running on a beach, a boy with a kite flying in the background. White picket fences maybe, clapboard houses with shingle roofs. A yacht on the sound, polo mallets clop-clopping against leather balls somewhere in the background. A kitchen even, with easy as they come, fresh-from-the-garden salads, a Thanksgiving turkey with all the trimmings. Beach pebbles and old shells on a stripped wood windowsill bleached in sunlight, kids hosing the $4 \times 4$ with dad got up in deck shoes and open neck madras shirt being a big kid like the rest of them . . . You get the picture? An aspirational lifestyle that fulfils many people's inner yearnings for a Disney safe, wash powder Monday world of happy people and bottle-free beaches. And by fingering these things, by crystallizing them, designers like Ralph Lauren or lifestyle architects like Martha Stewart formed narratives many people back in the do and dye 80s and 90s wanted to buy into.

Now Stewart's dream, very 'little duplex on the prairie' or Lauren's happy Hampton campers (in both senses of the word!) seem a tad out of step with a new mood that veers towards introspection, 'compressed spirituality', the one-off, individuality and inconspicuous consumption on one hand, and towards a 'let's party and be damned shiny surface, hairdresser's night out' on the other. Hence the rise and fall of the Gucci lifestyle. Our outer narratives then are shifting, taking us along new paths and these are impacting on our inner narratives – inexorably changing how we feel about family, class, culture, life, technology, food, science and medicine, but also how we report and categorize things.

Also how we feel about institutions like marriage, the monarchy, or McDonald's – a brand once favoured for its egalitarian credentials, its ability to bring good, cheap, easy-to-carry food to the hard pushed masses. Now it is a brand that has all but abandoned its clown Ronald because 'he seems inappropriate' they say; but also in these days of child sex allegations, son-of-Chucky spin-offs and worries about our children's safety, clowns carry faintly sinister undertones. McDonald's have also shifted away from its meat-only roots, its 'one burger, one world' mentality and in the process, we would argue, abandoned a narrative that was really old hat – imperialistic, didactic, bland, potentially unhealthy, boring, low brow – and replaced it with what?

One that is a narrative of many parts, a hapless hydra of irony, schmaltz and lo-cal buns with equally lo-cal aspirations. From McDonald's to McDabble in one fell marketing swoop. A brand, we predict, that is about to encounter hard times ahead because, like many brands in its position, it is not only failing to read its customer narratives, it is failing to understand its own narratives.

However, we must be sure that the narratives are true and not part of the mythical lore that seeps into our consciousness on a daily basis. It is important to see and hold them in context and perspective.

## ◼ Always look for the truth in the tale as well as the sting

The media, for example, talk of cloning and stem cell research in the way that they spoke of the first testtube babies created in petri dishes rather than wombs way back in the 80s. There was fear, disgust, loathing and the constant underlying idea that these children were Frankensteinian in conception, 'of the devil', as one paper put it, a travesty of science, against God's law etc. and so yawn.

In 2002, Elizabeth Carr, conceived in the said petri dish and born on December 28th 1981, marked the arrival of the one millionth in vitro birth by addressing a United Nations conference on infertility. She said quite simply that, as far as in vitro children are concerned, their way of arriving in the world was 'not a big deal'.

End of story. End of all those interminable debates among ethicists, philosophers, religious fundamentalists and geneticists determined to write their narratives (or their version of how the world should be shaped and how we should come into it) over others.

This is what is always worth remembering when looking at outer and inner narratives – those adhered to by the collective or the herd, and those we create for ourselves. They are only narratives, not fixed points. Just as people get bored with the same old story, so too are they intrigued by new ones.

> ** They are only narratives, not fixed points. Just as people get bored with the same old story, so too are they intrigued by new ones. **

# 37

# Narratives we live and die by –
## or when truth is relative

The uncovering of prosumer narratives is what forecasting is about in essence – locating and mining these new narratives, what the good profiler brings back from the field to the studio for assessing. The outer narrative – done through reading our networks, the visual snapshots, personal diaries and documentaries of the people we are profiling – and the inner narratives as they react and change against them. The latter 'decoded' or brailled from their on-camera, in situ interviews, or the cartograms our interviewees or edge dwellers allow us to create, but also the brand maps and garbage profiles they also bring to our attention.

We say in situ interviews because this is how all interviews of a core or emerging target group should be done – never in a studio, never in a focus group situation, and never in a place of your own choosing.

If you identify a new group, as we did in the case of our Grit Girls, then it is important to do all your interviewing in the field. You need to use what you see with what you've learned from your networks and from third party sources to inform your questions and the on-camera digging you need to do to get to the narrative they carry inside them. These, after all, give you clues to their self-actualized desires and to your brand success.

Grit Girl, a very powerful trend to come, came to our attention through a number of networkers who reported her presence in particular types of bars in London, Manchester, Leeds and Glasgow. They said she was loud, drank fairly heavily, consistently, wine instead of beer but also cocktails, whiskies (usually as a chaser) and obviously had money or fairly good credit lines.

She seemed to be conscious of her weight and in conversation she alluded to it. She was attentive to her looks, under thirty and seemed to be single. She had a close and closed circle of female friends and tended to 'pack' with them on nights out. She regarded men, at least in social situations, as fringe or bit players in her socializing. She wasn't however the 'mad for it', beer-drinking ladette of old, happy to dance on tables, shout 'off, off, off' at strippers dressed as policemen, or indeed fall into the gutter or a cab after one too many Archers. She was, we were told, in a far more refined and mercurial category.

In other words, unlike her *Loaded*-reading male counterpart, she had moved on and up. Maybe she wasn't even part of this band in the first place. She also read *Glamour*, instead of *Elle* (her second favourite read) or *Marie Claire* and was keen on beauty regimes, designer labels. She was also keen on reading, eating out, and travelling with friends, and not merely for sex. Informal interviewing and observational sorties took place in bars, clubs, gyms, shops, areas where she lived, jobs she worked at and the restaurants she frequented.

Researchers at this stage tend to work alone and always carry ID, copies of previous reports we've done, a small camera, a tape recorder and a small Sony Digicam for capturing what we refer to at this stage of the process as 'atmospherics', images that pinpoint the general ambience of the place or people being observed.

To capture the atmospherics of a venue over a longer period (important if you are attempting to address issues relating to how people shop, drink, party, or hang out over an hour, a day or a night), it's usually possible to buy or gain access to the venue's CCTV footage. If the project is issue-specific it might be possible, to establish a hide on site that uses hidden or in-house cameras appropriately trained to capture the atmospheres and activities you are keen to monitor.

At this point, we found our gatekeepers and used them to introduce researchers into the scene. Researchers, until they have established what a new trend or lifestyle remit is, carry out ambient or eavesdropping interviews at this stage. People know they are there and that they are working on a project about women's lifestyles, but the lifestyle itself hasn't been tagged, nor will our researchers discuss angles, theories or hypotheses. This is to ensure that they themselves don't contaminate or skew the project in a different direction by revealing 'their narrative' of what they are looking at.

Informal interviews and initial contacts suggested that this kind of woman was 'easy' or 'relaxed' in her conversational asides with men, that she talked to them straight on, 'chap to chap' as one of our networkers put it. If she was chatted up, engaged with the person concerned – in two cases other women – she was keen, but more times than not, easily and effortlessly extricated herself from the situation and returned to her mates, 'the girl not feeling bad about being turned down, the woman not feeling that turning her down was a problem'.

While some networkers were reporting back on Grit Girl's social networks, others were e-mailing or jpeging back visuals of the kind of wine bars or sofa pubs she was hanging out in.

## ■ Sitting rooms as the new drinking rooms

Bars that looked like sitting rooms, bars that were comfy and intimate, bars with cushions, footstools, modern bright colours and soft, atmospheric lamps and downlighters that made the spaces personal and customer friendly.

There were images of beers being drunk – tall thin glasses, goblet glasses with cloudy beers, Belgian pilsners. Also a particular variety of wines – Chilean, Australian, Californian and South African in the main; light, new world labels in other words, the favourites being Australian and Californian, chardonnay and sauvignon.

The images of the foods being eaten showed salads, tuna and marlin steaks, open sandwiches with healthy options, but a side order of thick, hand-cut chips with 'retro' label ketchup, old-style Colman's mustard, alongside grain or seeded varieties. The plates were large, white and clean making portions look smaller, more nouveau – in these things detail is everything.

But the thing that networkers noticed – these are the things you need to note when preparing for your formal interview sessions – was the ratio of male to female customers. These kinds of bars were used by as many, if not more, women than men, and also by a high proportion of blacks, Asians and gays – usually gay men.

Women came in groups, but also alone and always with a mobile phone – Nokias, Samsungs, the occasional Ericsson – always with paperbacks, carrying an under-the-armpit shoulder bag. They also had a bigger bag to take things home from the office or one that was good for the gym – Louis Vuitton, Hermès or a generic but tough looking granny bag. These were women who seemed to be there to talk, to hang out; women who seemed to use, live and take control of the space in the way that men normally do in more traditional brewery bar set ups.

## ■ Assembling a profile – keep your options open

While these fragments of information were coming in, researchers at the studio were hard at work using the visual information gathered to create what we call lifestyle cartograms. This is literally a wall of images – interiors, products, places, exterior views of houses, images of cars, beers, foods and brands our Grit Girl, on initial reading, seems keen on.

In tandem with this, researchers were also working on mining the culture for general trend shifts or demographic swings that might be playing a part in why she was behaving the way she did. Here they found that women are now living alone for longer. They are working harder and longer hours (averaging a 9.1 hour day), putting careers before children, cohabiting first and marrying, if they marry at all, second.

They were also delaying marriage till their late twenties or early thirties – 28 is the age when most women now marry as opposed to 23 in the 60s – and also delaying having children beyond that still – once women had their first child between 20 and 24, now the first child is born to women between 26 and 29 on average.

## ■ The big picture narrative

This kind of mining can be sporadic, wide ranging and general. At this stage, the team are simply colouring in the Bigger Picture as far as women are concerned, and then using this, along with the more personal details collected by networkers to create a thesis or framework into which more focused interviews can be placed.

It is important at this stage to gather all points relevant to the Bigger Picture scenario. We found out from the Family Policy Studies Unit, for instance, that 20% of women who are now 27 will be childless at the age of 45; from the Henley Centre, the fact that 74 per cent of divorces are now initiated by women and, worse (for men at least), that many speak to solicitors before discussing their potential break-up with their husband!

We also learned from Professor Richard Scase, whose book *Britain in 2010* is something of a handbook about the office, the fact that more businesses were set up by women in 2000 than by men, and that women's businesses are generally less likely to go bankrupt in their first year of trading because they have more lateral and pre-emptive ways of dealing with market stresses and pressures.

From the Government's General Household Survey, we gleaned that 14 per cent of UK households are occupied by single women, compared to 10 per cent in 1963; that less than half of the UK female population will be married by 2005 as a result of later first-time marriages, an increase in the number of cohabiting couples and a continuing rise not just in divorce rates but the reasons chosen for divorcing.

These snapshot images of what women were up to were equally revealing when we spoke to our networkers in the US. Books like *Late Night in Paradise: Sex and Morals at the Century's End* (Katie Roiphe), Susan Faludi's *Stiffed* and a flotilla of other similar reads were flagging up this new type of can-do, single, late twenty-something women – along with shows like *Sex in the City*, *Will and Grace*, the female characters in programmes like the *Sopranos*.

Bestseller lists are always a good way of checking the current pulse of the consumer – the singles chart, holiday destinations, drinks, magazines and heroes and heroines. These are barometers of where people are at, not necessarily where they are going to. This is why studying these lists or areas is about identifying the sleepers, the slow risers, ones that are hinting at where the next little big shift is coming from. All these help towards framing the general profile however, establishing a possible lifestyle narrative along which these women may be moving.

## ■ Trend and trend counterpoints

In tandem with the above, braillers across our network were picking up on the opposite kinds of vibes and feelings about men – increases in depression were being reported, more suicides and breakdowns; a sense that men were losing face or position and their understanding of place in what one of them had dubbed, 'the rise of the female century'.

In the EU, in 2000/01, more women than men graduated from university, more girls than boys did better at GCSEs; in America female admissions to university were as high as 56 per cent, while men's admissions rates were falling.

## ■ Always look at how one trend impacts on another

We were also hearing about male body dysmorphia – three million cases and rising in the US alone – about rocketing demands for male cosmetic surgery, and for the kinds of procedures that suggested and continue to suggest that men were and are having serious second thoughts about masculinity, and what it means in a twenty-first century world where women are at last demanding not just equality but a return to 'gender difference'. As one of our Grit Girls so succinctly put it in an interview, 'Who after all wants to be as stupid as a man!'

In one survey carried out by *Psychology Today*, more men (38 per cent) were concerned about the size and shape of their breasts (yes, their breasts!) than women (34 per cent).

All this suggested that our networkers' initial observations were right. That there was a gender shift taking place and one that reflected back onto women's lifestyles, and a particular kind of independent woman at that.

Also a particular type of man, for one must surely impact on the behavioural patterns and social, sexual and societal outlooks of the other. In this instance (the men we did for another project!), we were concerned with the kind of positive, upbeat, career confident, late twenty-something woman we now knew to be out there.

> **❝ Initial observations were right. That there was a gender shift taking place and one that reflected back onto women's lifestyles. ❞**

Time then to interview face-to-face – to unfold her narrative maps and brand cartograms. Oh yes, and to go through her rubbish for if we are what we eat, we are more truly the sum total of all those things we throw away!

# Open-ended questions –
## not probing, just fishing

The art of the interview is the art of the open-ended question and the 'in context' lateral lead. Good in situ interviews use these to unravel the many narratives the interviewee may be working to, but also to uncover their brand or lifestage ladders, their personal take on where and how a Big Picture trend might be impacting on them, or indeed where they – if they are one of our edge dwellers – might be impacting on the culture in a way that makes them the trend starter!

Open-ended questions help you achieve this goal because they act as prompts, links, bridges or threads to move you and the interviewee deeper into the issues concerned and the tasks and activities being observed.

They are questions designed to 'unpack' a conversation, to strip away another layer, to probe deeper or to break down into intelligible segments acts, rituals or ways of doing things that may seem strange to the observer or outsider. What is being sought here are the 'narratives that people live by' (and thus the things that make our products or brands more relevant and useful to them). So the interviewer should never use statements or make value judgments that they attempt to pass off as questions. In the case of the former, the interviewee will find themselves answering in shorter and ever decreasing terms; in the case of the latter, if the statement niggles or annoys, they not only become irritated, but find themselves responding 'yes', 'no', or 'I disagree' – a sure way of further closing off the paths to the kinds of things we are attempting to get out of them.

> **❝When people agree to be interviewed, they are in effect agreeing to answer questions, offer insights and open up their inner selves. ❞**

The point to remember is this – when people agree to be interviewed, they are in effect agreeing to answer questions, offer insights and open up their inner selves but they are not signing a contract of interrogation or an agreement to have their views challenged, or to hear your views superimposed on theirs.

Readers familiar with the Zaltman Metaphor Elicitation Technique, one of marketing's old standbys, will be aware of the frustrations that questioning like this can cause. In this process, and many of the more overt techniques employed by researchers, interviewees are encouraged to work through a series of stages that depend on their ability to interpret, or comment on images supplied by the researcher or brought to the 'control' venue by themselves. They will then use storytelling to create narratives within which the pictures being used have a purpose, or say something about them as people.

## ■ Lifestage ladders

The pictures may then be used to create a ladder or hierarchy of importance, sometimes known as a Kelly grid, to create a brand narrative that allows the interviewer to see how the consumer rates brands, or uses them to create a narrative profile that starts with their needs and works upwards towards their desires.

Questions are then asked about the images themselves – what do they mean? What inner thoughts, moods, desires and emotions do they represent? Then the missing ones are sought out, and the interviewee is asked to explain what these mean, how they relate to the 'I self', the mirror self, the extended self and so on.

It is about using unfolding narratives and our ability to visualize and recall images and confer higher meanings on them, or using them as a kind of shorthand or grammar to say much more complex things about the self or where it is going.

All of this is, to say the least, exhausting for both parties and depends as much on how good the interviewee is at recalling them (not very good usually) as how well the researcher using the technique is versed in probing deeply into the psyche of the individual involved, and also of the culture and value systems they live in.

It is a good technique and a valued tool, but it does not integrate and engage with the consumer in the deep way that forecasters require, or the way that brands need to do if they are looking for product solutions and design strategies, along with new brand opportunities.

The conversational techniques we are about to describe come closer than any others we know in providing answers to all facets of the questions that brands, forecasters and future-faced organizations need to ask – who are you? Where are you coming from? Where are you going? How does your journey impact on the bigger picture? How does the bigger picture impact on your journey? But also how can I make your journey easier, or use details from it to make other people's journey equally simple and clear cut?

## ■ To plug into the person, plug into their habitat

You can't ask these questions directly. They must be asked in context, in situ, and above all in a style that suits the context, not a style that suits the control group or the interviewee room situation.

Also – and this is a problem with other techniques – answers should come from situation and from context, not just as responses to the questions being asked. This may be wholly inappropriate anyway when you get to the field, or the bar, or the restaurant where you may be investigating a new trend towards one-pot dining (all courses being served from the same pot at the same time), cellular offices (yes, the closed plan office is on its way back), the tower block as fashionable bolthole (coming to a housing estate or housing project near you). Or worse, because of their narrowness, the questions may shield you from seeing the real truths or directions of the trend you are exploring. In many ways the techniques being used here are the same as those used to identify the D-factor.

## ■ Open-ended questions

This is why you should also avoid questions that appear to be judgemental in tone, or leading in character and intonation. Questions which begin, 'Is it true that . . .?' or 'I find it hard to . . .', or 'Your stance/outlook/lifestyle seems a little odd to the average person . . .' are certainly the kind to avoid for all the obvious reasons.

They are read by the interviewee – usually nervous and therefore overly sensitive – as judgements, challenges and, in many cases, as being a bit daft! If after all the interviewee is a 'straight edger', a 'hardcore skater', 'New Essentialist Shopper', 'consumanist', or 'culture jammer', their views, no matter how contrary, do not seem odd to them, so the good interviewer should never suggest this.

Nor should they pass a statement off as a question in an attempt to lead the interviewee on. 'Your car is red, red cars are usually driven by drivers with a higher propensity for accidents' – what can an interviewee say to this? Yes; no; I didn't know that; I disagree; are you suggesting I'm a dangerous driver?

Yet this kind of thing is the trick and trade of many marketers – 'Do you agree/disagree with the following . . .? Which tells you what? What they agree and disagree with, but what about all those other things they might want to talk about?

And is life that linear, that black and white? You can bet your irrational expectations model that it's not, so why go down that route when you are attempting to get insights? Online polls such as YouGov or those conducted by Mori on the telephone are the stuff of knee-jerk research and deserve to be used as such – a narrowcast, spur of the moment view that tells us little about the long term forecast and less about the realities, or indeed complexities, of the increasingly fragmented life prisms we live in. Whim is hardly a good way of reading the culture or basing sound, indeed long term, brand planning decisions on, yet increasingly we are beginning to go along this route – ask easy-to-answer questions for easy-to-produce reports or market surveys.

Another question favoured by the keep-things-simple brigade is, 'People believe that . . .' Again, a wrong move – if this interview is about what the interviewee believes (somebody you've identified as unique and different, or a firestarter in their category or area), what other people believe isn't going to be all that interesting. This is about them, remember – their belief systems, their values register.

Then there's, 'What are you doing now?' This is usually asked by researchers or ethnographers attempting to elicit insights that may or may not improve the design of, say, a kettle. This question was asked in one ethnographic survey we were conducting for a household goods manufacturer – and the reply? 'I'm filling it.' So much for staggering insights and questions designed to get people to open up, reveal and create product opportunities.

## ■ Solutions from narrative procedures

The kettle is a case in point. The man holding it was in his late seventies and the kettle was one of those jug designs, which are excellent if you are twenty-something, have 20/20 vision and arthritis-free wrists, but if you are elderly with arthritis and poor vision, it is a poorly-designed accident waiting to happen. Even our non-designer researcher noted the difficulties the man had in gripping it, in trying to swing it under the tap with his swollen wrists and knuckles and calcified joints.

Worse, the expression of pain on his face was all too obvious when the kettle began to fill, then overfill and flood since he couldn't see how much water was actually in there, despite the indicators (minuscule it has to be said) on the side. Then he had to return it to its base plate, and when it had boiled, remove it and pour the water into a mug without scalding himself – which he did, to his credit, but with great difficulty.

What the researcher wanted him to talk about – for the benefit of the manufacturer and its R&D and marketing departments – was the effect that gravity and the heavy kettle had on his wrists and coordination. And the strategies he used to avoid this – his attempt to roll the kettle away to the right only increasing the pain and pressure on his wrist and arm. But what we really wanted to find out by observation, gentle leading and probing was how the design of the kettle could be improved. Which, eventually, a more experienced researcher managed to do. How? By watching, observing, listening and then by using the context of what the man

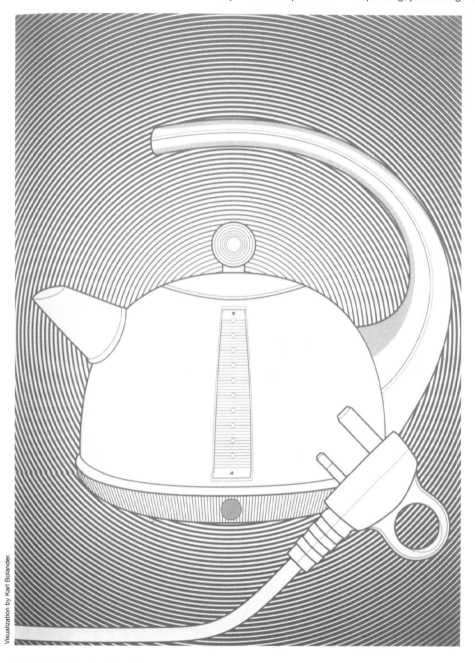

Visualization by Karl Bolander.

**Third age kettle: visualization of a kettle designed to be used by sixty-something consumers with failing strength and poor eyesight and body co-ordination.**

was doing to frame questions not just about the task, but also about his difficulty with it and how he seemed to be overcoming that difficulty. Only then were we beginning to see things as he saw them.

# Listen, look, jot down –
## let solutions speak for themselves

An observational statement with a question is a good way to cut to what you want the interviewee to talk about without making it seem that this is your only focus of interest. What we call the 'context, conflict, follow through and solution' model. These, incidentally, are the key components of a good story, play or narrative – the context or scene, then the conflict (character, plot, friction), then how these pan out (the follow through), and finally the solution, or the happy-ever-after ending.

You should see actions in this way – as narratives, activities that are, in essence, miniature stories or microdramas. That way you observe them more carefully and watch the simplest tasks – shopping, cooking, driving, buying a brand, even boiling a kettle – as events with their own rhythms and conflicts.

> ❝ It helps you to break down the most mundane of activities in a way that gives them weight. ❞

Why is this important? Because it helps you to break down the most mundane of activities in a way that gives them weight but also allows you to see how something is done – and how some things, tasks or products can be improved on, such as our kettle. This is also true of how you ask your question and use it to break down the drama or narrative of the act, but also to identify, follow through and resolve (as in how this act or design can be improved in a way that suits the end user).

So, 'I can see that filling the kettle (context) causes discomfort (conflict), but I'm sure you've considered ways of reducing this (follow through); maybe if you could tell me about it.' And he does because the question is open ended, one that invites narrative and participation (solution). You also generate insight for the man himself which generates an insight that designers can work with. Because he thinks about this every time he fills the kettle, and because it is about his pain and a possible solution to that pain, he will be more than happy to answer.

In this case, the subsequent answers flowed easily and created a verbal description of the blueprint for the kind of kettle that admirably suits the over-sixties and those partially impaired by health or age – a huge and growing market, as you can see from our Rainbow Youth trend. It also provided us with a solution to a new look mobile phone – larger pads, bigger displays, louder ring, easy-grip shape. Also a hammer designed to use gravity to better effect and also to improve the tool's safety features and the impact of the shaft on the hand and wrist as it was used to bang in nails.

Because our user's comments were on video, designers were able to share the pain, appreciate their problems and could empathize with their situation. Better still, even if this had been a high concept design idea about making, say, a kettle fashionable or turning a mobile phone into a designer object, designers could not dispute the evidence of their eyes or the comments of the end user. Function was the issue here and function, in this case, could be improved by altering the form of the kettle and its centre of gravity, as well as its shape and finish.

A new kettle was created – one with an old-style bow handle from which the kettle hung thus shifting the centre of gravity underneath the hand, making it easier to lift and pour. The spout was also readjusted – it was made wider to allow the kettle to be filled through it (the way most people do when in a hurry, but not how they would describe it if you asked them to recall from memory – most would say, 'take the lid off and then fill it'). The spout was also set at an angle to take steam away from the handle, and the holder's fingers, when boiling.

Again it was noted in video research that, contrary to what people tell you, most remove the kettle when the water was boiling and bubbling – in other words at its most dangerous – risking both spillage and scalding. A lip adjustment in the kettle's spout design further guarded against this. Also by making the kettle bowl shaped and adding a larger water level indicator – bright with big slides and big numbers – it also became a kettle designed to accommodate the needs of users with poor eyesight, rather than the whims of a designer.

A further innovation came in the form of a plug with a ring-pull moulded section that enabled it to be pulled from the socket with greater ease – an issue if arthritis has seized up the joints. A designer wouldn't think of this and a focus group interviewer wouldn't necessarily see it as part of their brief. Yet in the context of the home, and by observing how this man was using his kettle, a researcher could see that plugging it in or taking the plug out (it was noted that quite a few elderly people did this, fearing fires) was almost as difficult as using the kettle.

The researcher's questions were contextualized but also conversational in tone.

She asked questions – she had worked in radio – that began with 'Tell me more about . . .', or 'Describe the first time that . . .'. Questions like these, asking for description, more trenchant comment or encouraging revelation are excellent. Radio broadcasters and the best TV chat show hosts use them to incisive effect.

They are also asking for the narrative to begin – the story to be told, the inner life and feelings of the interviewee to be rolled out. 'Tell me', 'Show me', 'Explain to me', 'I noted that you did . . .', 'I was very impressed with the way you . . .', 'What were you thinking about when . . .?' Questions like these allow the interviewee to expand, open up and come out of themselves – it is here that the best insights are gained or lost.

Unfortunately, usually lost it has to be said, especially if the researcher (or client sitting in on the process) chirps up, 'Which reminds me of the time that . . .' or, worse, corrects the interviewee on a point that seems to be inaccurate or, as is often the case (especially with conservative clients and opinionated interviewers), with a 'Well, that's not strictly true' or 'Well, not everybody believes that.'

Photography by Sandro Sodano.

**The self-actualized consumer – photographic portrait of trans-brow learner. Here high-brow and low-brow reading and learning patterns are mixed and merged in ways that refuse to distinguish between 'high' and 'low' culture.**

## ■ This is their tale not yours

Whatever an interviewee believes or tells you, believe them! Accept it! Don't challenge it! Even if they erroneously suggest (as happened in one interview we were doing with anti-global demonstrators in the process of formulating our consumanist trend overview) that brands like Shell, BP and Coca-Cola are among the world's greatest polluters and users of child labour.

People carry myths with them – as in stories about rat droppings being found in beefburgers, or underarm deodorants being responsible for an increase in breast cancer for women (you mean men don't use deodorant?). These are sometimes key to understanding their deeper feelings or self-narratives, since these in themselves might reveal an entire, yet hidden, belief system or philosophy that in fact drives or motivates a particular group to do what it does.

It might, as in the case of the protesters we were dealing with, offer brand insights into how they should shape future policies, flag up future ethical, social or environmental initiatives or create challenge systems or networks to address claims that are blatantly untrue. The interviewer or researcher should be objective. They should also stage interviews in two parts – in the field while the target group is doing, interacting or being, and in a place of their choosing – a bar, a club, a street – which is emblematic of them – their retreat, their space, their milieu where they feel important, individual or in control.

These places offer clues to their characters and it is important to record them there, but also to take snapshots or video grabs of the place in question – what's on the bar or behind it, what's on the bookshelf, the table, in the fridge, on the floor and walls – so that you are capturing not just them but their spirit. Remember our 12 upper-middle-class couples and how much people could tell about them from their front rooms?

You can also use these video grabs or snapshots to add to your cartographic map of a person's life, so that you are always deepening your understanding of them, and this, more than anything, opens doors to the inner self – into what makes them what they are, but also where they want to go.

It is also important to remember that good field research is about observing the inconsequential as well as the consequential. On one of our Grit Girl tapes, we noted that one of our interviewees was walking along a street towards a wine bar she went to a minimum of three times a week – she looked into the doorway of a pub as she passed and, without realizing it (and, it has to be said, without our researcher realizing it at the time), pulled a face.

It wasn't a big gesture. On the Richter scale of social gurneys a 0.0000007, but when we viewed the tape back at the office, it was picked up and queried by one of our better trained researchers. He was intrigued and called the woman in for a chat. She was equally intrigued but knew straight away why she had pulled that face.

'Wasn't very PLU,' she told us.
    'PLU?'
    'You know, for people like us.'
    'What wasn't?'

A look that indicated the place she was looking into, the place she passed. 'The bar?'

'The Boar's Head' (a laugh here) 'which just about sums it up.'

'You didn't like the place?'

Fake shudder, 'Awful.'

'Can you elaborate on that?'

Another shrug. 'Just . . . well the whole thing. The warm beery smells at the door. All the city boys (sneers at this) in suits with their Head trainer bags (eyes rolling) on the floor, squaring up to the bar. Their pints (eyes rolling again), the carpet, the gaming machines, the . . . well just the general sense of staleness, and damp beer mats and bar towels and strict brewery measures the place gave off. And' (she laughed) 'you just know it's going to have a guest ale.'

'What's wrong with a guest ale?'

'Well it just says everything about the bar, the people who go there.'

She was becoming frustrated now, annoyed that she couldn't quite articulate what it was that bothered her, or whether or not it was right that these things should bother her.

'It seems so . . . well,' and then she said it, sighing, eyes rolling back slightly as her shoulders dropped in cold resignation, 'sad.'

Had she seen these things as she passed? Probably not, but a single fractional glimpse had set in train a series of emotions that had caused this lifestyle 'cascade' to be unleashed. Her attitude to 'beer', 'boys in suits', 'Head trainer bags', 'the guest ale' thing, but also to the design and attitude of the pub itself.

It also told us that she had a strong sense of 'them' and 'us', of PLUs and non-PLUs. As with all 'cascade' moments, we sent our researcher back to the pub in question to record interiors, customers and general ambience for screening and discussion during the closing stages of the project.

## ■ Cover all angles – narratives are about facets, not one-sided views

In all, 30 women of the kind we were keen to know more about were photographed, videoed or interviewed in situations we and they felt were pivotal to how they saw their lives – a typical night out in their favourite pub with their usual group of friends, a night at a favourite restaurant, a night in, an hour at the gym, in their bathroom observing their beauty regime (21 minutes on average), a shopping expedition, a car journey, a day at their place of work, a night or morning hanging out with their flatmates.

As well as booking out each interviewee with a researcher and camera person, all were asked to keep visual diaries or 'dream diaries' of key or significant events in their week – drinks with friends, a shopping trip, a club night out, a group, or single night in – what we call a snapshot map of places, people or things. These diaries can be simple affairs. They use disposable cameras to capture activities as they see them – like a photographic record of an evening out. As well as giving a camera to the person being interviewed, we give them to four or five others in their group or network to get a more rounded 360-degree version of what that event or activity is about to all concerned.

You manage to see other potentials like this, even perhaps other products. This was the case with IDEO when they identified an opening in the market for

Popshots cameras, which became the market's first single-use instant camera. Their ethnographers noted that on evenings out the emphasis wasn't on the camera (something the manufacturers were a bit miffed about) but on the experience, the event and how this event needed to be recorded.

The IDEO ethnographers noted that people liked to record fun, togetherness and the way the group interacted. This had to be done quickly in low light conditions with a camera that was easy to use and didn't require much thinking about in terms of cost and usage – point and click was the rule here. At parties people tend to lose things or, worse, have them stolen, so the product needed to be cheap, but also bright and upbeat because it was part of an upbeat event. They also noted that many people take

> **❝ If you don't know what a consumer's world looks like how can you create a product for it? ❞**

pictures but, once the event is over and passed from memory, forget to get them developed. So the camera was designed around an easy-to-follow, one-two-three-step process that walked users through taking photos and it also came with a return paid envelope which encouraged users to get films developed and to return the camera for recycling. A cash refund was also on offer along with major prizes to ensure that the return envelope was used.

The follow-up camera, the Izone, took this process a step further by allowing users to create small instant pictures that could be printed out and used as stickers on helmets, books, backpacks and each other!

This plugged into a number of key and concurrent trends – the desire to customize, to buy all things Japanese and kitsch, to plug into 70s colours and 70s sensibilities, to enjoy the cheesy aspects of pop culture – but also to create things that were about inclusiveness, about exchanging personal objects, about 'marking' one's networks by designing and making badges all could wear – what some trend forecasters have referred to as 'clanning'.

IDEO's industrial team and its human factors specialists then interviewed teenagers about their likes and dislikes – the kind of advertising they preferred, their personal tastes. They then photographed the shoes they wore, their clothes, the places they hung out in, their bedrooms, their friends, the kinds of stereos, phones, games and toys they bought. These were turned into storyboards, or brand cartograms, for designers to absorb, study and produce the kind of camera that wouldn't look out of place in such an environment. These lifestyle portraits are vital to any kind of product creation or brand building. If you don't know what a consumer's world looks like how can you create a product for it?

In the case of our Grit Girl work, we likewise asked them to photograph the brands they use. This can simply be a photograph of a fridge, or if it is a group where brands are seen in a negative light (our global protesters for instance), the people, places or personal things that fit this category. We also asked them to grade these in terms of value, and spiritual and emotional worth.

This can take about 30 minutes to do and again it is important that the researcher working with them doesn't lead or prompt, but observes how they make their choices and asks them why – homing in on images, or things missing perhaps, and recording this in their research log.

Sometimes, if the groups are wary of this process, we ask our gatekeeper to facilitate the session, or indeed run it. In this way we use their knowledge of the group, along with their knowledge of the person being questioned, to add new layers to the information being recorded.

We can't stress, however, the importance of keeping the researcher's presumptions and prejudices out of things at this stage. The micronarratives you are trying to capture should never just be your narratives nor those of your field team, but the aggregate of all players and viewpoints involved.

Likewise, field research notes should be done in two ways – the impressionistic voice (in the mould of our pop culture writers) and the factual one (the journalistic or ethnographic voice). This is why we employ lifestyle journalists, or ethnographers and researchers trained in key journalistic techniques, alongside art photographers, video makers, writers and poets to capture the inner sense of what people may be trying to communicate.

The researcher who is recording facts, however, should do just that and describe the activity under review in the most minute detail. This again is where the 'leverage' or real insights come from.

In a project for BMW, for instance, we worked with ordinary drivers (who saw cars as a way of getting from A to B) and BMW brand-obsessed drivers (who saw cars in terms of status) to see if their sense of car, or their poetics of car, was in any way different. As it turned out it was, and radically so. This is why field research wins out over focus group research. In the latter, people are speaking from memory, and selective memory at that, so their answers are dangerously unreliable. In the former, you are seeing them in the context of what they are doing, and this is where you realize that what people say sometimes has little to do with what they mean, and even less with what they are actually saying!

# Here in my car –
## when saying isn't telling

*Junction*, as we called the report, profiled 16 people from a variety of backgrounds and career categories – doctors, housewives, DJs, programmers, risk analysts and graduates. We divided it into two sections, our ordinary car owners (who saw their cars in terms of utility rather than status) and those who bought into the BMW brand.

> **We wanted to know if their cars had a personality, a sex, a spirit and a life over and above the one intended by the car's makers.**

In each section, we asked users to consider their cars in emotional, aesthetic and spiritual terms rather than financial – what we call the poetics of car ownership rather than the realities.

We wanted to know if their cars had a personality, a sex, a spirit and a life over and above the one intended by the car's makers.

To this end we used researchers to travel with non-BMW owners on important journeys – to work, to a business appointment, on a school run, for pleasure – since all of them held the view that their car was ALL about function, SOMETIMES about status, MORE times about space, but SELDOM about spirit or personality.

Researchers and photographers travelling with them found that this was far from the case. For example, Sally, our full-time housewife, described her car as 'nothing more than a runaround', a 'functional tool', 'a necessity'. Yet when asked during one key journey why she was smiling, she replied that it was because she was in her car – something she thought of as a quiet space. 'This is often the only time that I can sit and think without interruptions.' It was a third space for her, a temple of quiet and calm.

In this context then, and under careful and gentle questioning from our researchers backed up with photographic evidence, we learned that the car – even for ordinary car owners – did indeed have a personality, or at least a usefulness or 'hidden life' over and above the functional.

In contrast, on initial questioning, BMW owners said that their cars were ALL about these things – spirit, personality, space – but also about environment, speed, design, brand and status.

In their case then, rather than travel with them, we interviewed them and asked each to capture what these things meant to them via a series of personal visual diaries. We were, quite frankly, surprised by the results!

Image after image showed us clean hubcaps, pristine engines, streamlined steering wheels, sleek surfaces and foldaway tool kits with hardly any reference to people or the kind of detritus, day-to-day paraphernalia that suggest personality, spirit or emotion in the traditional understanding of these words.

In a separate study of European men, in association with Magic Hat, a research network operating inside McCann-Erickson Worldwide, we noticed similar contradictions coming out. When asked to keep diaries on the emotional side of masculinity, or rather masculinity as it was becoming, our networkers sent us written diaries full of the pleasures of men being more open, egalitarian and sympathetic to women, embracing the feminine and so on ad nauseam.

Yet when we asked them to photograph this process, we received images of TV remote control units, stereo systems, footballs, ash trays, beer cans and gadgets. No pictures of children, family, dogs or anything remotely soft, emotional or tactile. And girlfriends – only images of their breasts, their heads and faces chopped by the frame of the image! Always important then to visually check the textual, or the visuals with text!

## ▓ Poetics of car = the emotional intangibles at a product's heart

In our ordinary car users group we included Sally, a full-time mother with two children; Syed, an Asian minicab driver; Krishnan, a medical statistician; Anne, a graphic designer; Christian, also a graphic designer and Anne's husband; Maisse, a doctor; Ray, a drum and base DJ; and Martyn, a company director.

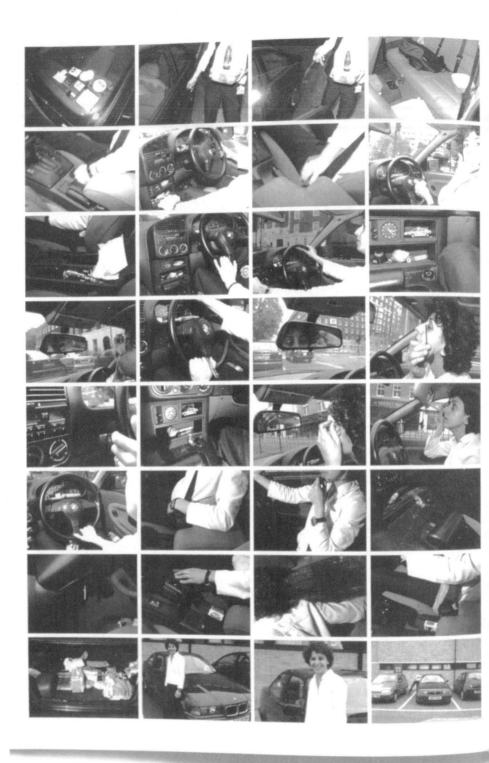

BMW and the Future Laboratory's ethnographic snapshot of how one female driver used her car as a 'third space'.

Sally, a housewife, had no articulated sense of 'car', but when observed during her key journeys, she demonstrated a relationship with her run-around that was very personal and intimate. It was a 'third space', a place to escape, and a friend to escape in.

Each was initially interviewed to find out what they thought of their car, of driving, of the place and position their car held in their lives. They were then accompanied on a major or important journey to see how their initial responses matched with how they interacted with their vehicle or 'sense of vehicle'.

This two-pronged approach to any kind of ethnographic work like this is important. What people tell you about a journey or a narrative (for this read using a product or a brand) and how they live out that journey or narrative invariably differ – sometimes dramatically so.

It is here in this information gap – between what a person says and how and why they do something – where true insight lies. It is about improving a product's design, a consumer's sense of delight, a supermarket or bar layout, how they see the future they may or may not want to inhabit. A future, as we found with this and other projects, that veered more and more towards the personal and the individual.

We were curious, however, to pursue the notion of personality, or rather of how people personalized their cars. Many of our respondents had said that they didn't personalize things, but as the project progressed this seemed far from the case. Initially 'personalization' conjured up for many images and twee associations that

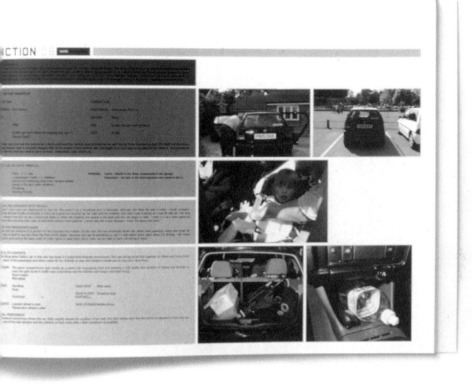

had nothing, as they put it, 'to do with them'. People who hung silly things from the rear view mirror, or gave their car a name were regarded with a certain contempt. One respondent, Christian, even sneered openly at that kind of person.

Krishnan, a second generation Asian medical statistician, was more open about his affections for his car. He called it 'Kasey', or KC as in Krishnan's car, and treated it accordingly – in a friendly, matey, easy going way.

Maisse Farhan, a doctor, despite not having a name for her car, referred to it as a 'she', her third bedroom, an extension of herself and her house. This was underscored by the way she personalized her dash space and glove compartments with make-up, tweezers, hand cream, playing cards, Tampax, plastic spoons, drinking straws, pens, shells from Norfolk, a toy BMW mini-police car, even a champagne cork memento of a recent night out.

> **❝ This is the key point to be remembered about behavioural research. How you define a term isn't necessarily how others define it. ❞**

Syed, the Asian minicab driver, personalized his car with his horny little devil mascot – a proud present from an ex-girlfriend. Ray Keith, the DJ, called his car his

Martyn Evans regarded his car as an extension of his office, 'a place to make calls' and 'to catch up on outstanding work'.

---

mistress and said he wouldn't customize it because it already had all the customized gadgets a man of his status could want – F1 steering wheel, Harman Kardon stereo $6 \times$ CD changer, heated seats, bass box in the boot, even a television and GPS navigational system!

Customization or personalization was seen to be a thing others did – and not a very good thing at that. But under observation most of our respondents indulged their cars in some way or other – even if they didn't realize that they were doing it.

This is the key point to be remembered about behavioural research. How you define a term isn't necessarily how others define it. Try to see it in their context, from their side of things. The empathic approach.

## ■ Brands are not always about personality

Brand- and status-wise, there were some very interesting contrasts between our ordinary car users and our BMW users. The former – with two exceptions – claimed

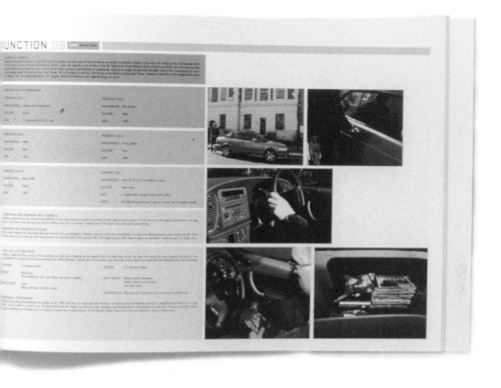

that the brand they had chosen said little or nothing about their status or personality, while the latter thought their choice said a lot about them in terms of personality and success.

In fact, among our ordinary car users there was the underlying idea that to be brand obsessed in this way was morally wrong, and that it was rubbish to suggest that the choice of car in any way related to sense of status or personality. Words like convenience, size, cheapness and, if pushed, design also figured, but the general impression given was one of nonchalant acceptance.

We found this to be true of many products as well as cars. Household goods, for instance, fell into this category. Many consumers who saw value as being more important than values or lifestyle. Consumers on low incomes or with large families tended to rank brand, personality and values low in their list of requirements, while convenience, volume, value and 'it does what it says on the tin' claims were very high in their list and scale of priorities.

A tip then for brands like Unilever, Procter & Gamble and for supermarkets – when selling products that people see as necessities or basic shopping require-

**Krishnan, a medical statistician, uses plastic toys, music, smell and colour to personalize the interior of his car in ways he himself wasn't even aware of. This is why observation is key to the brand or product awareness process.**

ments, price, performance and volume matter over all else. Own brands, or 'do-brands' are best here – brands that suggest performance and effect. But be careful – even if a product is cheap, convenient and brandless, it shouldn't look cheap, convenient and brandless. Consumers don't want to be fobbed off or be seen to be cheap in front of other shoppers – brash graphics, flashy look-at-me stars with low prices on them, or packs finished in red, blue or yellow graphics may be noticeable but they still suggest cheapness. Many consumers are waking up to this so design is still important – a product's packaging is something that can sink or save it.

Drug manufacturers have been particularly adept at identifying these surface signifiers and how they impact on our sense of product. Pills, for instance, designed to look large are believed by consumers to have a 'bigger effect'. Red pills are

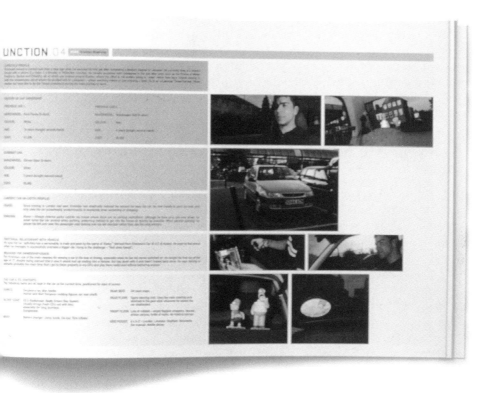

thought to be more effective than white ones, blue pills more likely to improve sleep, four pills taken regularly better than two regardless of strength. Likewise, capsules are seen be stronger and contain more slow-release ingredients than hard or opaque pill formats. Hexagonal shapes are considered more likely to impact on performance and strength, lozenge shapes are related in some way to the mind or chemical imbalances, and so on.

We know that green, yellow, brown, beige, pine or mauve colours on packaging suggest to consumers that the brands wrapped in these colours are somehow safer for the environment, or have organic properties. Yet, as our own work with consumers shows, the more they know, the more complex their relationships with products become. So if your brand is sold as a basic, it stops being a brand and any attempt to increase price or improve the brand's value (seen as another way of increasing price) is doomed to failure.

This is the nature of generic brands. They appeal to a consumer in a very basic and price specific way – in other words, they see them as cheap and they expect them to be cheap. Generic brands appeal to the pocket rather than to the emotional needs of the customer. If, on the other hand, they see the brand as a vital part of their life – which cars are, even if this is demonstrated rather than articulated – it may be that surface qualities (design say) are important even if they do not say this. This is why it is vital that you look at their past purchases, or if you are a food manufacturer or seller of white goods, that you look at products they already have or have previously enjoyed.

## ■ Our sense of brands may be located in our sense of 'past'

In the case of our car project, even those who said that design wasn't all that important (unlike our BMW owners who thought it vitally so) or that it commented on your personality in any way weren't really telling us the full story, as we found out when we examined these statements against their previous choice of cars. For Keith it was a classic Mini, a classic Morris Minor, a TR7, a Ford Escort Mark II and an old Saab. For Martyn Evans, an original Austin Mini, a VW beetle, an MGB, a Ford Zephyr and a Saab 9000. For Anne, who does not own a car but drives her husband's, has supreme faith in the VW brand, owns a Vespa scooter and says her ideal car would be a Volkswagen Beetle or a new Mini Cooper. Christian, a devout VW fan, has also owned a Citroën, yes you've guessed it, of the 2CV standard issue graphic designer variety. All these classic, designer originals and 'personality' cars and yet they say they are not interested in brands or status!

> **As our respondents became more relaxed with our researchers and photographer, they became more open about how they saw vehicles in emotional or spiritual terms.**

So even if people say they have no sense of brand, no belief in brand or no understanding of brand, it is important to dig and to look back into their past. Here you will find something that tells you what brand means to them. Dependability, longevity, tradition, continuity, nostalgia, dependence were just some of the words that came to light when we asked an older but brand-suspicious group of shoppers what they thought about products that they bought again and again.

But when we asked them what 'brand' meant they said costly, bright, brash, superficial, fashionable, transient and vulgar – nothing at all to do with the first set of characteristics. Yet they were the ones chosen by brand strategists and marketers when we asked them to select words from a list that described their sense of brand!

As our respondents became more relaxed with our researchers and photographer, they became more open about how they saw vehicles in emotional or spiritual terms. Words like 'escape' were used to describe what their car meant to them if we eliminated obvious activities such as driving to and from work, or the shops or the school run.

Likewise, phrases such as 'a third bedroom' (Maisse), 'a place to think' (Sally), 'a place to work and make all my personal and social calls' (Maisse), 'to listen to music properly' (Krishnan), 'to socialize in with friends' (Syed), 'to catch up on business calls' (Martyn), 'people watching' (Anne), 'speeding, chilling, getting into the right mood with music' (Ray), 'a useful way of learning about a place' (Anne) – like tactile brands then, ones that enable, empower, involve.

Their sense of car also had certain romantic and sensual attachments – it made them think of faraway places, of travel, of possibility. It also made them feel in control – something public transport didn't do – although, perversely, all admitted that work journeys made them angry, and inevitably late because of the traffic, other drivers and the chaotic state of UK roads.

## ■ The aura of brand

The BMW users, on initial interviewing and on viewing their visual diaries, seemed to have an entirely different attitude and outlook to how they saw and related to their cars. Because they were enthusiasts – and chosen as such – they had clear and definite reasons for wanting the brand. Or at least five of the eight did, the rest saying that the brand, in the sense of what BMW stood for, had little to do with their choice.

All agreed, however, that the car's perceived environmental credentials were good reasons for choosing BMW – likewise design, and speed or, as one put it, performance. Design could, and in fact did, mean anything from slickness to the fact that the car had lots of stowed away gadgets and boy's-own style tool kits.

While the ordinary car owners seem to live in a fairly chaotic, jumble-rich environment where cars were cleaned irregularly ('once a month', 'a couple of times a year', 'when I can no longer get into it'), all but two of the BMW owners cleaned, hoovered and polished their cars on a weekly basis, if not twice weekly. Again this over-attentiveness was reinforced by visual diaries which contained cleaning fluids, chamois leathers, tins of polish and wax, and rag boxes. Boot areas were seen to be exceptionally tidy ('anal' was the actual term used by one of our ethnographers), with glove compartments, interiors, seats and dash areas equally free from the usual paraphernalia in a car that is well used and 'broken in.' Other terms used by our ethnographers included sterile, soulless, bland and characterless.

Few in this group had personalized their cars. One had named his 'Noggy' after nogara silver, its colour – but others thought this kind of affectation was 'just plain wrong'. Unlike the ordinary car users, who contradicted this view in terms of what they actually did when they were in their cars, BMW users seemed not to indulge in making things more comfortable or personal. They liked the absence of detail, liked the idea of the car being devoid of too much personality.

Smell was the other area that stood out. While the ordinary owners seemed not to consider this as a major issue – most mentioned body odour as the predominant smell – BMW users spoke of their cars smelling of 'leather', 'fresh pine', 'smelling clean', 'lime air freshener' and 'faintly of cleaning products'.

Photography by Mischa Haller.

Usability patterns and usage of space, seats and passenger environments on Eurostar, 2002. This kind of visual document will tell you far more about how we use seats or engage with public or public/private spaces than any amount of questioning or focus group work.

## ■ Record the unseen, pin down the invisible

The good researcher or ethnographer should always note the atmospherics of a place – its smells, sounds, music. They should be recorded rather than described. In addition they should record its unseen atmospheres, its hollowness, its air of depression or heaviness – capture things not just as they are but as they resonate. Think about playwrights such as Samuel Beckett or Harold Pinter, painters like Howard Hodgkin and Mark Rothko, musicians like Ives or Terry Reilly, poets like Raymond Carver, architects like Ando and Meier, film's like Derek Jarman's *Blue*, or Warhol's time lapse images of the New York skyline. It is not what is said that is important, or indeed seen or heard, but what is absent.

> **ff This is what good ethnography does. It charts journeys and offers us narrative maps – spiritual as well as visual. 55**

In the BMW sample this sense of cleanliness, of things being antiseptic was picked up on by our ethnographers when looking at the visual diaries. They noticed that the focus was on polish, finish, fluids, clean carpets, car mats (something indeed most of our BMW users classed as accessories or personalized touches they liked!) and cleaning utensils.

They were slightly puzzled by the antiseptic nature of the diaries. By how, given the fact that all respondents were asked to photograph a 'poetic' or 'spiritual sense' of car, they had chosen to focus on such neutral and, as one put it, 'faintly cold and inhuman things'.

There were few personal artefacts shown – such things as books, clothing, papers, toys, sweet wrappers – while only one set of images actually featured another person, or references to other people in them.

There was the sense that these cars were prize cars, show vehicles, fetishistic objects to be looked at, admired and be proud of but not necessarily to be related to emotionally, spiritually, irrationally or poetically. Worrying traits, our ethnographers and researchers felt, since the latter are the very things that connect us with brands more and more. This is what good ethnography does. It charts journeys and offers us narrative maps – spiritual as well as visual – but it also offers us bigger insights on what brands are and what they can become without this being the intended path of the brand builders. Insights like this are vital to the continuity and longevity of a brand – but the best kinds of insights can be found in the most unusual of places.

part

**Cultural footprints:**
using 'aftermaths' to create
brand maps

# A load of rubbish –
## discarded dreams and how to read them

Garbology isn't new – archaeologists have been sifting through the shellfish deposits and table middens of our ancestors for hundreds of years, learning much about their daily diets and day-to-day social routines as a consequence. Campbell (soup) for instance, keen to discover who the typical tinned soup user was, went though people's bins at the turn of the last century and found to their surprise, that soups pitched at the upper classes were instead being consumed by the lower-middle classes who wanted the lifestyle of the rich, but couldn't afford the cooking staff, so easy to prepare soup seemed like a good solution!

Despite such forays, the use of garbology in the consumer insight business is still fairly marginal – although über-fan and celebrity stalker A. J. Weberman used it to now infamous effect when he scoured the trash cans of Bob Dylan and Neil Simons, to emerge with such celebrity artefacts as soiled diapers and half-eaten bagels. Followers of the *Rockford Files*, *Law and Order* or the recent paternity case surrounding actress and single mum Liz Hurley will also be familiar with the routine – rubber gloves, a quick delve in the refuse bins of the suspects involved and presto! An incriminating note, a bloodied fabric swatch, dental floss containing the DNA of our father-to-be.

Intrusive, smelly, fanciful, revealing? Probably all four, but certainly a much better way of building a forensic profile of a person's financial well-being and ongoing lifestyle habits than sitting them down and asking them questions about how they shop and what they earn.

### ■ What goes in, always comes out

Experian, for instance, discovered that 20 per cent of UK bins contain a whole credit card or debit card slip with card numbers that can be linked to an individual name or address – 11 per cent of these slips contained an expiry date and signature. 72 per cent of bins examined also contained the full name and address of at least one household member, while a significant percentage of bins contained an account number and a sort code that could be linked back to an individual bank account.

Bins also contained blank cheque books with unsigned cheques, till receipts from the week's shopping, credit card slips of meals out, service till receipts showing the last withdrawal made, mini-statements showing an account balance and the last five places where money was spent including how much was spent.

In our own searches, we've uncovered fax rolls with details of a person's tax returns, VAT claims, scribbled notes to accountants, bank managers and business colleagues giving detailed and very intimate information on recent financial transactions, and in many cases (especially to accountants), confessed improprieties!

We've also found discarded bank statements, personal receipts – for taxis, restaurants, shopping, drinks, buses, tubes – itemized phone bills, utility bills, bills for clothes, toiletries and bathroom products. All of these allow you to produce a very sophisticated financial portrait or cartogram of the person being profiled – from annual earnings to monthly household outgoings, to spends on food, hygiene, toiletries and essential as well as luxury goods.

> **20 per cent of UK bins contain a whole credit card or debit card slip with card numbers that can be linked to an individual name or address.**

Household finances are only one facet of the profile available. From a person's refuse bin we can learn much about their diet, about their notions of luxury, of self, of aspiration, and sense of emotional, physical and spiritual well-being. The BBC's *Money Programme* asked us to analyse a bin belonging to a typical shopper (who the producers refused to identify). We were able to tell that the bin belonged to a woman (brown hair dye tube, surgical gloves to protect hands from dye stains, *Take a Break* magazine, Tampax box, Simple moisturiser, Boots lipstick tube) with one or possibly two children. One was aged about 7, the other 10+ (economy pack crisps, fish fingers, beefburgers, McDonald's cartons, Burger King cartons, sweet wrappers, Kellogg's Coco Pops, two six-pack T-shirt packets from Asda, one for 5–7 year olds, the other 12-years plus). One of them suffered from health issues relating to hyperactivity (paperbag with an adrenalin pen which could only be got on prescription).

We also gauged that the woman was on a low income (lots of the food stuff prices had been reduced, marked up as two-for-one offers or were low cost own brands). She was possibily on income support (dates on the product suggested that things were bought frequently rather than in one big shopping trip). She shopped around for bargains (most people shop at one, possibly two, supermarkets tending to be brand loyal but in this bin we found products from Sainsbury's, Marks & Spencer, Asda and Somerfield with no one brand predominating). She lived in an urban rather than metropolitan area (Somerfield's stores tend to stay out of big cities, but the fact that there were many different retail brands in the same bin suggested that all were within walking distance, not that common in a city like London, Manchester or Edinburgh, but certainly in a town like Brighton or Hastings one tends to find these patterns). She was not particularly brand loyal but promiscuous in her shopping habits (the large number of own brands found in the bin, the fact that no one brand predominated, the fact that all seemed to be chosen for value, over values, for bulk over quality).

## ■ Note what's missing as well as what's there

We guessed her age as late 30s to early 40s (the hair dye, according to the packet, was designed specifically for grey hair). She was certainly on a low income but could also be on income support or unemployed. There were no bank statements in the bin, no till receipts, no cheque book stubs, indeed no financial records, no bank circulars or letters from credit card companies offering a new credit card or loan facilities (all highly unusual, unless the bin owner is unusually careful about destroying financial records and circulars but common enough if the person does not earn enough to qualify for their name to be added to these lists). Likewise, there were no 'heavy' meat products in her bin – steak, sausages, pies, bacon, pork – no beer bottles, although there were a number of Smirnoff Ice bottles, few vegetable peelings and little or no evidence of fruit.

There were, however, cigarette butts from low tar Spanish cigarettes with lipstick on the filter. All of this suggested that she was a woman living alone with her children, so either unmarried or separated. The Spanish cigarettes suggested a recent holiday or a purchase on the local black market (which turned out to be the case).

Our profile was accurate in most respects, except for the two children. There was just one, a boy, who suffered from a hyperactive disorder, but the other (we guessed that there was another from the larger size T-shirt pack) was the mum buying the larger T-shirts for herself.

But what did this bin tell us about the woman and her son apart from the obvious – that she needed food to be cheap, convenient, close to where she lived and not too exotic? It told us quite a lot. Her sense of loyalty to brands was low, not because she didn't value them but because, in many ways, they didn't value her – or attempt to woo her in anything but the most lumpen and patronizing way.

She did, for instance, try to buy food that was healthy. There were a lot of lo-cal purchases (our anomalies) and she was attracted to anything organic, lean or with a reduced fat, sugar or additive content. All of this suggested that she not only read labels carefully – which people on limited budgets invariably do – but that she was making (despite what the number of retail brands bought suggested) clear and calculated choices about what she was buying. If things were inside her price range she tended to buy well, to choose healthy products, organic ones, and those that came with a 'values' proposition – free range eggs, organic bread, fair trade coffee.

So even if her habits were conservative or safe, she was willing to try things that were aspirational in that they were allowing her to buy into, and to contribute to, good causes and make a contribution in terms of how she saw herself – not just a shopper but a good citizen.

It is our contention that most of the brands she was dealing with did not allow her to do this. Freedom foods and organic foods are generally more expensive, and targeted at the aspirational, high spend, 'educated' shopper, which is good for their ego and self-actualized sense of being, but not for the low spend shopper who may want to partake in this process but find themselves excluded – or as they see it, victimized by retailers who are really saying, yes we want your money, but we are not really keen on your long term loyalty since you don't have a lot of it . . . A shopper faced with subliminal messages like this will shop around rather than remain loyal, but they take away with them, as we shall see later, a poor sense of brand and, worse, a poor sense that they pass on to others.

A properly constructed refuse bin audit allows you to see this visually as well as statistically and texturally. Visual audits, particularly, permit you to create a brand or lifestyle profile of a consumer in a way that offers up real rather than ideal insights of their day-to-day activities, their personal lives and private prejudices. (See our opening images of rubbish from Future Laboratory members on pages i–iii of this book.)

Researchers are very familiar with the fact that most people talk ideally about their diet, quoting reading material or lifestyle habits when asked specific questions on these areas, few ever really tell the truth about how much fat or carbohydrate they eat over protein and healthy or vegetable foodstuffs – or indeed which papers and books they actually read, as opposed to which they think they should be reading.

In one audit, carried out during that part of the last decade when all those in the know in Europe and the US were talking lean cuisine and all things healthy and low in fat or added cholesterol, a bin scour discovered that this was very far from the truth. People consistently under-reported how much fat or fatty food they ate, and over-reported how much healthy food such as fruit or diet soda they had in contrast. In this audit, 94 per cent under-reported the amount of sugar they ate, 81 per cent on chips and popcorn, 80 per cent on candy, 80 per cent on bacon and 63 per cent on ice cream.

In contrast, keen to demonstrate that they had all bought into the trend towards a healthier lifestyle, all over-reported the amount of cottage cheese they ate by 311 per cent, on liver by 200 per cent, on tuna by 184 per cent and on vegetable soup by 94 per cent!

Our own household bin surveys are forever pointing up these anomalies. Most people believe they eat far healthier foods than they do. Most also claim to cook more than they do, while takers of Sunday papers will tick serious papers like the *The Sunday Times*, *The Telegraph* or the *Observer* when asked what they read – more times than not they have ignored the copy of the *News of the World*, or *Sunday Sport* found in their rubbish. When confronted about it, many will say they read them for a laugh or a bit of light relief.

## ■ People want to be seen to do good

This revisionist view of household activities is universal. Even mothers or heads of households who do the weekly shop and prepare the main family meals tend to err towards the 'ideal' – and when confronted with the reality of their day-to-day cooking habits, or household activities as deduced from their rubbish output, are genuinely surprised by the results.

Horace Schwerin and Phalen Golden, who perhaps kick-started what has become known as garbology, noted similar discrepancies in how our ideal sense of diet and lifestyle activity was challenged by the reality of the refuse we discard. In 1941 they spoke to US recruits about aspects of army life they disliked most. Sergeant Bilko fans will know the answer straightaway – food! But before they could find out why, Army brass told them that surveys of this kind were not permitted under military law. Rather than question the men,

> ❝ similar discrepancies in how our ideal sense of diet and lifestyle activity was challenged by the reality of the refuse we discard. ❞

Schwerin and Golden hit on a better idea – they decided to look at the food that was thrown out or left in the mess hall uneaten. Not surprisingly this turned out to be a hell of a lot – 2.4 million man meals were studied, of which 20 per cent were thrown out. Most of this was due to overestimation which in turn was due to cooking foods most of the men had no interest in – soups, kale, spinach – causing 65 per cent of those dining to leave food on their plate, while desserts were universally liked – cakes, cookies, canned fruit and ice cream especially, which was consumed completely no matter how much of it had been prepared.

What Schwerin and Golden also discovered – and this perhaps is where the real benefits of garbology lie – is how the environment impacted on the nature and amounts of food consumed. They noted, for instance, that soldiers ate more of everything if they were allowed to smoke in the canteen or mess hall. They also ate more if they were allowed to dine directly rather than having to queue. In particular, if they were allowed to eat when they wanted to eat, they ate much more than when they were ordered to do so.

Simple insights like these were used by the army to improve menus, diets and ways of dining – and also to prevent wasting 2.3 million pounds of food annually. But there are bigger, much more insightful lessons to be learned from studying people's public and private refuse, as we shall see.

# Waste not, want everything –
## bin-to-brand cartograms

Initiatives like the Garbage Project, set up by archaeologists in the University of Arizona in the wake of the 1970 Earth Day summit, have taken garbology a stage further. They prove that our waste really tells us more about our dietary and lifestyle habits than we would like to admit. However, they also reinforced the point that linear economic models, or notions of rational expectation and outcomes, are never the way they should be when you look to the realities of people's behavioural patterns, rather than to their ideals, or to how we are told markets should and do perform.

Pioneer garbologist and one of the cofounders of the Garbology Project, William Rathje noted this in 1973 when, during a beef shortage from March to September, household rubbish outputs did not conform to the pattern his collection and research term were predicting.

They were keen to see if red meat shortages would impact on the kind of waste being put out – would people buy more vegetables for instance? Increase their pasta intake? Buy more fish, or fowl? All logical assumptions – the kinds of things folk wisdom and economic analysis of a market under short supply of a particular item would suggest. The absence of one product would suggest a shift to another, or perhaps the bulk buying of red meats and a staged, but rationed, approach to their use and subsequent appearance in the nation's bins.

During the year commencing Spring 1973, bins were monitored and the results collated. Insights, says Rathje, were very surprising. Prior to the shortages, the amount of beef wasted or thrown out ran to about 3 per cent of the beef actually purchased, while during the months of the shortage this shot up to 9 per cent. In other words, there was three times as much wastage during the period of rationing as there was either side of it! Rathje and his team hypothesized that this had to do with the fact that consumers had stocked up on as much red meat produce they could get their hands on, regardless of the sell-by dates on the package, the kind of beef they were buying, or indeed how the said beef should be prepared. Consequently, sell-by dates came and went and the beef had to be thrown out. More was thrown out because householders who were used to preparing red meat products one way had little or no knowledge of how their recent purchases should be prepared.

## ▓ Trust your eyes, not the experts

Economists, dieticians and market research groups naturally disputed Rathje's findings. Sales were up, people had bought new types of food and in the process had experimented with diet, so the Garbage Project's findings must be flawed in some way. Rathje's team rejected this, but it wasn't until the sugar shortage of 1975 that they could prove their original findings to be right, and establish one of the first principles of garbology.

In 1975, the cost of sugar and high sugar products doubled. Rathje's researchers – again monitoring the levels of waste being thrown into bins, this time of the residents of Tucson, Arizona – discovered that sugar waste doubled during the period it was most difficult to come by!

This time they found whole cakes of the product in bins. Much of it had been bought by panicking Tucson residents in Mexico, 60 miles south of their town, only to find that the sugar, less refined than American sugar, behaved differently when cooked, and reacted differently in the local climate so it dried out quicker and caked into unyielding, unusable lumps.

> ❝ The more repetitive your diet, the more you eat the same things day after day, the less of it you waste. ❞

From this, and from interviews with Tucson residents, Rathje was able to formulate the often quoted home economics axiom that the more repetitive your diet, the more you eat the same things day after day, the less of it you waste.

Simple, stupendously so, but a base observation that has led lifestyle garbologists to some very keen and telling insights about a household's character. Also about how households and householders reveal themselves, not just by their purchases or lack of them, but by the conspicuous gaps or sudden shifts in household tastes that suggest that we are becoming a nation of recyclers (some evidence of this), keen to eat more vegetables and lean cuisine meals (more evidence of this in the south of England but not the north, on the coastal rim of the US but not in the middle or southern states). Also that we are keen on bingeing (the pleasure revenge principle); drinking more at home (wines mainly but also increasing our intake of vodka, gin and, of late, whisky – indeed we predict that whisky is about to make a big comeback as the cool drink of choice for late twenty-somethings); buying more fruit, more carbonated waters, fresh vegetables (courgettes and peppers), more fresh herbs (parsley, coriander, dill, sage), more fresh pastas (linguini and ravioli with the over-thirties, spaghetti still popular with those under-thirties from poorer income households). And yes, there's even a shift back to retro or 'memory' foods – Heinz beans, KP sauces, chips, white bread, steak and kidney pudding, custard, treacle pudding; and familiar olde worlde household brands like PG Tips, Colman's mustard, Kellogg's Corn Flakes and Marmite – all among forty-something bin holders in aspirational addresses or postcodes where loft living, or driving a people carrier or MPV or having a child called Zac, Zoë or Jack might be de rigueur, but so too is having a foothold in the past as their bins and trips to the bottle bank indicate.

Here, despite superficial nods to health and healthy eating, full fat milk bottles are deposited. Likewise, bottles of more traditional French wines (as opposed to the new world lighter varieties served by many of the restaurants targeting them), Bulgarian reds and as many burgundies and 'meaty, boeuf bourguignon' style bordeaux their Sainsbury's, Tesco or Waitrose carrier bags (never M&S, never Safeway, Iceland, or Somerfield) or Hermès, Selfridges, Liberty, Harrods, Harvey Nicks or Gap, CK, Hennes or FCUK store bags can carry. The latter, we note, are deposited in the paper bank or communal bins, the former (Selfridges, Liberty, Harrods and Harvey Nicks) carefully refolded and tossed back into the car boot. Recycling Jim, but only as garbologists really see it.

> **What's the point, after all, in telephone polls or focus group research if they are not even telling you the truth?**

For this is what good garbology is about – seeking out the oddities, creating clear and vivid garbage audits, or brand and lifestyle portraits of the household, householder or postcode concerned. An audit or portrait that is really an extensive and exhaustive list of a person's bin contents broken down into solids, slops, financial information, basic foodstuffs, luxury foodstuffs, fruit, vegetables, treats (sweets, chocolate wrappers, dessert containers), toiletries, fragrances, household cleaners, tinned goods, clothing items (basic wardrobe needs), fashion items (aspirational wardrobe needs), paper products, plastics, bottles, jars, meat, fish, poultry, bread, pastas, grain products, newspapers, wrapping papers, packaging, cereals, pet food containers, and so on and so forth.

This is done to pry certainly. But also to make the process of consumer profiling more accurate and truthful. What's the point, after all, in telephone polls or focus group research if they are not even telling you the truth? Even on something as trivial as beer consumption, as Garbage Project researchers discovered when they interviewed family members about how much beer they drank – some were honest, others claimed that they drank no beer at all yet in every case beer bottles were found, and in all cases the amount consumed was far higher than the amount admitted.

## ■ Creating a brand or bin cartogram

Doing a bin trawl or creating a brand cartogram from a consumer's rubbish does require a certain tact (gloves too), but it also provides a way of checking discarded rubbish against what consumers believe they have thrown out. It is important to interview all participants in the project at the start of the research programme – to get them to talk about their lifestyle, their diet, their alcohol or liquid intake in general terms and then to match this with what you find in their bins, refuse sacks or recycling containers.

It is also recommended that you photograph the contents of a participant's fridge and freezer, bathroom cabinet, beneath their sink where they store household cleaners and hygiene products, the dry goods cupboard, tinned food section, their wardrobe, their toiletries, magazine racks, drinks trolley, drinks cabinet, drinks in the fridge, bookshelves, the contents of their handbag or rucksack . . .

This means that you can check what goes into the bin against what was in, or remains in, their cupboards and food areas. You need to do this to ensure that your findings are accurate but also holistic in insight.

You should therefore create an itemized list broken down into food, finance, fruit, vegetables, brands, bottles, tins and jars, etc. Along with photographs of the contents of their bins that show each item laid out in a way that resembles an evolutionary map of their shopping purchases, from the cheapest items progressing to the most expensive; from small to large. We also produce brand maps or cartograms – strip photographs of all the key brands in their weekly shop, laying these out according to price from the cheapest to the most expensive.

In this way you create a brand ladder or brand hierarchy and by studying it, and by talking to the consumer involved, work out what is missing or what you think they need. One of the offshoots of doing this is noticing just how similar people are in terms of their basic shop within social or ethnic categories, and how consistent they are in terms of the kind of things bought over a year.

Bins or shopping baskets photographed by researchers at different times of the year show little in terms of seasonal variation, which says a lot about our homogenous, trans-seasonal lifestyles – and tells us that most people have in their head an automatic shop of basics, topped up occasionally by sudden shifts in food or wine tastes that speak of a trend, TV programme or lifestyle-driven health or food fad that tilts the average basket beyond the £45 mark, but seldom alters its basic composition.

What retailers don't understand, however, is that most of us refuse to take note of this as shoppers, believing instead that we are ever the hunter gatherer, trying new things and seeking out new mouthwatering sensations. So the retailer spends heavily on promoting new regional cuisines, new world wines or new types of pasta when most of us buy the same old things week after week.

Yet here's the rub. Few of the shoppers we've interviewed believe themselves to be consistent. Indeed most insisted against it – consistency was seen to be boring, in food terms at least – and when confronted with cartograms of their shopping baskets over a six-week period were genuinely surprised, embarrassed and determined to break their old habits.

Which many did when we looked at their shopping on subsequent occasions. Which proved a point that one of our researchers had suggested to a retail client during a Trend Briefing – instead of targeting shoppers with new and unfamiliar things, a campaign telling them how average, dull and workaday their shopping baskets were might be a more successful way of getting them to splurge out on foods and tastes new!

Although we admire consistency in others, we tend not to want to admit to it ourselves – especially if doing so suggests a lack of adventure and originality. Certainly when you show a customer a bin or shopping basket cartogram, their reaction is always, 'But I'm sure I bought more of this and this.'

When you break the dietary content down, or show them how similar their basic shop is to someone in a social category they see as being above or below them, they are equally nonplussed. All middle-class people – if such categories still exist – would like to believe that their baskets are healthier than those of working-class people, or twenty-somethings more discerning than the over-forties, or Londoners more health conscious than those up north. To a point this is true but overwhelmingly, the basics in all shopping trolleys are the same, even if the colour of the bread we choose is slightly different.

But here's a thing. If we photograph middle England bins when their owners know about it, there is an instant shift in what is bought and discarded. Breads once white become brown or laced with sun-dried tomato and onion; pastas once fusilli transform into linguinis and herb-rich raviolis; bananas are abandoned in favour of more exotic fruits – kiwi, prickly pears, starfruits – that are never normally eaten; and herb and bistro salads replace the usual three leaf mix.

> **The point is that sometimes it is better to be covert than overt.**

Cheeses too become various. Usually it is Stilton, a hard tasteless Chedder and a grim but stalwart Wensleydale – now it is goat's cheese laced in a herb rind, or runny cheeses in wooden tubs, or a beer washed, yellowing rind type, smelly and thus all the more discerning and classy for it. Once the trawl is over, the return to type is sharp and sudden, like an old dowager forced to be modern and health conscious for a day, the strings of the corset are pulled and it all hangs out once more, dreary Paxo stuffing and all.

The point is that sometimes it is better to be covert than overt, better to watch from afar than to announce your intentions – for shopping, like sex, is better done when we think we are doing it in the privacy of our own world.

# Garbology maps –
## an atlas of prosumer desire

Bin cartograms and photographs of shopping baskets tell us a lot about lifestyle shifts and where we are heading. Recently, for example, we noted an increase in the number of people buying 'freedom' or free range foods, organic products, ethically-produced coffees and teas, and meats from approved sources. There was also an increase in the purchase of shampoos, face products and body washes with herbal extracts, or with the claim on the packaging that they have not been tested on animals or were in some way 'natural' (not the same as organic but a claim 'clean' enough to convince some consumers of their worthiness), or less damaging to the environment.

Fewer households seemed as concerned about eco-friendly washing-up liquids, washing powders or dishwasher detergents being safe for the environment. This suggests that, in certain categories, there is an element of environmental fatigue or 'concern blindness' – which our own research indicates takes place quickest among products that are basic to our everyday needs and do not require a high level or thought, or shelf interaction.

In other words, we can make a point about buying our Cafe Direct or free range eggs because it demonstrates choice visibly and has a clear human or humane dimension or dinner party anecdote attached to it – we are seen to be supporting the rights of small coffee growers in Puerto Rico, or condemning the use of battery farming. On the other hand, the benefits of using a detergent that is softer on the hands or less damaging to the environment seem somehow less obvious, less appealing – in other words, its narrative appeal is lessened by its ubiquity.

Notions like these are easily confirmed when bin contents and consumer cartograms are shown to the owners of the bins they have come from. More times than not we've found that those claiming a high awareness of environmental issues in conversation rarely exhibit it when it comes to their household waste.

They may take papers to the paper bank, or bottles to the bottle bank, and in many cases they may even buy 'ethically sourced' supermarket products, but this does not make them better recyclers overall as an examination of their household rubbish invariably reveals. They still throw out things that should and could be recycled, and they still waste vast quantities of food, washing-up liquid, cardboard, paper, plastic and glassware. In other words, those who claim to be high recyclers, or have a high or 'keen interest' in the environment, are only marginally better than the average household which claims to have 'some interest' in these things.

## ■ Make people's principles easier to realize

This is good news for retailers, manufacturers and brands that truly want to be part of the triple bottom line process – it isn't just middle-class consumers who care but all of us; it's just that most don't want to make the effort. They want you to do it and, no, they are not willing to carry the cost – again that's your job. Most consumers are not convinced that environmentally sound products should cost more since they are recyclable so they assume that, as well as helping the environment, they are also helping manufacturers and retailers to save money. So if 'freedom' goods cost more, they think retailers are actually profiting from the consumers' efforts to be more thoughtful shoppers. Some groups – especially our New Essentialist Shoppers, low income students, single mums and first-time house buyers operating on a strict budget – have the idea that retailers are, perhaps, cynically profiting from their environmental credentials at the consumer's expense.

There is suspicion that if, for example, organic food doesn't need all those chemicals to grow, all those hormones and fertilizers, why are we paying more? We have also found that foodstuffs packaged in environmentally suggestive graphics or colour schemes – blues, greens, beiges, mauves, browns, off-yellows – are likely to grab the attention of the environmentally conscious consumer even if no specific environmental claim is being made.

When this was pointed out, many felt that a trust or understanding had been broken. They trusted the retailer to flag up a product's environmental credentials on the understanding that this would in fact be the case, rather than being a straightforward marketing ploy – and a dishonest one at that.

> **Again there was the feeling that they were being conned – and because they themselves cared, cynicism was now setting in.**

We noted a concern that health and beauty products fell into this category. Many of the environmentally aware shoppers we spoke to had quite a lot of non-environmentally safe shampoos, body lotions and conditioners in their rubbish. When questioned, they said 'if they (the manufacturers) didn't care why should we?'

Again there was the feeling that they were being conned – and because they themselves cared, cynicism was now setting in. However, a brand, brand range or retailer that establishes itself as a genuine environmentally aware, socially acceptable and ethically sound product with appropriately designed packaging will succeed – so long as it can compete on price with those other non-environmentally sound retailers and brands. Furthermore, the product, dare we say it, still needs to look sexy – a dull, worthy looking bottle or carton with faded colours, lumpen packaging and 'granola' sensibilities isn't the way to go. Long gone is the idea that the baggy jumper and dangly earring brigade are the only people who want to buy into a caring or 'citizen brand' promise. We are all saviours of the planet – most of us will do it happily in a stylish and less ugly way. Even recycling should be fun.

## ▨ Why should people pay more for less?

It is wrong to assume, as many retailers do, that people will pay more for products that contain fewer additives, or have been less processed and refined than their competitor's. Retailers who charge more for organic foods are finding this out to their cost. Customers see such charges as a conscience levy, or as a cynical way for retailers to make money from them because of their efforts to be better citizens when they shop.

The advantage of bin trawls or bin cartograms is that they provide you with all these things, but they also reveal everything from dietary details to brand hierarchies, to how the reality of someone's life differs from how they want others to see them. Bin trawling can be intrusive and it can be abused – especially given the amount of uncensored financial and intimate personal data people throw out. But if it is regulated properly few people complain.

Rarely, in fact, does a client need to know personal particulars about an interviewee. It is often sufficient to find out postcode specifics or the bin demographics of an area. If they need people's names, we tend to give them suitably appropriate nicknames which can be cross-referred to back at the office if they need to be reinterviewed later, or if they are part of an ongoing programme.

Bins also offer insights into new product areas, categories or brand stretch. Currently, food markets in the UK and US are stumbling along with about 2 per cent growth. Brands are finding it difficult to identify what consumers want, how they want it and in what portions – or so it would seem when you look at supermarket shelves. Bins, however, tell us that consumers want more chilled but 'fresh' and ready-to-prepare foods – not lumpen but colourful, not just mediterranean – although there is still a huge demand for southern Italian, French and Spanish cuisine and also North African and, of late, UK regional dishes.

Chilled foods alone saw market growth of 8.9 per cent in 2001. This could be further encouraged by chilling dishes with ingredients that are fresh and light – to be cooked within ten minutes if it is a pasta-based recipe (anything longer and people complain that it takes too long to cook!) and within twenty if it is a winter oven-based dish.

Consumers now have less time than ever to eat lunch – the average time spent eating a desk lunch is 20 minutes in most city offices, according to our researchers. So why not bento boxes? Or ready-made lunch boxes that can be bought from the supermarket, or corner shop containing not just the three items we favour most (chicken tikka sandwich (on brown), freshly squeezed orange juice, and a packet of vegetable or parsnip crisps) but micromeals, lean bites and a high calorie indulgence dessert packed in a way that makes it convenient and comforting to throw into the briefcase or shoulder bag in the morning – or to carry out from the fast track aisle of the local supermarket during the lunch hour rush.

## ▨ Spiritual hygiene offers

Current stress levels have also caused an increase in sales in the personal care, pampering, beauty, calming lotion and fragrances market. More bins now contain more of the kind of products we associate with bath and body, smell and skin pampering. Indeed some bins suggest that people are spending as much on nourishing their outer selves as they are on food and wine – but there is still a long way to go before brands and retailers understand the needs of customers.

Household products are still sold in terms of hygiene, health and the removal of household odours, while the real market shift is towards the spirit and the senses. Indeed, as we go to church less and less, we frequent our bathrooms more and more. Our bathrooms have become bigger, our baths deeper and longer, our use of water more therapeutic, holistic and imaginative – we have personal spas, jacuzzis, plunge pools, power showers, acupressure showers, steam showers. We use these not just to wash, but to relax, destress, escape and realign our senses.

Bathrooms have become a third space – temples, inner sanctums, panic rooms – where we can retreat with candles, essential oils, coloured waters, skin balms, face creams, body butters, massage oils, face masks, scalp relaxants, feet coolers, foot balms, immersive therapies. But only at the top end of the market – among high ticket brands and haute luxury items – are these shifts best catered for.

For the rest of us, there is an array of badly packaged, evil smelling, cheap-on-the-skin oils, lotions and butter balms that leave residues on the bath, the body and on the bottle and container caps we find – which suggests that these things that claim to relax us are doing nothing of the sort.

We also find many containers that are thrown out with a third of their original contents, which would suggest that they have not lived up to their claims and the consumer has noted this. There is another factor which we feel is of particular importance when it comes to designing and selling products into this sector. Many of them are badly conceived and come with flash graphics in shapes that are reminiscent of Domestos and other household cleaner bottles rather than items which are going to be on public display.

Does this matter? Photograph a consumer's bathroom and you will see that it matters very much. Simple, clean, austere or easy-on-the-eye products are universally on display – plain bars of soap, glass bottles, scented candles, sponges, toiletries, flannels and soft fluffy towels that suggest pampering, preening and a sense of enveloped, tactile luxury. While, hidden in cabinets or placed out of view, we find basic needs products like Head and Shoulders, Mr Matey, Radox crystals (we may use them and we may like them, but we don't always want to acknowledge their presence). This tells us much about how consumers see brands, but also how a brand can communicate better with consumers in the way they want – by looking at where they are putting their products and designing them accordingly.

## ■ In matters of the sensual, design is almost everything

For instance, in all the time we have been doing bin trawls, it has been a rare consumer indeed that has thrown out an interesting bottle shape or container belonging to a luxury brand. And when we photograph their bathrooms what do we find? The bottles still on display, long after their contents have been depleted or, if they are refillable, filled with cheaper or look-alike products.

We have also found bottles, flasks and fragrance dispensers that are empty but still out on display – trophy like – in the way we have noted student households keeping wine bottles lined up on the top of kitchen cupboards after parties to mark their drinking abilities – and also their transition from drinking beer to more adult wines, whiskies and liqueurs. If the need for design is there and the demand, we wonder why manufacturers are so keen to ignore it?

Amid all this bin searching and soul searching, people invariably ask the same question, 'Do we take bins from people's doors without telling them?' The answer is yes. Sometimes this is useful if you are attempting to braille an area for a consumer type – bin trawls in East London, Brixton, Bethnal Green and West Kilburn have been done purely to create generic or area cartograms – to look at brand purchases, changes in household or area diets, to establish which retailers are the most popular, what brands are selling (and by inference which are not), what food types people like, whether people are recycling or not. But they are less useful and less telling about people on a personal level than trawls done with permission and before and after interviews. This allows you to use what you know (before) to extract as much as you can from their bin contents (during) in terms of text and subtext, and then use these to delve further when you compare findings to their previous statements and comments on their lifestyles and life aspirations.

As mentioned before, all this should be examined in tandem with photographs of bathroom cabinets, freezer contents, fridge contents, food cupboards, etc. For these reasons alone it is important to work with consumer clusters or project-specific groups. The more you tell them, the more they will tell you.

Even if you don't interview consumers, their bins still offer up very keen forensic and consumer profiles – are they lifestyle orientated? A needs liver? And how far do they travel from their postcode area to shop? If they do travel, which areas do they travel to? (This is usually established through packaging, carrier bags, product types, etc.) How frequently have they done this?

You are also looking for anomalous purchases – the product, package, food, fruit, beauty or skin care product that tells you where they are shifting to next on their needs versus desires shopping ladder.

## ▧ Social and life prism footprints

So it is not the Hermès, Armani, Tiffany regular you are necessarily keenest to know more about, but the 'needs' shopper – a Lidl regular, say, with a shoebox from JB sports and double meal deal Pizza Hut box along with empty cans of Tennants, foil Chinese and Indian takeaway containers (usually meat dishes), kebab wrappers, and pizza bread remnants – who suddenly starts discarding not Lynx or Gillette G2 deodorants (the most popular with teen boys and twenty-something males) as previous cartograms or trawls have led you to expect, but Clinique sloughing creams and Clarins skin care lotions, Black and White hair wax, empty bottles of chardonnay, vegetarian pizza boxes, roach ends from cannabis spliffs and shopping bags from FCUK, Hennes, Space NK and Selfridges foodhall.

A new tenant? A new flatmate? A new sexual partner? And if so, male or female?

The point is, with bins, as with our networks and urban hide or prosumer surveillance programmes, it is not always in the ordinary or the routine that you find the insights you are looking for but the anomalous, the unusual, the freakish, the deviant – a character or culture shift.

The footprints we consumers leave behind, the rubbish we discard, the visual changes we make to the landscape or how we craft and shape our personal environments or living spaces – all these can and do tell us much more. And in most cases it is all very public, very open, very much there for everybody to read and decode but very few companies we encounter do it, preferring instead to collect data by asking questions in ways that reveal very little.

**❝It is not always in the ordinary or the routine that you find the insights you are looking for but the anomalous, the unusual, the freakish, the deviant.❞**

Yet in most cases, the information gained from people when you question them is never as insightful as the information already available when you apply the processes of the good researcher to the mix rather than the antiquated methodologies of the traditional marketer.

To your bin cartograms, your videotaped interviews, your behavioural research projects, personal diaries and networker reports, you can add LAD stats (Local Area Data details) to further enhance the depth of your visual and textual material.

## 44

# Visual goes factual –
## matching images to words

Five years ago, getting the kind of localized detail that made garbage trawls useful quantitatively as well as qualitatively was almost impossible. Now the very government and local authority systems brought online to make it easier for policy makers to track down low income 'shadows', or zones of social exclusion, can also be used by garbologists or insight teams to add extra levels of detail and household information to their localized researches.

Under schemes like the Government's Neighbourhood Renewal Strategy, and ongoing work by the Department of Transport, Local Government and Regions, it is possible to access neighbourhood data by postcode that includes the number of people employed, the number not working, those paying VAT, the nature of businessestrading in the area, the types of shops operating, household incomes, their key household budgetary spends. Cross-referencing with the Office for National Statistics: Neighbourhood Statistics database makes available online Inland Revenue Data, Customs and Excise figures, local crime figures, household types and details on religion, sexuality and even shopping, career and leisure preferences and predilections.

# ■ 360-degree area snapshots

It is now possible for profilers to create the kind of 360-degree snapshot of an area that is a more powerful and rounded picture of its inhabitants, and the trends likely to emerge from that sector, or key consumer demographic.

Remembering our power hub principle, and the fact that people herd, hoard or hang together is enough to suggest that certain patterns you note in an area may be blossoming into a trend, or that sales of a particular type of product or the arrival of a particular look is a symptom of a much bigger, or indeed more trivial, mood swing in the culture.

Don't ignore what your eyes tell you, what a visual trawl of the culture suggests – data adds value, depth and the small tonal nuances that make things more coherent, but rarely does it add insight or tell you where things are going.

The cartogram, however, does and is key to this process of future mapping or brailling. When assembled correctly, it can be used by your research team working with chosen consumers to identify what it says about them – their brand purchases, life needs, hidden desires and what, if anything, is missing.

Rarely when people are confronted with the evidence of their day-to-day lives – on video, in their wastepaper baskets, in photographs – do they resort to the consumer ideal but, with gentle probing and with a researcher who has worked carefully on all aspects of the project, they will happily talk you through areas you might want to know more about.

This is because they want to know more. For many, this kind of approach to trend brailling or product development is so unique, so unusual, that they learn as much about themselves as you learn about them.

Most people, as long as the findings are revealed to them and all the processes of the procedure explained, will do far more for you than they will ever do in a focus group, or in answering a questionnaire or taking part in controlled usability studies. But you must always be honest. You must always explain what is required and how the information you acquire is to be used, and just what it is that has been acquired – a debrief in other words.

This can be as simple as identifying, via the cartogram or bin profile, the fact that the interviewee who claims to be keen on health and physical well-being actually consumes all the wrong kind of foods. You might then ask them why they think this is. A matter of packaging? A routine that is sedate, stressful, full of pressures and lacking in any real challenges?

Or maybe you notice that they are single and male – 8 million people will live alone by 2004, 40 per cent of them will be men – and that many of the food items they've purchased during the period under review have been wasted? Is this because they can't judge portions? Can't cook the chosen items? Tend to do the week's shop and then eat out with friends? Work late?

In the case of our Grit Girls it was noticed that many of the bin trawls contained a larger than expected number of wine bottles, also vodka and tequila, ready-to-cook meals (some with 'enough for two' labels on them, but with the second portion still in the package). There was evidence of rice and pasta-based dishes; tuna but also chicken; very little red meat but a lot of calming or herbal teas including peppermint and camomile. There were very few breakfast cereals, own-label supermarket coffees (3 and 4 strength cup versions for cafetières were among the favourite), quite a lot of local or corner shop brands and foodstuffs, and easy-to-use fridge-to-mouth packaging for Cheddar cheese, meat slices, sausages, sliced bacon, tins of baked beans and eggs. Also chocolate wrappers – Mars bars, Boosts, Twix bars and, in a few bins, high sugar NutriGrain cereal bars.

In other words, a nutritionally quirky, have-it-now, can't-be-bothered-cooking kind of diet that suggested a lifestyle lived to the full, but also one that harboured stresses and pressures – the wine, the spirits, the high strength coffee, sugar-fix confectionery bars and, at face value, 'contradictory' calming and herbal teas – and a routine that was more fraught or busy than it was calm or balanced.

The presence of local shop purchases in many of the bins suggested this – 'No time to go to the supermarket,' as one put it, 'just enough time to pick up a few essentials on the way home, or down the local 24-hour garage.'

> **' 'No time to go to the supermarket,' as one put it, 'just enough time to pick up a few essentials on the way home.' "**

This concurred with interviews and network feedback that suggested a frantic, ever busy, ever on the move, multitasking late twenty-something doer who had little time for life's more spiritual moments – although quiet and calm are obviously the kind of things that this growing group of female consumers needs.

But it also suggested other patterns or anomalies that told us about more significant shifts in taste – that the institutionalized big shop or weekly trip to the supermarket, or shopping centre is in decline. People were and are shopping more and buying less. They are making more visits to their local corner shop and buying food that will last for a day, or freezer food that lasts for a week or more, but avoiding the kind of perishable goods that may have to be thrown out if they are left for two days or more.

People, we found, were able to gauge short term social arrangements, but because their time had to be increasingly flexible, or at least social calendars more malleable, they found, more times than not, that nights planned in were usually nights spent out. Sell-by dates told us a lot about this pattern, many buying things on a Saturday or Sunday which were subsequently in the bin by Wednesday morning.

This group, our Grit Girls (and their male equivalents, Lone Wolves) had a lot to say about supermarkets when we interviewed them about their bin contents. They believed, for instance, that most supermarkets pitched their offers at the 'sherpa shopper' or the traditional family, despite the fact that in urban areas at least this group was in decline.

Our own researchers bore this out. Interviewing people and photographing their shopping in a number of supermarkets in London and around the UK, we managed to identify a plethora of alternative family types or social groups that we felt were not targeted by supermarkets in the way that they targeted the traditional family or shopper. These included:

■ Lone Nesters – singles in their mid-twenties

- Late Nesters – married or cohabiting couples in their late twenties/early thirties
- Negotiated Families – *Friends* style households in which students or young couples lived together to pool resources due to low incomes and high rents and mortgages
- Beanpole Families – in which parents had divorced and remarried, bringing to the new marriage children from previous relationship
- same-sex families
- Rainbow Youth couples – over sixties, high income, high spend on luxury goods and indulgence foods
- our nuclear family – now down to 1.3 children instead of 2.4.

All these new family types shopped differently but all felt they were penalized or 'marginalized'.

Many complained, for instance, that there were too many checkouts for bulk shoppers and too few for single-basket ones. Likewise there were comments about air miles or discount points that favoured those who bought more, while single portion items, ready meals, and 'serves two' or 'one' foodstuffs were substantially more expensive than economy or bulk buys when costed out.

There was the feeling too – especially among students, the young, single and starter home shopper – that they were not only marginalized, but that their custom wasn't necessarily appreciated, despite the fact that many, shopping four to six times a week, were spending as much in some cases if not more than those who did bulk shops.

Our single basket shoppers, we noted from their rubbish, were more often than not drawn to luxury items – treats or pleasure rewards – depending on the kind of day they had had. Three bad days (not uncommon) meant more wine was bought, luxe ice cream, chocolate, a comforting video, expensive cheeses, and if their shop had been a relatively healthy one (as was usually the case with younger singles and couples in their twenties and in urban areas), crisps and dips.

> **Only if variety is improved, prices held down, more brands introduced, more indulgence foods sold and the interiors made more welcoming.**

Looking at their rubbish, interviewing them, following them on their shop, it is all too obvious what is needed – a fast-track aisle that contains multiple shop essentials, smaller portions, lower prices, a shelf with pleasure-revenge specials, a takeaway meals section or charcuterie where food is cooked ready to be taken home, or better still delivered. Happy that the evening meal is sorted, our non-traditional shopper can shop the fast-track aisle and get to a fast-track checkout (lots of these) and still have time to spare.

This is key to understanding and pleasing this group – buying them time, making things easy, not keeping them standing around (their biggest complaint against supermarkets). Some said they were so fed up queuing and being treated shoddily that they had cut their weekly trips down and opted to shop locally instead.

Which is good news for the corner shop, but only if variety is improved, prices held down, more brands introduced, more indulgence foods sold and the interiors made more welcoming, less cluttered and, as one shopper put it, 'Lose the strip lighting and the man that follows you to the back to see what you're doing.'

In fact this is the only reason many of these shoppers stay with supermarkets. Not to do with loyalty but with choice and cost, but if a corner shop chain gets it right – the look, the variety, the service, the pricing structure, the food (organic, local), reflecting the best of Britain's increasingly multicultural palate, and the home delivery service – then the big five supermarkets (in urban areas at least where single households are on the increase, families and married couples in decline) will be in serious trouble. And you learn all this from the humble dustbin.

# Insight into strategy –
## when the visual becomes flesh

Using these techniques – garbology, bin cartograms, brand maps, reflective interviews, overt and covert ethnographic and video surveillance – helps to deepen the consumer profile you are attempting to construct. In tandem, or individually, they also act as ways of gathering live and tactile knowledge about consumer tastes as they are, and also as they are set to become.

At this stage, however, it is important to take a step back and, with your network, attempt to map these personal insights back into a bigger picture or narrative to ascertain what these things are saying about the general direction of the market.

Whether we have been looking at Grit Girls, for instance, or Rainbow Youth or a shift away from a service economy to an ideas culture – your microtrends as identified in studying the activities and attitudes of a select group of edge dwellers or a consumer group running against the prevailing trend – it is crucial to explore what these are saying about the bigger picture.

### ▧ Beyond laddism and geezer bird culture

Our Grit Girls are a good example of this. Identified by our network as a small but increasingly visible splinter group (from those typically described as ladettes or geezer birds), they were seen to be part of a much more long term and significant shift in how women are reappropriating and redefining not just their sense of femininity, confidence and purchasing power, but their voice and visibility in the bigger culture.

Having identified the group and having identified what we've termed as 'Regendering' and 'the female century' – two macrotrends, one relating to men and women and how they were redefining their roles, and the other relating to women themselves and how they were redefining their goals and life strategies – we then

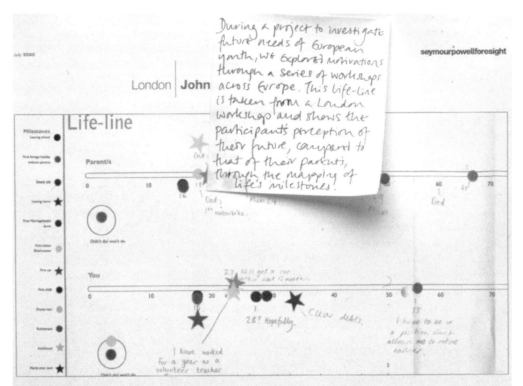

Life style mapping – teenagers compare their life maps and narrative pathways with those of their parents. Sample from Seymour Powell's on-going Life Stage Analysis report.

looked at how and what would be the implications for brands, retailers, leisure and the financial services sector.

To do this you need to identify

- a group's core characteristics or underpinning philosophy (the narratives that drive it – money, empowerment, spiritual well-being, love, lust, happiness . . . )
- the nature of its visual environment
- the texture of its emotional environment
- what it needs as a group to define itself
- what it desires to extend these needs
- who are its heroes and heroines
- what are its career choices, relationship goals – and the key tools they feel are needed to achieve these things.

All of these we uncover during our fieldwork – from interviews, diaries, a group or person's visual diaries, our own photographs, videos, field notes and sketches. It is crucial that all these are displayed on your trend wall or trend map to ensure that a group or tribe's inner and outer worlds are visually articulated. This is vital – no amount of number crunching, data gathering or telephone polling will give you the kind of 360-degree picture you will get if your map or tribe cartogram is produced properly.

## ■ Consumer cartogram

This is your consumer 'forensic', your snapshot of their lives and loves, their inner and outer yearnings – a wall that shows you who they are, what they think, who they associate with, how, where, why and when they do these things.

It is a visual and textual diary of their lives. It should be created along five lines or parallel stages. Lines of images literally that run across your trend wall or consumer map from left to right, from that cluster of images or Post-its or scribbles that represent the whole person (the things that define, that make them unique) to that cluster that symbolizes what they wish to become – images, notes, reflections, asides, usually gathered by the consumers themselves and collected as part of their ongoing dream diaries or personal diaries.

These two points – where they are coming from, where they are going to – are connected by our five narrative paths:

■ the first framed by family and friends
■ the second by emotions
■ the third by relationships
■ the fourth by careers
■ the fifth by life prisms.

Along each line, images are pasted along with facts, comments, observations – all selected to say something about the person or group sense of what family and friends mean to them – emotions, relationships, careers and so on.

We do this visually because using visuals is a better way of realizing the inner self, also because it allows people to play, to be creative and to use images, for instance, that may not be part of their life but inner articulations of something they have dreamt about, a mood or a place or a thing they have no actual words for.

Through the use of images – cutouts, photographs, collages, words, graphics, hand-scribbled notes – people can feel liberated enough to put together very complex and sensitive portraits of what and how they would like to define themselves. Sometimes consciously, most times unconsciously, but at all times revealing in a way they would never reveal themselves on paper or in a face-to-face interview.

What you get here is a phenomenally insightful snapshot of their sense of culture and defining characteristics in a microcosm. You see their world, its shapes, its colours and textures; the rooms they inhabit, the products they use, the dreams they have, the heroes they venerate; the career, financial and emotional markers that make these things possible.

This is Bacon's studio again – a world defined and pinned down in a way that makes it easier for all your insight team to share in its collective understanding.

This way there can be no missing out on what this woman or man looks like, how this group defines itself – and as a consequence what intangibles or tangibles might be missing, or might be required, to make this picture fuller, or to simplify it and thus make their private and public goals more attainable.

> **❝ The point about this level of intimacy isn't to uncover their needs and exploit them accordingly, but to establish unequivocally what they want. ❞**

At all stages, the consumers or people working with you must be involved. The point about this level of intimacy isn't to uncover their needs and exploit them accordingly, but to establish unequivocally what they want and how you can best help them achieve it. Exploiting a person's dreams is not the same as facilitating their desires – one is about profit, the other is about privilege, about enabling, facilitating, smoothing a path. The brand or organization that does this will capture the consumer's heart, and also their loyalty.

## ▓ Supersonglines and happiness superhighways

Along the bottom of our narrative or consumer trend map, we sometimes run a sixth line – what we call our supersongline or, as one of the office wags has dubbed it, the 'happiness superhighways'. This is the line we ourselves work on with consumers, using the detail found along the previous five, to produce this sixth visual line that takes us from where people are to where they may want to go – emotionally, spiritually, financially, sexually, physically. This line is our ultimate marker for determining what they want, how they want it and how a company or brand can best crystallize these wants and desires:

- ▓ as a product
- ▓ a brand
- ▓ a service
- ▓ a place
- ▓ an ethos or philosophy.

These are the core and vital things you seek. The things that will make your relationship with the customer unique and long term.

# Songlines and dreamlines –
## future narratives now

To make the visual real, you need to take the lessons learned from our section on narrative planning, and use this to create a story or tribal narrative that can be mapped back into, or tested against, the bigger trend picture.

This is the real work of your insight network or team – to match the microshifts into and against the macro. Using all the refractive, reflective and network details gathered to produce a script, or narrative document, that creates a brand plan, or brand strategy or tactile philosophy along which decisions need to move.

> **What we are doing here is refining the bigger trend now that we know more about a single facet of it.**

Our approach here is hands on and tactile. The team assembles to study the consumer forensic in much the same way as key players in a criminal investigation gather in the incident room to sift through, or be surrounded by, the visual, textual trace and personal statements, or documentary profiles and evidence assembled by researchers and unit directors.

At this point we compare our bigger picture trends to the consumer group trend or edge dweller trend we have been exploring – see our Trends Briefing in Part 12 for details of this.

What we are doing here is refining the bigger trend now that we know more about a single facet of it. Having explored Grit Girl culture, spent a week living with members of our Rainbow Youth group, or socializing with Sunshine Teens or the Beanpole Family, we then use our findings to add depth, texture and character to as much of the macrotrends they have sprung from as we feel is appropriate.

## ■ The micro is a symptom of the macro

It is important, however, to remember that the microtrend is a symptom of the macrotrend. Not necessarily the macrotrend in itself – our Rainbow Youth, as a group, might be affluent, articulate, over fifty, well educated and determined to be players, determined to exploit their incomes and assets for luxe leisure ends and new experiences, but they are not necessarily typical of all men and women in this age group.

The macrotrend then might be an ageing population, of which our Rainbow Youth group is a micro spin off. They are, in their own way, edge dwellers but could become, if they are visible, vocal and appealing as a niche group, the macrotrend of future years – a taste of things to come as they lay the pathway for other less adventurous members of their tribe to follow.

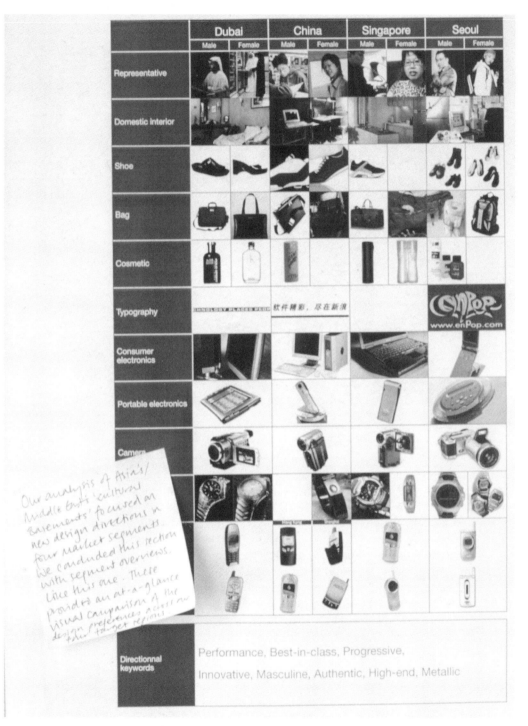

A short history of trends: Seymour Powell uses a cartographic approach to offer clients a quick and easy way to reference past designs and how they are likely to impact on current projects and consumer expectations of new products being taken to market.

Photography by Mischa Haller.

**The waiting game: ethnographic study on the impact of men shopping with their partners and wives, UK 2002.**

As a sub or microgroup, however, they may also fit into a much broader macrotrend, not related to age or to generation, but to a cultural drift towards a more leisurely view of life, or a sense that we need to redefine how and why we work the way we work. So they might, in effect, be part of our 'slo-gro' trend, our 'experience culture' trend; part of the shift away from dumbing down to brightening up, or what we term the 'content society'.

This is always difficult for marketers and traditional clients to understand – that trends can exist within trends, that we can no longer be defined by such characteristics as age, income, class or traditional, social and intellectual background. A woman in her fifties can, and usually does, have as much in common with a woman in her twenties (or a man in his twenties) than many of her own peer group.

This is what you notice when you take clients out into the field. These things are obvious, visible to the eye, but training and traditional assumptions about how markets and consumers behave prevent them from seeing it – clients have target markets we've discovered, and they see everything in relation to this.

Suppose they are a drinks distiller attempting to create a new brand or 'get down' with their target demographic (usually a client trying to flog yet another version of an alcopops drink or cannabis-laced vodka, 'Kids like that kind of thing'). We take them to the bars we think they should see, and the only thing they actually see is their existing target customer and what they are drinking – usually their competitor's brand.

What they don't see is a bar where age groups have merged. Where a 25-year-old man talks to another in his fifties – one drinking a pint of real ale and the other a glass of sémillon. Or two women, one black and one white, both in their early twenties chatting to a group of guys, mates rather than potential dates – the women on pints and the men on sauvignon blanc.

There are black guys here – traders – an Asian woman, an estate agent, men in suits with mauve shirts and purple ties with fat city-broker knots; there are guys in T-shirts, Acupuncture trainers. There's a mum and daughter on a girls' night out, both wearing brands and labels from the same shops – Morgan, Oasis, Kookai, Mango, shoes from Pied A Terre because they shop together, fit the same clothes and like the same styles – mum's on the vodka and Redbull and daughter's on the sea breezes. There's a gay couple, women in their early twenties, so-called lippie lesbians – MAC lipsticks, Mabelline face products, hair colours, mahogany and plum with bronze highlights, all by l'Oréal – with their heterosexual friends, the men on pints of Guinness and the two women on shorts.

All this. And all the client can see is the fact that there are only ten of his demographic types present, and four out of the ten are drinking lattes.

So what's he thinking? Not about all those other people. Not about the six that are drinking his type of bottled beer, but how can he convert the coffee drinkers!

Could he, for instance, come up with a coffee-flavoured vodka, or even a flavoured beer that contained coffee beans, real coffee beans? No questions about coffee culture, about the cultural merging and intermingling going on about him, about our shift away from lifestyles and into life prisms; none about our personal networks opening up and out towards cultural and social secularism, about our increased use of swing time encounters (a term coined by our network to describe the speed and dexterity with which we switch between business and play, social and personal, in the course of our day or evenings out, thanks to increased connectivity); nothing about the growing number of weak tie contacts we make on a day-to-day basis and the opportunities these are throwing up for brands and consumers alike; about the fact that it's midweek and so many people are drinking (Wednesday night in urban areas is fast taking over from Thursday and Friday as the big night out, while Monday nights have unofficially become same sex evenings out, as men and women meet in their own peer groups to discuss their weekends). Only this fixation with target market and target market conversion!

This is why taking the microtrend and mapping it back into the macrotrend is useful – it offers you more measured insights about the market generally. It reminds you that bigger trends aren't defined by age, income, geography (although they can be) but by attitude, outlook and an increasingly complex merging of ages, ethnicity, sexuality and social and cultural backgrounds that will make people more difficult to define and understand if you do not study them visually, and on their own turf and terms.

## ■ A watched trend never boils

It is important to do this on an ongoing basis, however. You must use your network to eavesdrop on key and core cultural shifts (the macrotrend). You must use these to identify, frame and define smaller microtrends – the ones that help you in your particular market – and then to work with this group to understand them, learn more about them and to use these understandings and insights to create the things they need, but also to inform your bigger picture.

The reasons for doing this 24Seven are simple. People live, so too do trends and, as complex theory and complex adaptive systems tell us, just as macrotrends spawn microtrends, so too do microtrends impact on the macro and in the process create new trends and subtrends of their own. This is how you must read trends – see them as snapshots of the bigger picture, or as microtrends that refract back on bigger changes.

Read them, then read them again as you map your own products, brands, ideas or service offers against them. Is there a fit? Is there dovetailing? Overlap? If not why not? Is it because you are producing things that are lagging behind these trends, ahead of them or outside them? And if you think your product fits but still isn't selling, how does it rate against our critical threshold model?

> **❝ Understand them, learn more about them and use these understandings and insights to create the things they need, but also to inform your bigger picture. ❞**

Well? Poorly? Just so? Is this because your customer is resisting it, or because you are ignoring the information from your customers? In which case live with them, work with them, watch how they use your products and services and turn those comments, criticisms and ethnographic observations into workable strategies.

Better still, set up your own insight team, give it its own studio, allow it to function independently of brand policy or company strategy. Let it make the market central to its mission statement, not the company's mission statement the thing that dictates to markets.

Ensure that all sectors of your company have access to this federally, and not just on a need-to-know basis – this kind of insight corralling or shielding is anathema to the tactile corporation. Ensure that they are all part of the network, all aware of what the network is doing, how it works, why and, more importantly, why it is live and there for feedback and input from all areas as well as to help you eavesdrop on the future.

Ensure that trend maps, cartograms, trend walls and edge dweller videos, dream books, views and comments are there for all to see, all to dip into at will. A prosumer map room, or cartographic trend room, is always a good idea. Make field research for all members of the company compulsory, and make it interdepartmental. See data as secondary, information as a poor substitute for live market knowledge and core consumer insight.

## ■ Doing is seeing – understanding the pathway to insight

In the tactile world, doing is seeing, seeing is understanding, understanding is the pathway to insight, insight is the way to gain consumer trust, collusion, approval and loyalty. So your marketing department – and we advise against you having one – should rarely be seen at their desks. They should be in the field, on the go, living the life of the customer as the customer lives it.

And if your customer is located north, south, east or west of where you are, this is where your insight team should be. Too many brands or organizations we speak to are located in London, New York, Paris or Amsterdam when their target market is far away from these places.

To operate remotely is to be remote. Be clear about this – you cannot know your customer until you live with your customer. Any marketer that says differently is lying or lazy, but usually both. Data gathering creates another layer of digital smog to penetrate when attemping to see what the market is doing and where it is going. We can guarantee that an hour in the field is worth a month in the office slaving needlessly away at dull terminals and dead keyboards. Customers are loyal only when you observe them – take your eyes away and they are gone.

> **This way, when the future happens you'll know about it.**

Remember too that a truly tactile company goes beyond category definition and product generation – it goes to the heart of the consumer and operates from there out. This requires transparency, trust and the notion that we are 'in this together'; that goods, services, brands, even profits are federally produced and collectively and collaboratively monitored. That there is no end to this process, only ongoing dialogue and engagement. Living not with the enemy as many corporations see consumers, but as their friends.

This way, when the future happens you'll know about it. When the next little big thing appears you'll be ready – better still, you'll be making it!

If you don't or can't or won't then perhaps the following pages created from our Lifesigns Network report will help you reconsider – especially if you are unfamiliar with all or some of the points we are about to make.

You shouldn't be – they're all out there, in your own sector, your own country, your own profit patch. So why isn't your marketing department picking up on them? Why aren't you picking up on them? Why are you sitting here reading this? You should be looking, listening, recording, learning . . .

That man or woman opposite you – their face, their clothes, their shoes, the bag they are holding, the book they are reading. Those odd little anomalies – a suit but no tie, shoes but no socks, a PDA but no mobile, why? What does it mean? What's happening? What's new? Why not ask them?

Better still, why not follow them? Who knows, you may learn something . . .

part

# 12

# Trends briefing

Four times a year our network assembles – academics, designers, architects, fashion designers, marketers, economists, DJs, writers, thinkers, doers, seers, housewives, scientists, biologists, futurologists, musicians, videomakers, photographers, web designers, ethnographers, programmers, teenagers, betweenagers, rainbow warriors, third agers. Four times a year it considers the future by asking that question more and more of us are now asking – What's new?

Every quarter, the answers change – not drastically but fractionally, as each new and incoming event leaves its shadow on the previous quarter's findings. Updates for those who want regular bulletins from the future can be had from **www.thefuturelaboratory.com**. For those who want the bigger picture, here it is, for the moment at least.

# Citizen brands –
## the truth wins out

In his book *Citizen Brands*, Michael Willmott presents one of the strongest cases ever for reinventing brands. In 2002, for instance, a Harris poll in *BusinessWeek* magazine showed that two-thirds of respondents agreed that 'having large profits was more important to big business than developing safe, reliable, quality products for consumers', while only a quarter felt that business was excellent or pretty good in 'being straightforward and honest in their dealings with consumers and employees'.

Brands were seen to be 'squeezing out local business' and 'reducing local variety and culture'. Most worryingly, there was a perception of an increasing dislocation between the interests of business and society generally, with the proportion of US citizens agreeing that 'what is good for business is good for most Americans' declining from 71 per cent in 1996 to 47 per cent in 2002.

## ■ Brands are untrustworthy

Research for the Future Foundation's nVision service showed similar attitudes among UK consumers. Those who agreed that most companies were fair to consumers have declined over the last 20 years, down from 58 per cent in 1980 to 36 per cent in July 2002. Half of those polled agreed that 'you can't trust large multinational companies nowadays', while three-quarters believed that such companies either 'have too much power and should be stopped now' or that they 'need to be policed and controlled more than they are at present'.

## ■ Customer loyalty down

In such circumstances, it is not surprising that customer loyalty seems to be falling too. US advertising agency DDB reported that the proportion of consumers saying they stuck with well-known brands was down from 66 per cent in 1975 for 20–29 year olds to 59 per cent in 2000, and from 86 per cent to 59 per cent for those aged 60–69.

The public perception of some of these big brands is poor too. In a recent survey in Britain by the Industrial Society, Nike – the archetypal 90s brand and one of the best known globally – had the lowest trust rating bar one. Under a quarter of respondents said that they trusted the brand either 'a great deal' or 'mostly' – a figure way below those achieved by the likes of The Body Shop, Virgin or high street chemist, Boots.

## ▓ Ruthless cola

As mentioned in Chapter 3, in an earlier survey, from a preset list of 30 adjectives (some positive, others negative), the adjectives most often associated with Nike were ambitious, aggressive, greedy, exclusive and cynical. Those for Coca-Cola were similar but with secretive and ruthless replacing the last two. Marlboro was also seen as heartless and deceitful. Brands then are in trouble – and Willmott's *Citizen Brand* concept suggests a possible way out. But he's not alone. Many companies such as BP, Shell, Nike and Esso have been developing their own versions – Angel Brands, Truth Brands, Ecobrands – and bringing in-house the kind of attitudes and self-auditing systems hitherto found only in ethically, socially and environmentally aware NGOs.

## ▓ Triple bottom line

This triple bottom line method of accounting is, however, the beginning of a far longer and far more painful process – one in which the remaking or rebuilding of brands will have to start not with an idea from the advertising agency or marketing company handling the account, but from within the very heart of the companies who own these brands and products in the first place. To do anything less will only continue to jeopardize a brand's true worth. In the past, poor communication systems, a compliant consumer and the relative absence of politically active NGOs meant that, internally or externally, all dirty linen could be washed or dumped without discovery. Now internet vigilance, blogg sites, company moles, whistle-blowers, share of shelf-activists and an increased intolerance of excessive profit or unfair treatment of a company's labour force are leading to a situation where companies are being independently audited, whether they like it or not. Better then for companies and brands to do this themselves. In doing so they will, eliminate problems before less forgiving consumers or NGOs stumble onto them.

## ▓ What it means for brands

For companies to be 'Citizen Brands' in the way the term demands it, they must also introduce 360-degree reporting on their employment methods, manufacturing, distribution and marketing. They must also ensure that all the companies they deal with comply with this method of working. The concept also demands that brands treat their customers fairly, honestly and demonstrate transparency of purpose at all levels. So, no excessive profits for shareholders to the detriment of employees, no fat cat boardroom payouts, no using unscrupulous corporate tactics to freeze competition out or to keep prices artificially inflated.

## ▓ Good commercial logic

There is, as Willmott says, good commercial logic to this. 'Being a good corporate citizen helps to build reputation and trust, it has the general effect of increasing perceptions about the quality of the company's products and service. Secondly, it creates what might be called a 'goodwill' bank – a depth of feeling for the company that will make customers more disposed towards it, even to the extent that they might overlook occasional lapses. Both of these lead to increased loyalty and higher value and more profitable customers. In this way, corporate citizenship could well become a crucial part of branding, an integral part of brand equity.'

Willmott continues, 'But this only makes sense if you accept the argument that brands have become detached from society. But if brands encapsulate values, intangible attributes and the relationship between a company and its customers, then they are surely social constructs that must reflect and embrace the operating environments the company lives in.'

# Blur –
## no cause, only effect

The blurred economy is a market place, as Stan Davis and Christopher Meyer of the Ernst & Young Centre for Business Innovation explain, 'Where the exchanges between customer and company, manufacturer and distributor, employer and employee happen in continuous, ever compressing and multiplex time.' It is an economic model few of us have grappled with successfully. We talk of 'just in time' delivery, relationship marketing, the impact of the net, mobiles and handhelds on how we trade and connect brands to the consumer without really knowing what this means. Likewise, we use terms like connectivity, time-based competition and connectedness in our conversations and interagency e-mails, without really comprehending what true connectedness is.

### ■ Compressed living

A few random facts show just how blur has changed the way we communicate, sell and live. Between 1965 and 1995 in America the average news soundbite imploded from forty-two seconds to just eight. In 1979, the average length of a *Time* cover story was nearly 4500 words, today the same story and its ideas must be told in 2800 words. Even journals like *Scientific American* have cut the length of standard articles by 20 per cent.

Our ability to communicate and transact information has similarly speeded up. Napoleon famously built a series of semaphore towers that stretched from Lille to Milan, from Brest to Metz, a fantastic piece of connected communications technology that allowed his generals to receive information over distance at the then phenomenal speed of 0.5 bits per second. Today, an ethernet link carries about 100 million bits in the same amount of time, while BT now carries more data transactions per year than it does voice traffic.

## ■ Fast action finances

The same is true of finance, and how we assimilate new ideas and technologies. In 1977, about £0.7bn worth of foreign exchange was traded every day. Today that figure stands at £1 trillion and it continues to compress itself as our 'agency horizon' (a scientific term that describes our abilities to extend the speed and distance at which we travel, connect and work in time and space) increases. Likewise, the way we acquire and use connected technologies like the internet or e-mail has speeded up. It took 40 years for radio to reach 10 million users – the internet had 50 million users in five years, Hotmail had 50 million users in one year.

## ■ Blurred trading

These are just a few pertinent examples of what blur does to how we communicate, behave and connect. It not only speeds things up, but causes them to overlap, collide and merge into new areas of market activity. Equally, a campaign can no longer be rolled out regionally, or a brand owner take a decision in America, which isn't communicated unilaterally in every relevant chatroom or rant site that feels that people should know about it.

360-degree coverage – all angles of a story reported at all points in the story chain and from all points of view, regardless of how a brand or business feels about such coverage – is now a reality of corporate life, as are extranets that allow consumers to make inputs into the manufacturing and product cycle earlier and earlier.

All of this has led to a culture of schizoid possibility. We now talk of speed dialling, transumers, com.sumers, loop feedback, knowledge economies, bottom-up brands, hypermobility, tension gradients, compression travel, hurry sickness, plexi-tasking and backgrounding. We do a number of tasks simultaneously, prioritizing one, then another as the situation changes.

## ■ What this means for brands

Oddly, it reminds us of why we need brands in the first place – to simplify things. To bundle products, categories and services together, but also to act as pathfinders and scouts to aid our journey through this data and communications fog which the age of connectivity has blanketed us in. So, far from the brand being a useless concept, or less needed in a world of the connected prosumer or consumanist, it has a new and vital role to play.

Not just as product focusers – on the Fortune 500, the top 200 companies now trade in ideas rather than objects – but as knowledge givers and ideas enhancers. This is the true way forward in a blurred world. They must add value at all points, both spiritual and physical. They must also offer services or products that enable; lifestyle options that clarify and cushion. They must become protectors – create firewalls when we need them; corridors of escape when more are required – but at all times keep us informed.

## ■ Loop feedback

For this is what the blurred consumer requires first and last. Loop feedback, availability of ALL information at ALL times – and that means information which is held about your company and employees as well as information held about the consumer.

In the blurred world, information exchange must be a multiplex act – all you have the consumer must have, and vice versa. Blur isn't a one-way transaction – enabling technologies and connectivity engines means that in the future the consumer will know as much about you and your strategies as you know about them and their desires! Finally, blur demands personalization and customization on a scale hitherto avoided by brands.

## ■ Personalization

Car companies such as Rover, Nissan, BMW, Porsche and Morgan all offer customized services to high paying consumers – likewise Adidas and labels like Gucci and Levis; and stove makers like Aga and Viking. But more and more customers on the high street are making similar demands for a more personalized service and few are expecting to pay for it.

We've seen the rise of bespoke fragrance makers, apartments by Richard Rogers, John Pawson and Norman Foster for first-time buyers, made-to-measure clothing lines, the increased use of personal shoppers, personalized ringtones, desktop systems that can be configured for a single family or a single end user. At stores like Urban Outfitters we can even download our own DVD selection, while the Apple iPod allows us to customize our own soundscape. But these are only hints of a truly interactive world to come and few brands have really grasped this. In the blurred world, uniqueness will not only be expected as standard, it will be the beginning of the relationship with the consumer, not the end point.

# Slo-gro –
## living in the quiet lane

Post-September 11th, many brands are having to rethink their policies. Designers are moving back to notions of sustainable design – about reinvesting value and meaning in products rather than planned obsolescence and novelty. Marketers are beginning to think once again in intellectual rather than celebrity and no-brow terms about the world we live in. Carlo Petrini's *Slow Food* movement and Silvio Barbero's *Slow Cities* in Italy are two aspects of this mood towards restoring positive values to the word 'slow'. According to *Time* magazine, consumers now associate quality and individuality with the small, artisan workshop, or with slowness rather than the anonymous shelves of remote, one-stop shopping centres. More American companies, the magazine suggests, should embrace these principles if they are to win back consumer confidence, but also convince the rest of the world that American brands and brand values are still worth buying into.

## ■ Anti-global outlook

Likewise, governments are beginning to question the notion that globalization is the only way forward, or that a 24Seven work/profit economy is necessarily the best for improving the lifestyles and quality of life of its citizens. In France, for instance, the working week has been reduced to 35 hours (compare the UK average of 47) with a significant impact on productivity levels. These have not only risen, but now outstrip those in the US where the average worker spends 1706 hours of their year in employment compared to their French counterpart who has reduced theirs to 1558.

## ■ Work less, live more

Companies like Volkswagen have also discovered similar benefits by introducing a 28.8 hour week – employee satisfaction levels have rocketed along with production output. In the UK we work harder, faster and longer than our European neighbours – one in seven men works a 60-hour week, while 37 per cent of married men work for 47 hours – and we are seeing government and public sector initiatives such as the Work–Life Balance movement being set up to claw back time badly needed for improving the quality of the way we live. Some brands, such as Whitbread, Airtours, Scottish Coal and Nationwide, are declaring themselves to be 'decelerated' companies and are introducing shorter workings days, flexitime work packages, good food initiatives and e-mail-free Fridays (the average UK worker now spends 90 minutes a day answering and sending e-mails) to re-establish a sense of lifestyle priority and well-being for overstretched staff. Generally, more consumers are questioning the notion that globalization, or economic success, means speeding things up or making accessibility quicker. Yes, this flies in the face of the idea that we live in a connected economy, but no, it does not contradict the notion that connectivity is wrong. It merely challenges the nature of connectivity – how we connect, why and what responsibilities total connectedness demands of us. It is what we call channelled connectedness – the idea that in some areas connectivity should and will be excluded or metered, while in others it will be welcomed and wooed.

## ■ Slow inside fast

Indeed in many ways, slow culture has been made possible by the speed at which we conduct our business and discover things about the world. The Italian *Slow Food* movement and others in France happened as a consequence of fast food activity –

the arrival of McDonald's made a French farmer and an Italian food critic hyperaware of the need to nurture slowness and to re-establish what 'slow' meant in terms of cultural values and social activities such as cooking, dining, talking and travelling.

However we look at it, slo-gro, where slowness is the profit centre (slow towns have reported as much as a 15 per cent increase in profits for local shops and industries), will become a desired norm for many harassed and overworked consumers – whether it is a village, a country, a place or product – and brands, again, are best placed to facilitate this shift.

## ■ Inconvenience foods

Watch out then for the rise of slow dining, inconvenience foods, farmer's markets, artisan products, slow contracts. Watch also for slowness zones in shops, towns and public sector buildings where people will be encouraged to talk, walk, listen or wait. Retailers are already exploring the idea of introducing slo-go zones to help customers chill a little when they enter their store. Shops like Zara, Top Shop, Selfridges, Waterstones, Borders and Bluewater Shopping Centre have all established chill-out areas or 'hanging' zones for customers to have coffee, a back massage or simply to read and relax.

## ■ What this means for brands

The return of the artisan look, the quality moment, product or service that exudes a meditative, poetic approach to trading. But also the creation of zones for people to escape into (see Blur, Chapter 48) – the boutique hotel, the organic supermarket, the handmade suit, the hand-built car, the anthropometric office, the factory or workplace designed around employee needs rather than for the ergonomics of profit.

Think wellness brands – brands and products that offer us 'smoothness' of transaction. Slowness, true slowness, is about relationship management, about being a good neighbour – brands in the slow sector need to be this more than anything else.

## ■ Remembered experience

Brands need to be facilitators, comforters, arbiters of taste, bringers of craft, insight, the remembered experience. They need to keep people at their heart and, dare we say it, be at the other end of the line when customers call to talk – no more automated routing systems, no more, 'Hello, do you mind holding' responses when customers finally get through.

Slo-gro is part of a greater move towards an economy based on people (humanomics) as opposed to one obsessed with numbers and profits.

Brands then need to reconsider their brand poetics and what brand noise really means They should also seriously consider the idea that some slow brands will become tactile brands because of their invisibility – their absence from the brandscape, rather than their presence.

'Slow' demands stealth as well as ingenuity and integrity of product – and it demands it all the time, consistently, smoothly and without reserve. Quality cannot be metered out, nor can good craftsmanship be done on a shoestring or by cutting corners. If you enter this market, and many will choose not to, you have to be in it for the long haul, not the short return.

# The pleasure hide –
## the party-on generation

An estimated 657 million people went on international tourist trips in 2002, making travel one of the world's biggest industries – it employs 10 per cent of the global workforce and is worth £300bn annually. Despite the events of September 11th, the travel market continues to expand – the European market alone is set to double by 2020, up in net worth terms from £60bn to £120bn. Today's travellers, whether business or pleasure, are accustomed to speed, convenience and what the industry now calls immersive luxury. 'There has been such a rapid increase in affluence over the past ten years that, for many people, the primary concern isn't financial but being well looked after,' says Philip Grierson, marketing manager for premium tour operator Cox & Kings. 'People are becoming more ambitious with even their secondary holidays, and this will be an ever increasing market.'

### ■ Online leisure

Internet bookings too are up and the no-frills traveller booking online, says Forrester Research, is currently spending £592m annually. This figure is set to rise to £3.7bn by 2005 as more routes are opened and discount airlines record month-on-month increases for bookings – making online transactions represent 14 per cent of total airline ticket sales. Package holidays continue to be key to wooing customers at the cheaper end of the travel market, while cruising continues to attract older, more affluent consumers. However, since the events of September 11th, even these areas have experienced significant demographic shifts. Generally, a number of new types of travel experiences and trends have emerged which operators in this sector need to know about.

### ■ Immersive luxury

Even traditional hotel chains like the Hyatt, Sheraton and Le Meridien groups have spotted this. Noting an increase in the number of customers demanding 'fast-forward style with fast forward service', many have taken a leaf out of the books of boutique hoteliers like Ian Schrager and the Costes brothers and used architects like Skidmore Owings & Merill (the Shanghai Hyatt) or London's Real Studios to create rooms which Juergen Bartel, Le Meridien group CEO, refers to as, 'Combining the latest and fastest technology available with good design and elements of the arts.'

## ■ Compression weekends

Leisure can also be hard work. One of the strongest current travel trends is towards short breaks packed with activities. According to the *European Travel Monitor*, short trips of between one and three days accounted for 27 per cent of all holidays taken in 2002 – six out of ten trips now last a week or less. Eastern European cities such as Tallinn, Riga and Krakow are growing in popularity, while the club scene in Reykjavik, Copenhagen, Helsinki and Stockholm continues to attract young, hip tourists. Even long-haul flights are gearing up to the boom in compression breaks. Weekends in New York have been established for a long time, so people are now travelling to Cape Town, Moscow, Hong Kong, Singapore and St. Petersburg and even Sydney for Friday to Monday weekends.

## ■ Getting the knowledge

Travellers are not just taking more city breaks, they expect to be entertained and even educated while they're there. People want more out of a city than just sightseeing – like fabulous food or their favourite music. Hence the rise of opera circuit holidays, or gastronomy weekends in Lyons which culminate in an evening meal at the restaurant of the original celebrity chef, Paul Bocuse. Dennis Bederoff, research director at the Swedish Tourist Authority, says that 'everyone I know who has visited London over the past year has gone to see *Mamma Mia!*, the musical tribute to Swedish supergroup Abba.'

## ■ Shopping and surgery safaris

Shopping trips are attractive to the cash-rich, time-poor generation. We're now seeing people taking long weekends not only in Paris, Amsterdam and Rome but in Prague, Boston, Toronto, Marrakesh, St. Tropez, and St. Petersburg. In this mix, many are combining visits to shops with visits to plastic surgeons. Indeed some tour operators are now offering surgery and shopping breaks to Cape Town, Moscow, Miami and London, with many tourists taking advantage of low travel rates, plummeting surgery costs and a chance to recover in five-star hotels away from the maddening gaze of friends or business colleagues.

## ■ Futurist breaks

In their words and images, manifestos and paintings the futurists gave us a brave new world of surging towers, Marionetti angles and architecture that hummed with new technology and wondrous building materials. Now fast-forward tourists are booking holidays to buildings, railways stations or travelling on high-speed trains – anything that offers them a glimpse of tomorrow.

Included in this list, of course, is the Bilboa Guggenheim, Valencia's City of Arts and Sciences (Ciudad de las Artes y las Ciencias), the Petronas Towers in Kuala Lumpa, Cornwall's Eden project, the Shanghai Museum and Foster's Reichstag building in Berlin. Indeed Berlin's Potsdamer Platz has become a must-see Dan Dare destination for *Time Machine* tourism. Here you can see works by Gehry, Piano, Helmut Jahn, Richard Rogers, Arata Isozaki and José Rafael Moneo among others. Michel Saee's Turku Library in Finland has also become a place of pilgrimage, and Slovenia's University Sports Centre by Sadar in Vuga Arhitekti that looks like a giant piece of Andre Bloc sculpture.

## ■ Supertrains and fab stations

Superspeed trains and the stations that house them have also become traveller attractions in their own right. The Paris to Marseilles TGV has seen bookings quadruple as passengers pay to enjoy the train as much as the places it goes to. Germany's ICE 3 supertrain with its hyperslick lounges and Neumeister Design interiors with glass-floored cabins that allow passengers to watch tracks whiz beneath at 330 kph is similarly profiting from this trend.

Likewise the luxury class Crystal Panoramic Express that operates between Montreux and Lenk in Switzerland. This comes with observation cars, glass roofs, curved interiors, UV filter glass windows and an in-cabin service better than airline executive class. But if trains have plugged into the future and the golden age of luxury travel to boost their appeal, so too have structures like Norman Foster's Hung Hom station in Hong Kong, Terry Farrell's Inch'on airport station in South Korea, or Bernhard Tschumi's station in Lausanne. However, Eurolille with its awe inspiring works by Jean-Marie Duthilleul, Christian de Portzamparc, Claude Vasconi, Jean Nouvel and Rem Koolhaas still remains one of the biggest and most visited transit hubs in Europe.

## ■ Decelerated living

The opposite of the frenetic minibreak is the more sedate luxury of the cruise. Cruising may be less strenuous than trying to 'do' a city in three days, but ocean-going holidays have shrugged off their moribund, geriatric connotations. While the very top end of the market remains ultraexpensive, a record number of British holidaymakers went cruising last year – over 850 000, an increase of 16 per cent on the previous year; and French and German numbers are also rising. Between now and 2005, cruise lines will be launching 70 new ships, some able to carry 4000 passengers round the Mediterranean or the Caribbean. Many will be equipped with skating rinks, saunas, theatres, gourmet lounges, luxury goods malls and sports facilities. Others will offer themed trips such as wine tastings, archeological expeditions, or year long hop-on-hop-off cruises for retired couples anxious to 'boil off' funds before squabbling taxmen or family members can get their hands on them.

## ■ Spa living

Another radical repositioning is that of the spa holiday – now known as the wellness break. Stressed out careerists can spend time out of the office chilling in desirable destinations such as Cyprus, Sumatra or India. Holistic therapies such as Ayurveda and aromatherapy have cast off their alternative, hippy image and are now seen as mainstream activities which are particularly popular with the young and well-heeled – Thomas Cook, Kuoni and Cox & Kings all report an increase in sales.

## ■ Obscurity travel

There's a cachet in holidaying somewhere the neighbours haven't been – or, prefer-ably, even heard of. 'More affluent holidaymakers seek lesser-known, more remote destinations as the standard tourist sites become overcrowded,' says Philip Grierson. 'For example, the Golden Triangle was a prime destination in India, but now it's very well-trodden. We are moving into areas like Kerala in the south, or old palaces in Rajasthan.' In Peru, the north is becoming more popular instead of Machu Pichu and, despite the events of September 11th, there is a growing market for holidays in Syria, Libya, Iran, Iraq and Cuba, and Middle East destinations such as Dubai are also taking a slice of the cake. 'This kind of break is largely dependent on the available infrastructure,' says Grierson. 'Our clients expect a certain level of comfort, decent roads, hotels, communications.'

## ■ Adrenalin breaks

More intrepid travellers who don't expect home comforts are also a growing group. The market for extreme holidays has grown by 15 per cent in the last year, and even mainstream travel agencies are offering bungee jumping, rapids rafting and the like, as well as diving, surfing, cycling and tennis, and all kinds of activity holidays. We're also witnessing a growth in 'seen-it all travellers' booking trips to war zones (Kabul, Beirut, Belfast, Jerusalem), earthquake areas, and social and environmental flashpoints (Indonesia, Sudan, East Timor) to boost their sense of danger and extreme expectation.

As one our network members touring Kabul puts it, 'It's no longer fun to bungee jump or ski down mountains when so many ordinary people are at risk. But to participate in that risk, well that's an adrenalin rush at its most aggressive.'

## ■ Urban safaris

Watch out too for the growth in multidestination packages, those that allow you to stagger and select destinations at short notice over a year – so-called 'pix and mix' holidays – and urban safaris. The latter are proving popular with city dwellers from cities like Tokyo, New York, London, Paris and Singapore who book with so-called PSOs (personal service organizations) such as the UK-based Quintessentially who offer them everything from VIP party access to getting a table at the Four Seasons, to persuading a city's most inaccessible dinner party host to have you over for dinner.

More noticeably, hotels in London, Paris, New York and Moscow are seeing a significant increase in the number of same-city residents booking in for 'at home' weekends or, in the case of London, Paris and New York, for corridor parties, clubland's latest craze.

# Cellular lives –
## new millennium families

The structure of families is changing on a Europe-wide scale and this is set to have a huge impact on how we create products and sell brands in the near future. European divorce rates are already rising to meet those in the UK, where one in three marriages now ends in divorce. In tandem with this, there has been a similar decline in the number of marriages. Single parent households in Germany with a male head now stand at 63 per cent, while those headed by a woman have risen by 31 per cent over the same ten-year period. In France, divorce rates have increased fourfold since 1965, while the number of adults deciding to opt out of marriage altogether has risen by 12 per cent since 1980. In Italy divorce rates are up by 30 per cent since 1990, while birth rates have dropped to just 1.2 children per woman. In the Netherlands, 23 per cent of children are born out of wedlock. In the eastern bloc, births in Poland have almost doubled in the past 20 years, while in the Czech Republic marriage rates have fallen by 23 per cent over the last decade.

## ■ Single person households on the rise

In Great Britain 65 per cent of people with dependent children are married but this is changing. In 1983, 3.7 per cent of children in the EU lived in single person households but by 2000 this figure had increased to 9.7 per cent. Generally, over the last two decades the number of people living in single parent households has tripled across Europe, but the pattern has been significant in the UK, where figures jumped from 6.4 per cent in 1983, to 19.8 per cent in 2000. With less than half the UK population set to be married by 2005, this figure will increase even more dramatically. Taken in isolation these figures seem mere statistical blips, but when taken together they offer a glimpse of a far more sexually and socially diverse landscape than ever seen in Britain or the European mainland before.

## ■ Nuclear meltdown

Even the figures on the nuclear family are telling. Down in size from 2.4 children to 1.3, with couples marrying later (at 28) and staying with their careers longer and, increasingly, delaying having children to their late twenties or their mid- to late thirties. All this has created an entirely new set of family types for agencies and brand owners to cope with.

## ■ New family types

These include:

- Lone Nesters – people choosing to live alone to avoid families completely.
- Late Nesters – yes to families but only in their late twenties and early thirties.
- Single Dads – on the rise, dedicated and keen but lacking in support and help.
- Teen Mums – the UK still has the highest percentage of teen mums in the EU, second only to the US.
- Shared Parent families – more couples reaching amicable coparenting agreements after divorce or separation.
- Step-parent or Beanpole families – large families reappearing as an increasing number of couples remarry, taking children from previous relationships.
- Double Income Lone Kid households – a growing trend; careerist parents, a lone child, high disposable income.
- Single Income Now Divorced – separated men and women who are 'time poor' and indulgence friendly, with 1.2 to 2.3 kids usually living with their mother but sharing quality time with their father.
- Alpha Mothers – high earning careerists with serial partners, one child and a lifestyle where marriage is not an issue.
- Same-sex families – EU-wide legislation to legalize partnerships and the adoption arrangements of same-sex couples is likely to increase the number and diversity of this hitherto invisible family type.
- Negotiated families – more single and cohabiting couples with or without children choosing *Friends*-style living arrangements as increased house prices, college fees and low pay entry points to the jobs market make it increasingly difficult for people in their early twenties to go it alone.
- Extended families – more middle and lower income couples are choosing to live with parents for financial and childcare reasons.
- Nuclear families – still key but getting smaller in number, richer, divorced, and/or married later, average size is now mum, dad, and 1.3 children.

## ■ What it means for brands

These changes are set to have a profound impact on brands and how we promote them. Such diversity means there can no longer be 'ideal' family arrangements in our print or media campaigns. This is a generation that will demand financial, health, tax and social welfare packages that reflect their changing and individual status. Advertisers will be penalized for non-representation, or for targeting one family type over another. Likewise, brands, services and product categories will be expected to have a more human face and voice. In an increasingly single and fragmented society, brands that encourage and allow relationships with this new type of consumer landscape are more likely succeed and prosper.

## ■ Brand simplification

There will also be a greater demand for brands that simplify – that o.
holidays, 'time out' facilities, 'life stage' financial, health and educatio
that reflect the unique and changing status of these new family types. Many of these
types describe themselves as 'highly vocal', 'sensitive to overt targeting', but 'welcome
honest, open dialogue' and agencies and brand managers should remember this when
creating campaigns for this market. Like our New Essentialist Shoppers, they expect to
be treated fairly, not marginalized or charged extra because they are perceived to be a
lucrative minority. In ten years they will be the dominant force.

# Branded youth –
## the repackaging of childhood and beyond

Our concerns here were threefold:

- how much cash kids have
- how they spend it
- and how they structure their social lives.

All of course are interlinked and each impacts on the other, but in ways that
surprised even us. Yes, girls are different from boys and yes, parents do matter in
how money is spent – although, oddly, not when it comes to trainers – and despite
shifts in our attitude to class, such things still matter in how children from higher
and lower income families behave.

## ■ How much they're worth

Children between 7 and 14 are handed about £59m annually in pocket money –
equal to about £6.09 per week. This increase in spending power, however, has not
affected the value of other gifts from their parents. 'Pester power' has also risen in
the past five years. 43 per cent of parents (7 per cent more than five years ago) say
their children pressure them into purchases, and the lower down the income scale
you go, the more likely it is that pester power works!

## ■ North–south spending divide

Research has also disclosed significant regional differences concerning our youth.
Scottish and northern children receive more pocket money than their traditionally

more affluent southern peers. London children received a weekly average of £5.14 last year, while young Scots got £6.37. Social trend experts say that parents' longer working hours could be pushing up spending by and on children. Phil Evans, a Consumers' Association spokesperson, believes that, 'A lot of this is down to parental guilt. We work for so many hours that we try to make up for it by endlessly buying our children things.' Eight in ten of all 7–10 year olds also have a bank or a building society account – differences by demographic subgroup are fairly small, but there is some evidence that girls get the savings habit slightly earlier than boys. The majority of children (more than six in ten) say they opened their first account when they were aged 6 or younger.

## ■ High income, mean parents

Children from ABC1 families are more likely than C2DEs to have a bank or building society account and generally have more money saved up. However, C2DE parents are more generous in terms of pocket money, with more than half of their 7–10 year olds, compared with four in ten ABC1s, receiving more than £2 a week. Similarly, 20 per cent of C2DE children, but only 12 per cent of ABC1s, say their parents buy them everything they want.

Spending habits change between ages 7 and 10 – especially for girls, although sophistication levels have clearly not advanced so far as to remove toys and games from the top of their spending list. 65 per cent of 7–8 year olds and 57 per cent of 9–10 year olds say they spend their money on them. Another traditional favourite category for pocket money spending is crisps, sweets and chocolate. The more adult tastes of 9–10 year olds are highlighted by the fact that CDs and other recorded music make up their third highest spending category (more than four in ten buy them) but these are still very low down the list for 7–8 year olds.

## ■ Age influences spending

A change takes place in spending habits at around the age of 9 with a much wider range of items competing for their pocket money than is the case for 7 and 8 year olds. Older ages tend to shift purchases from sweets, etc. to magazines and comics; from drinks to computer and video games. Gender heavily affects how older group members spend. Young boys are more likely to spend their money on toys, computer and video games, and sports and hobbies. More girls than boys buy magazines, CDs, clothes, toiletries, cosmetics and presents for friends.

## ■ Changing spending habits

The spending habits of girls change more between the 7–8 and 9–10 age groups than is the case with boys. This may well reflect the fact that girls, who tend to reach puberty earlier than boys, begin to show signs of sophistication at an earlier age. Almost all 7–10 year olds, in all demographic subgroups, say they go shopping for clothes with their parents. Parents are more likely than children to be the decision maker when it comes to purchasing jeans, but children clearly have more input into the purchase of trainers, with 63 per cent saying that they chose their latest pair themselves. There is a strong male–female division (which reflects that found among adults) in terms of attitude to shopping for clothes – half of all boys agree that shopping for clothes is boring but only 13 per cent of girls do. Children become increasingly body conscious as they move through this age group – by the age of 7–8, 37 per cent have used deodorant, 31 per cent hair gel, and 25 per cent body spray. By the time they reach 9–10, this has increased to over half in each case.

## Shifting social bonds

For the under-10s particularly, the changes in family structure brought on by longer working hours, increased divorce rates and the number of single person households have ushered in profound social changes. Likewise, the increased focus on school work. Among 7–10 year olds particularly, school work and examinations figure far more prominently in their conversations and their reasons for feeling stressed compared to similar groups a decade ago. Eight in ten 7–10 year olds now agree that it is important to work hard at school and 45 per cent already have ambitions to go to university. Perhaps because of the academic pressure, enjoyment of school is by no means widespread – less than half of all 7–10 year olds (42 per cent) agree that they enjoy going to school, and around one in five actively disagrees.

## Nuclear family versus the 'negotiated' family

The value of family life to children in this age group is very clear from the fact that eight in ten agree (and only 1 per cent disagree) that they like spending time with their family. However, as traditional family structures break up, many are creating alternative family-style units among their friends and peers. Being part of a group is very important to 7–10 year olds as a whole – six in ten agree, and less than 1 per cent disagree that this matters to them more than anything else. However, conformity to the group does not necessarily extend to wearing the same clothes as their friends. Girls are rather more likely than boys to want to be different in this way, with 37 per cent (as opposed to 32 per cent of boys) making an effort to wear clothes that are different. However, only 13 per cent would go as far as to say they are more trendy than their friends, and only 14 per cent claim the distinction of being the first to try out new things.

## Non-influential TV

Although 38 per cent say they like to buy things they have seen in television advertisements, rather fewer than this (one in five) say that they like the advertisements themselves. Younger children tend to be more appreciative of advertising than older ones, although they don't necessarily see that they are being sold a product. Nearly half of 7–8-year-old boys but only three in ten 9–10-year-old girls say they like to buy things they have seen advertised on television.

## ■ Shopping and looking

Six in ten of all 7–10 year olds buy CDs and 85 per cent listen to the radio. Interest in music is more widespread among girls than boys – for example, nearly eight in ten 9–10-year-old girls buy CDs but only 56 per cent of boys. However, their interest in music does not necessarily extend to knowledge of the Top Ten, with only 12 per cent saying they always know what's in it. Although more than half of the total sample say they enjoy reading books, this drops to 36 per cent among 9–10-year-old boys. Among girls, in general, 63 per cent enjoy reading, with 7–8 year olds being the most prolific – 67 per cent of this age group enjoy reading and more than four in ten have read more than 20 books in the past six months. Girls are considerably more likely than boys to buy books for themselves with 46 per cent, compared with about 33 per cent of boys, saying they do so. Boys in this age group tend to spend their money on games, videos, CDs and trainers.

## ■ Tween tensions

A high proportion of 7–10 year olds (72 per cent) identified themselves as being very worried about cruelty to children, and only slightly fewer than this (67 per cent) said they were worried about cruelty to animals. The dangers of smoking cigarettes, and of other drugs, also figure highly in children's anxieties – a total of 88 per cent are either 'very worried' or 'a little worried' about the former, and 86 per cent about the latter. Brands-wise they had no particular views on brands that were perceived to be damaging, unethical or indeed cruel to animals. They showed little awareness of issues being covered in newspapers concerning brands which use sweated labour, test their products on animals or have negative ratings among adults.

## ■ Mobile lives

Ownership of mobile phones is relatively low with only 13 per cent of 7–10 year olds having one of their own (although when shared ownership is taken into consideration, this rises to 22 per cent). Parents are the most likely recipients of calls from their children's mobile phones, followed by friends and other family members. Around three in ten phone owners send text messages to their parents with a similar proportion texting their friends. Use of the home telephone by 7–10 year olds is also still at a fairly low level – even though half of all respondents had used their home phone in the previous week, the majority of these made only one or two calls. Girls' use of the home phone tends to be higher than for boys, and older children use it more than younger ones.

## ■ Techno-savvy

Use of computers is almost universal – more than eight in ten use one at school, and two-thirds use one at home. There is a strong bias by socio-economic groups in respect of home usage of computers – 80 per cent of ABC1s but only 53 per cent

of C2DEs do so, but C2DE children who do have one at home
ABC1s to be the main user.

Video games and TV are more important to boys than gir
tion (84 per cent) of all 7–10 year olds play video games, w'
in their bedroom. Although three-quarters of girls do play '
cent have bought any in the last year, with only 33 per cent
which ones to buy. Boys are more interested, with 92 per cent playing, ￼
having bought in the last year and 63 per cent saying they are the decision make.
A total of 62 per cent of all 7–10 year olds have a television in their bedroom – this
is clearly more important to boys than girls, with 76 per cent of all 9–10-year-old
boys having one compared with 60 per cent of girls.

## ▧ Techno-friendly

Network research also indicates that 85 per cent of children say that they
understand the latest interactive technology and enjoy the process of learning
online, as well as using their computers to play games, etc. In fact, many see the
computer as a social tool and tend to use it with other kids present – unlike adults
who treat it as a tool to be used when alone. They also see the internet and their
home computer as a 'portal' learning tool or a 'knowledge enabler', while adults
saw it as a way of checking information. Most children also see things like mobiles,
laptops, image mobiles, Handsprings, PlayStation 2, Xbox and interactive TV as
everyday familiar tools for communicating, playing games or accessing information online and couldn't quite understand why their parents had such negative
views about technology generally.

## ▧ Thumbs not fingers

More interestingly, work at Warwick University's Cybernetic Culture Research Unit
shows that under-10s physically relate to technology differently. For this group and
their older brothers and sisters brought up on GameBoys, PlayStations, Xboxes and
SMS texting, the thumb has replaced the index finger as the most important and
most muscled digit on the hand! The study, carried out in nine cities, showed that
more young people used their thumbs to work keyboards, play games and send
messages than adults – and were doing so in way that was completely altering how
they related to a technology environment where keyboards were designed to be
worked with fingers more frequently than thumbs. These *oya yubi sedai* (thumb
tribes), as we said earlier, work keyboards more rapidly than those using all their
digits, and now even use the thumb to do tasks traditionally carried out with the
index finger.

## ▧ What it means for brands

Generally under-10s want products to be inclusive not exclusive. Brands should
contribute to their peer and group dynamic and not attempt to isolate them in any
way. Although childen want to be different, they don't want to stand out. The

interactive' or 'connected' the product the better. Fashionability matters individuality and peer endorsement matters much more, especially in lower come groups, than TV advertising. At this age, hardware design is less important than software content and interaction, although in the mobile phone sector, design is always mentioned as a key purchasing influence – for girls it's about colour, convenience and lightness; for boys it's about shapes and designs that make them look more adult. Keyboard design is important to both groups – designed not to be worked by the fingers but by the thumbs. Indeed boys tended towards more 'visible' mobile designs (as in larger, chunkier handsets) and were just as keen on characteristic ringtones as girls.

## ▣ Parental heroes

Parents were seen as heroes and heroines across all social categories and their opinions mattered on clothing purchases, but not on trainers or logo tops – these were heavily influenced by peers, and older brothers and sisters. Honesty was important between age groups, but also in ads and offers targeting them. All liked brands, products and retailers that gave them free things and added extras. Few had objections to being e-mailed or receiving text messages offering them 'stuff', so long as they were getting something in return.

# New Essentialist Shopper –
## keeping it real

Shoppers who spend £100 plus on their weekly shopping bill are key to keeping supermarket profits buoyant, but New Essentialist Shoppers could be key to keeping their long term profits healthy. The trouble is that many supermarkets are unwilling to woo this kind of customer because they see their weekly spends as too low and their social and ethical stances too hard to address.

## ▣ Low average spends

These shoppers are also less keen on impulse purchases, tend to buy smaller sized portions, spend between £22 and £80 on their average weekly bills, think carefully about the social, ethical and environmental impact of supermarket ranges but are unwilling to pay extra for foods containing an organic stamp, or 'freedom' tag. Consequently, the top five supermarkets tend to ignore them. This is bad news indeed, since these are by far the fastest growing and among the most vocally active of all consumer groups. Although they spend less, their spend increases, on average, by 3.9 per cent annually.

## ■ Loyalty counts

More importantly, they are loyal to the stores they shop at, and are less likely to swap stores just because one is advertising cheaper prices than another. Yes, value is important to them – and many criticize the stores they use for targeting the family shopper with bulk buys – but they are still high on 'values' and if a store seems to care about the way it sources its food, this matters to them a lot. Unlike the more affluent shopper, however, they will not pay more for organic produce. Partly because they can't, but mostly because they don't believe it should cost more in the first place. Research tends to bear them out on this.

## ■ Student shoppers

Although many New Essentialist Shoppers are first-time careerists, the student population makes up a sizeable portion of their overall numbers and a look at this sector alone offers clear indications of how much this market is potentially worth, if nurtured properly. According to Mintel, students eat out more, use more beauty products and go to gyms and health clubs more often than the rest of us. They are also 'twice as interested' in designer clothes, luxury watches and foods, and generally enjoy shopping – any sort of shopping. They also take more holidays than they used to – 500,000 booked with STA, the youth travel specialist, last year. According to the Student Living Survey published in 2002, two-thirds of students have their own computer, a figure that has risen significantly in the past 12 months. Many are happy to spend grants and part-time job incomes on Nike trainers, Diesel jeans and mobile phones – for which they unblinkingly pay £100 in monthly bills. Food is, of course, a high priority and they are keen, even on limited budgets, to try new food types and product categories – although basic foodstuffs still include bread, pasta, milk, sausages, cheese and bacon.

## ■ Values versus value

In terms of stores favoured for value, our network researchers learned that New Essentialist Shoppers rate Asda head and shoulders above the others in terms of low prices and value for money. The more upmarket Waitrose was second for value but unbeatable for quality and choice. Tesco was rated third on prices, followed by Somerfield, then Sainsbury's, which was praised for its quality and range. Bottom of this survey of six stores was Safeway. Generally, they wanted to see more regional produce in stores, a greater emphasis on localized sourcing and more detailed information on food packaging on whereabouts items were sourced and how they were packaged.

As with most consumers, they are anti-GM, worried about irradiated foodstuffs, and are more likely, following recent media coverage of CJD and foot and mouth disease, to buy fish, white meat, lamb and pork over red meat, pies and processed animal foodstuffs.

## ▓ Feel victimized

Although loyal to retailers, they believe retailers are far from loyal to them. Value foods, they say, look cheaper and make them feel mean and excluded when they buy them. Cheap prices, they say, shouldn't mean cheap packaging – New Essentialist Shoppers feel excluded by poor packaging, flash graphics and '5p for a can of beans' type offers.

Their spends are low because they are students, graduates or newly cohabitating couples, not because they fit into traditional low income socio-economic categories.

## ▓ Honest advertising

They expect brands and retailers to be honest, clear and concise in their advertising and marketing campaigns. Demanding luxury products, but unable to pay for them, they would like stores to introduce 'try out' days on traditionally expensive goods rather than award people storecard points, which they say favours high income/high spend shoppers over them. They would also like stores to wine and woo them more – larger shopping trolleys, home delivery services, nappy changing facilities and bulk purchase ranges seem to favour family groups or affluent married couples, and in many ways they see this as unintentional discrimination.

## ▓ Essential foodstuffs

New Essentialist Shoppers would like to see fast-track aisles containing essential foodstuffs, more express checkout tills with dedicated packers, luxury goods offers targeted specifically at them, more late night openings, improved food labelling (they are keen on nutritional, ethical and environmental information) and more fruit and vegetables that have been sourced locally. Unlike many shoppers who regard door-to-door leafleting as an irritation or would be 'put out by a telephone call or e-mail from their local store about a special offer or upcoming bargain', the New Essentialist Shopper is very keen to know more, especially if the store demonstrates in its offer some knowledge of their circumstances and life choices. Relationships matter here – friendliness, not just to keep them spending the amounts they are spending, but to keep them coming back when their salaries increase and they no longer fit into such a narrowcast category.

# Gated luxury –
## new wealth decade

Our increased need for security, and a growing gap between rich and poor, and middle and low income households, have created huge social and psychological divides that many companies, brands and private sector security firms are profiting from. A simple fact illustrates the extent of the problem – 1 per cent of the world now has an income equal to the poorest 57 per cent. In Britain a similar pattern has emerged – since the 80s, more millionaires have been created than were created from First World War business activities.

Despite this, poverty levels have rocketed and the gap between rich and poor has become even greater. To this end in 2003 the Government and the top four clearing banks are setting up the Universal Bank to help millions of socially excluded consumers to come into the financial fold by offering them subsidized and very basic banking facilities.

## ■ The most watched nation

In tandem with the growing number of people classed as socially excluded, we have witnessed the rise of gated communities like Wentworth, Poundbury, Wynyard Woods, Repton Park, Virginia Park and Canary Riverside, while key lifestyle groups such as the New Affluentials, Bobos, Lone Wolves, Middle Rich and the aptly named Lager Toffs are buying into a range of luxury apartments, private housing schemes and 'model villages' where security gates, cameras, porters and security guards, according to a *Sunday Times* article, are sold as standard. Private cameras used to be installed in about 20 per cent of the enclosed apartment blocks in London, says London Residental Research, but now the figure stands at 65 per cent. CCTV-wise we've become the most watched nation on Earth. Currently there are one million CCTV cameras in operation around the UK, with the Government set to spend a further £100m on 250 CCTV systems in our town and city centres.

## ■ Zoning Out

This need to gate and cloak ourselves from the everyday has given rise two key trends – Zoning Out and the Limelight Syndrome – and new groups of money-rich consumers – Bobos, New Affluentials, Lager Toffs, Middle Rich and Lotto Rich – all of whom place a high value on security, and status-orientated brands and apartments. This is reflective of a cross-sector mood that has seen our desire for luxury-end products that swaddle and pamper increase over the past year.

## ■ Luxe living

Consumers are now splashing out one-third more on going out, holidays and entertainment than on eating, drinking and health. This luxe-life shift – or Limelight Syndrome, the need to be treated like a VIP or celebrity, as we have called it – is the biggest shift in spending since records began 50 years ago. Spends on restaurants, entertainment, leisure and holidays reached £110bn last year, dwarfing the £80bn spent on essentials such as food and drink, household goods, toiletries and medical services. In 1991, Britons spent £60bn on food and drink, household goods and health, compared with £56bn on 'fun'. By 2002, that situation had reversed. Allowing for inflation, overall spending on luxuries has risen by a massive 50 per cent over the past decade while spending on essentials was up by just 7 per cent. Spending on some basics – notably food, general household goods and clothes – has fallen in real terms.

## ■ The leisure hive

We have become a nation of leisure seekers and at the pinnacle of this we are seeing the emergence of groups like the New Affluentials, the Bobos, the Middle Rich, the Lotto Rich and Lager Toffs. In the financial world, the richest groups among them have been dubbed 'hinwis', an acronym which means high net worth individuals. In income terms these are worth between £200 000 and £1m a year. In 1995 there were 372 000 of them, now this figure stands at 746 000. Those who earn between £70k and £200k are called the mass affluent. Add to this the fact that 74 000 millionaires were recognized as such last year, and that those earning between £30k and £200k now stands at 3.7 million and you are, according to Datamonitor, talking about a combined new wealth of £313bn. Within these broad brush strokes of wealth however, a number of subgroups lurk – and these are the ones we are keenest on.

## ■ Money maketh its own class

Our network indicates that the Middle Rich earn £80k a year, are conservative, keen on classic brands and tend to live outside our main cities and towns. Lager Toffs earn an estimated £70k plus and are keen on gated Georgian-style mansions, Barratt-style homes, enclosed leisure or golfing communities and spend heavily on status brands, holidays and cars. New Affluentials are high income, high flyers who earn £100k plus, but see themselves as 'middling rich' and prefer to think that they keep quiet about their incomes. Like the Bobos (Bohemian Bourgeois to give them their proper title), they are keen urban dwellers. They live in converted churches, old Victorian schoolhouses or gentrified Victorian terrace houses but prefer classic or quiet brands in terms of clothes, cars and household products. Bobos earn £150K plus and work in music, media, marketing and design. They are keen on new technologies – the Handspring, Pogo and DVD minidiscs can be seen in their one-shoulder rucksacks first – new start-up ventures and are core readers of magazines like *Wallpaper*, *Fortune* and *National Geographic*.

# Lotto Rich

The Lotto Rich, worth £5m plus, are keen on conspicuous brands, gated dwellings, villa-style houses in the Home Counties, the coastal areas of Spain and take, on average, four holidays a year. They are traditionally conservative, keen on brash luxury brands such as Gucci, Prada, D&G and Louis Vuitton.

The newest arrivals, the Super Rich, are estimated to be worth £10m plus each, most are under 30 and work in the areas of technology, sports and the top-end creative sector – usually the three Ms; music, modelling and media.

The Middle Rich, Super Rich and New Affluentials are less concerned about brand status, but more keen on a brand's worth and quality intangibles, in terms of what they know about it rather than what it necessarily says about them.

## ▨ Boutique lives

All groups spend a minimum of £6000 on travel annually, between £150 to £400 a month eating out, and will spend from £250 000 to £1.4m on property. Bobos and the Super Rich are particularly keen on treatments, places and products that are designed to pamper and cloak them. They call it Zoning Out – using their money and influence to escape. And escape they do – to the burgeoning number of spas, wellness centres and boutique hotels that have sprouted throughout Britain and Europe to accommodate their needs. Indeed, these two groups have been highly influential in bringing new standards of luxury and exclusion to the market, making their influence felt from hotels like the Delano, the Hudson or St. Martin's Lane, to more downmarket traditional venues like the Le Meridien and Hyatt which have converted whole floors, in some cases entire hotels, to woo and win their patronage.

## ▨ Ascetic luxury

Eschewing traditional trappings of wealth, the Bobo, New Affluential and Super Rich are, as one survey respondent put it, 'Happy to go economy if I can stay in a superluxe hotel.' They also like low-key labels, classic or outdoor brands, not 'new money' labels like D&G, Versace, Prada and Gucci, and prefer to drive tried and tested cars such as Volvos, Volkswagens, Morgans, Land Cruisers, Saabs and small city equivalents such as the Smart car.

Lotto Rich, Super Rich and Lager Toffs are deeply concerned about brands and status. They want to be seen in the right labels, right cars and right neighbourhoods. To do this they will happily spend more on property – from £375 000 to £4.5m – and are obsessed with security, walled enclosures, CCTV and villa-style dwellings in the Home Counties, Cheshire and Southern Spain. Married, with very traditional views on family and social position, they spend £500 plus monthly on eating out and prefer cars such as Ferrari, Porsche, Jaguar, Rolls-Royce and Aston Martin. Their most wanted labels include Versace, Dolce & Gabanna, Gucci and Galliano.

## ■ What it means for brands

Careful positioning is key. Bobos, the Super Rich or New Affluentials will not touch brands tainted with 'brash luxury'. All however want their brands to seem exclusive and to be slightly aloof. The Limelight Syndrome is a trend bought into by Lager Toffs, the Middle Rich and Lotto Rich, who want loud glamour, ostentatious service and 24Seven attentiveness in their chosen hotels, resorts or restaurants to Zone Out in. They like the concept of the VIP bar, the guest list attitude (as long as they are on it) and the 'white stretchlimo moment'. So they are keen to hear about brands, places, products or service categories that fulfill these things.

## ■ High flyers who demand low visibility

Bobos, the Super Rich and New Affluentials are in many ways opposites. Zoning Out is their favourite trend – a mood or moment that is about escape, the rainforest hotel, the ascetic spa weekend, the cross-desert trek – while their version of the Limelight Syndrome is to go unrecognized, remain undisturbed, melt in. Because they are high flyers and visible high income earners, they demand time out and social invisibility – which isn't really about invisibility at all but about products, services, hotels, people and brands that create the illusion of isolation and exclusion around them, without actually excluding them! They too demand 360-degree service, 24Seven access and a level of luxury that in many ways is more demanding. For them a hotel or a product or a spa, or indeed the layout of a room, can be wrong and therefore not 'them' because it has grouped the wrong ambience together, placed the right furniture designers in the wrong setting or has created a stealth brand but sold it in a vulgar and flash manner.

## Keen social history

Unlike the Lotto Rich, the Middle Rich or Lager Toffs, the Bobos, Super Rich and New Affluentials carry in their heads a keen social and aesthetic history that makes them one of the most difficult groups to target, but one of the most lucrative in the long term. These after all are the antennae groups that are the first to acquire the products that will crowd tomorrow's mainstream markets.

# Regendering –
## men on the turn

Men are in crisis – or so the media and books like *Bowling Alone*, *On Men* and *Stiffed* have been telling us for the past two years. Suicide rates are up, likewise male depression, impotence and anorexia, while in Britain and the US there is a growing sense that men are now the second sex. Although anxiety levels among men are indeed rising, our own researches and those done by Magic Hat, part of McCann-Erickson, show that men see these things in a far more positive light than initially appears to be the case.

## ▓ Euro-males rising

In a cross-Europe survey, most men in the sample believed that these changes were not only necessary, but beneficial to men as well as to women. Longer paternity leave was welcome, along with shared parenting. Few men were resistant to the idea of a female boss and most saw equality as desirable, even if they recognized that more work had to be done to make this happen. Yes, there were resentments – those showing it we called Resisters – and many of these centred around a perceived loss of masculinity, because of women's growing importance. But even among this group, change was seen to be inevitable. In the UK, such shifts were quite noticeable, with Adapters and Resisters defending their side with equal vigour. (Adapters are men who can adapt and change as the needs of a time or trend shift require.)

## ▓ White Van Man

The notional groups or types we've created more than demonstrate this. Male Himbos who are obsessed with cosmetics, fragrances and pamper and preen themselves; Adonis Men who exhibit an unhealthy obsession for working-out and body building; Lone Bowlers who believe that women have taken over and are neutering men in the workplace and at home; Cosmocrats who are high-flying, high-earning transatlantic executives; Hedonists who have careers that begin with 'M' – media, modelling and music – and like to party and take pleasure in travelling, holidaying and hanging out; Samurai Men who are extreme sports enthusiasts who use such activities to reinforce the sense of masculinity; and Lone Wolves, the bachelors of the new century who enjoy home comforts and living alone. Male Himbo, Adonis Man and Lone Bowler see and sell themselves as Resisters – Cosmocrat, Hedonist, Samurai Man, Lone Wolf and, surprisingly, White Van Man sees himself in the latter category. Indeed White Van Man, for all his male posturing, seemed to be the most positive and upbeat of all groups interviewed by

Future Laboratory researchers. A firm follower of the *Sun*, the *Star* and Sky Digital, he was nevertheless approving of equality in the workplace, shared responsibilities on the home front and, of all the groups, took the strongest interest in his children and felt it was important to do right for and by them.

## ■ Living alone

Lone Wolf, among the most affluent and complex of the types in the sample, had no issues with equality and treated male and female colleagues with equal regard. He viewed women as partners 'in and out of bed'. He was, however, wary of marriage and even of cohabiting, preferring to live alone and to keep his finances, friends and personal space detached from any romantic liaison he might be involved in. He also believed that women in his social group should do the same. Similar patterns were apparent from the replies of Samurai Man, Cosmocrat and Hedonist, although all were far more egalitarian when it came to romance, cohabiting and children. All of these were desirable and they all viewed their chosen partner (male or female) as a friend, a lover and a co-adventurer.

Our Male Himbo, Lone Bowler and Adonis Man all shared similar negative and gloomy outlooks. Lone Bowler saw any kind of equality for women as wrong and viewed it as a threat to his masculinity and sense of traditional values. He tended to be didactic in his outlook and fundamentalist in his opinions. Male Himbo and Adonis Man were equally upset about female successes in recent years, but only because of the increased levels of insecurity it caused for them.

## ■ Adonis complex

To combat this, Adonis Man saw his role with women as a take-them-and-leave-them Lothario ('they'll do it to you sooner or later') and used everything in his armoury – from brash labels to male fragrances, to 'his passion wagon' – to achieve his set ends. Male Himbo, on the other hand, gave himself over to body-building and working out to the extent that his issues shifted from being mere social symptoms to the psychological. Adonis Man derives his title from the 'Adonis complex', a term coined by Dr. Harrison G. Pope to describe 3 million plus US males suffering from acute body dysmorphophobia syndrome, a psychological illness brought on by feelings of inadequacy, and one that causes sufferers to become obsessive body-builders. The first cases have now been diagnosed in Britain, and Pope believes it will become as serious for men as anorexia has been for women.

## ■ Living with mother

Although the categories differ, there are a number of statistical similarities worth considering. If cohabiting or marrying, most of these men are doing so later than those a decade ago when marriage or partnership arrangements happened in their early twenties – now it is around 28. White Van Man, Adonis Man and Lone Bowler tend, as a group, to remain in their parents' house until their late twenties (for the sake of income and social convenience), and have salary levels ranging between

£19k and £22k. For White Van Man, who is a keen saver, hard worker and enjoys going out, living with his parents is more to do with saving money and enjoying his home comforts than any fear of the world at large.

## ■ Toiletries spending up

Adonis Man, Lone Wolf, Hedonist, Cosmocrat and Samurai Man together make a powerful market force to be reckoned with. Collectively, they have been responsible for pushing toiletries sales up from £431.5m to £580.4m between 1995 and 1999, and driving market growth in key areas such as technology, home computers and music systems. Because their views towards women have altered somewhat over recent years, sales of magazines traditionally targeted at this market – such as *Loaded, FHM, GQ, Esquire* and *Maxim* – have plummeted. However, recent research shows that magazines such as *Esquire* and *GQ* (having rebranded themselves as 'intelligent' reads) and newcomer *Jack* have all managed to increase monthly sales and to attract a more affluent and discerning reader to their brightened up mix of reportage, investigation, insight and fewer laddish fashion spreads.

## ■ What it means for brands?

Although brands should avoid being sexist or pejorative in their targeting of these new male consumer types – White Van Man, Adonis Man and Male Himbo do not view themselves in an ironic or marginal manner – equally they should avoid the notion of being unisex. All groups spoken to had little or no interest in a unisex brand or product and saw such an idea as negative and vague, rather than something that necessarily diluted their sense of masculinity. Indeed, when asked if a brand could be male or female, many of our 100 plus panel agreed that it could, without it being seen as a negative thing in itself.

## ■ Male and female brands

Volvo, for instance, was seen as a masculine brand, but also a car that could appeal equally to a woman. Likewise, the Smart car was thought to be female (as in a small, compact, ergonomic, status-aware vehicle) in terms of its brand characteristics, but Cosmocrat, Hedonist, Samurai Man and even Lone Wolf saw no problem in driving it since these characteristics were equally appealing and positive. For men generally, brands, services, products and retail outlets need to explain themselves carefully and clearly. Simplicity is key to all communication with the male consumer – likewise, deals and strategies that enhance his status and sense of self. While he accepts, or will eventually accept, equality as a given, he still fundamentally believes that men and women are different and that these differences can be positive and beneficial.

## ■ Loyalty first

He values loyalty, trust, fairness and honesty, and he expects this from his brands. Professional and social relationships are important, and brands that sell themselves in this way retain his loyalty. Indeed, he tends to buy his car, computer equipment, mortgage, sound system, holiday package and furniture from places that have been recommended – he in turn, if satisfied, recommends these things on. Such relationships keep hassle to a minimum and they make him feel more at ease when making a buying decision.

# The genome century – G-strings and DNA

We are all familiar with GM foods, Dolly the Sheep and recent media coverage on designer babies, stem cell technology and human cloning. Few of us will have really considered the implications of these phenomena for society as a whole or to the branding and advertising sectors in particular. Which, for instance, will be the first agency or brand to run the anti-GM gauntlet with ads for GM breakfast cereals? Or farm produce containing not just modified plant genes but animal and human genes?

## ■ Biobrand futures

Which agency, or retailer, given the current resistance to all things genetically modified, would handle the accounts, or products, of companies like DuPont, Norvartis, Monsanto, Calgene, Myriad and Genzyme? And if they were asked to promote or sell transgenic meat – knowing the damage that this could do to their own brands – would they be happy to do it? Or to sell cloning kits? Or to promote 'pharms' where skin is cultivated instead of fruit, vegetables or animals?

## ■ Bioeconomics

If this seems far-fetched, as our Lifesigns Network points out, the biotech sector already produces these things and currently makes a £10bn profit annually from doing so – and this is just the tip of the iceberg. Jeremy Rifkin, head of the Foundation for Economic Trends, says that the biotech century will usher in changes as profound and shocking as those brought in on the coat-tails of the Industrial Revolution. Terms such as pharmetics, transgenics, xenotransplanting, biofuels, biomedicines, cloning and stem cell technology will become commonplace and the Fortune 500 and the FTSE 100 will, by the end of the next decade, be dominated by biotech names and biotech brands. There are now 1300 active biotech companies in Europe and the US, and this number is expected to double over the next five years as patents are realized and first generation biotech trials brought to fruition.

## What it means to brands

The ethical, social and moral implications are immense. Despite the inevitability of such changes, fundamentalists, activists, ethicists, consumer groups and many European governments will target the more visible and ethically challenging brands or companies in the way that they have already attacked names like Monsanto and Aventis for creating so-called Frankenstein foods. But these changes, especially in the food, biofuel and biomedical sectors, are already happening (six UK and ten US companies now offer genetic screening to couples who want to create the best conditions for conceiving a 'perfect' child) and it is important that brand managers, marketers, creatives and planners develop strategies for dealing with them.

## Social philosophers

A few forward-looking companies and institutes in the US have already appointed social philosophers, ethicists or have established knowledge units to look at how these things can be best sold to the consumer. Others have started trials to validate the safety claims many biotech companies have made about their products. Short term, however, foodstuffs carrying GM ingredients will certainly come with GM labelling attached, according to Norvartis, who say that 93 per cent of consumers they spoke to in a survey want such labelling. In the clothing sector, source-of-origin marks seem to concern the consumer less. 80 per cent of all US cottons are now genetically modified, while the first genetically enhanced superwools (designed to be softer, longer and more durable) will be available in our stores over the next four years.

## Countering objections

Although consumers object to GM food, early research among patients waiting for heart, liver or kidney replacement shows little resistance to the idea of genetically manufactured organs. According to Saloman Brothers, the Wall Street investors, over 450 000 people will spend £6 billion plus having a xenotransplanted liver, kidney or heart by 2010. It is perhaps in the areas of fashion, medicine and biofuels that biobrands will enjoy their earliest successes. From here, say our Lifesigns Network, they can establish best brand practices or promote their brands in a way that will make them more acceptable, or trusted, when it comes to entering areas that people have strong ethical doubts about.

## Do GM people dream of GM foods?

As one networker put it, 'Who will seriously object to GM cornflakes on ethical grounds, if they are able to eat them thanks to a GM heart!' Perhaps, but who will purchase a luxe brand of pasta or a choice tuna steak when it comes with the strap line, 'Contains over eight variant animal and fruit genes including cow, sheep, pig, apple, elephant and human.' You see why advertising agencies will be needed more in the future than they've ever been needed in the past?

# Rainbow Youth –
## coming up guns and roses

The baby-boomer generation have come of age – the so-called third age. This is not a sedate sector of the population but a group set to turn previous ideas of age, and ageing, upside down. Fitter, wealthier, happier and determined to live longer than their forebears (British male life expectancy will rise from 75 to 79 by 2010 with a corresponding increase from 80 to 83 for women), thanks to improved diet and healthcare procedures. They are also determined to go out fighting – especially against policies, designs, institutions and services that exclude them or patronize them for their status and wealth. Unlike their parents, who were happy to conform, to make do and mend, this group is proactive, politically astute, brand aware and status conscious and has the one thing governments, brands, pensions and financial service providers want more than anything – money.

## ■ Crock of gold

This group, Rainbow Youth as we've called them, own three-quarters of all financial assets and account for half of all discretionary spending power in developed countries, according to SeniorAgency International, a consultancy specializing in marketing to the elderly. The US Census Bureau paints a similarly positive picture – poverty rates among the over sixty-fives has dropped from 35 per cent in 1960 to 10.2 per cent today, compared with a fall from 22 per cent to 11.3 per cent for the population as a whole. Over two-thirds of this group in the UK and US own their own homes, three-quarters of which are unencumbered by a mortgage. In America, they control four-fifths of the money invested in savings and loans and own two-thirds of all shares on the stock market.

## ■ Stage not age

Preferring to see retirement as a third stage rather than third age, this group will become one of the most active, travelled and consumer-aware demographics ever. Over the past two decades, consumption patterns for the over fifties has increased three times as fast as that for the rest of the population. In industrialized countries, Rainbow Youth buy about half of all new cars – many of these are sports utility vehicles and all are top of the range. Even Harley Davidson says the average age of its customers now stands at 52 plus.

## ■ Testing the waters

Brands and businesses are only just beginning to cater for this sector's needs. Last year L'Oréal recruited the 57-year-old French actress Catherine Deneuve to promote hair care products to this market; Estée Lauder meanwhile is using Karen Graham, a 70s supermodel, to sell its face creams; while Unilever, noting that margarine products were in decline, launched its Proactive range – designed to spread easily and also to reduce cholesterol – and it was responsible for turning round Unilever's then ailing margarine division. Danone have likewise entered the Rainbow Youth market with its calcium-rich Talians mineral water, and in Japan NTT DoCoMo launched the Raku-Raku range of phones with bigger displays, bigger key pads and louder ringtones which sold over 200 000 in less than two months. In Paris too, having consulted with older customers, map designers produced an easy-to-follow Metro map which was so successful with old and young alike that it has now been adopted as the new map in all stations.

## ◼ Designs for our future selves

Japan, along with the US, is way ahead of Europe when it comes to working with consumer groups in this sector. With 25 per cent of the Japanese population now over sixty, 17 industrial associations in Japan have formed the Kyoyo-Hin Foundation – the foundation for universal products – whose purpose is to create designs that are inclusive and ergonomic to all age groups. Fiskars, a Finnish company inspired by this approach, has created the 'soft touch scissors', and Oxo developed cooking utensils designed for those suffering from arthritis – all of which are big sellers among the young. Even car maker Ford has created a suit for its designers which simulates the restricted movements of many of those in their sixties to help develop cars that are easier to operate.

## ◼ Bridge careerism

Far from going riotously into this good night of their old age, Rainbow Youth has also become a major player in third stage business start-ups (or bridge economics), according to Ernst & Young, who say they are now responsible for 15 per cent of all business start-ups in the UK alone – a 50 per cent increase over the past ten years. 27 per cent of entrepreneurs in Britain are now over 45, while the highest survival rate among start-ups is, says Warwick Business School, by those who set up their companies between the ages of 50 and 55. All of this has caused banks, businesses and loan companies to rethink their lending and start-up strategies.

## ◼ What it means to brands

It means trouble unless you design, produce and sell goods that are inclusive, optimistic and enabling. As brands like Lancôme (who ditched the 42-year-old Isabella Rossellini because she was deemed too old) or Gerber (who launched a line of food products called 'Senior Citizen' which resembled their baby food range) discovered to their cost, Rainbow Youth have no wish to be patronized or treated as frail or infirm, even if dexterity is an issue. They are active, outward looking and determined to enjoy life at all levels. Travel is crucial, the pleasures of the table and of the great outdoors are key to understanding them. Even Saga, once keen to offer trips to the Cotswolds or cosy cruises in the Mediterranean now cater for sixty-somethings who are keen to do elephant trekking, scuba diving and take trips up the Mekong River. In the US, Grandtravel and Family Hostel have noted this generation's ease with their own children, their grandchildren and with friends in their thirties and forties and they are offering intergeneration deals to those who want to travel with friends of many ages to places where three or more generations can be catered for at the same time – giving rise to a whole subtrend for transgenerational travel.

# The wellness century –
## the health bubble rises

US consumers spend $1.4 trillion on health, or 14 per cent of the gross domestic product. Within a decade, this figure will rise to $3 trillion, or 17 per cent of the country's national output. By mid-century medical care alone will absorb almost one-third of the US economy. In the UK, health-related issues are expected to cost the government £50bn over the next 30 years, while increased life expectancy could add a further £20bn to this as men and women live longer – as commented on in the Rainbow Youth section.

### ■ Times set to get bleaker

Much negative reporting has accompanied details on how this shift will be funded. The head of the National Association of Pension Funds has warned that working from 25 to 55 will not generate enough money to sustain those retiring at 55 and living on until 95, while another survey from UK investments analysts say that those retiring at 55 will need a least £1m in assets and cash to keep themselves in the lifestyle they have grown accustomed to. Meanwhile the Institute of Actuaries in the UK has calculated that while there are now 3.5 people of working age to fund a pension for each person over 65, this will be down to 2.4 by 2036 – this points to serious trouble ahead for those in the population known as Middle Youth.

### ■ Every crowd has a silver lining

All this, of course, assumes that things won't change in terms of how we work our lives or live our work. Already more of us are investing not just in pensions, but in property, the stock market and our own businesses. We are also choosing to put off retirement (because we have to, but more and more because we want to) and engage in 'bridge careers', thus creating what our forecasters call a bridge market or bridge economy – a second, even third, boost in our personal income profile. The pessimists are also overlooking the obvious, that the health boom isn't just to do with supporting an ageing society, but about those in their forties and fifties (Generation Flex) who are more determined than ever to buy into preventative medicines, alternative therapies and the burgeoning wellness sector to stay healthy for longer – but also to make health and wellness a strategic and vital part of their lifestyle agenda.

## ▓ Working out to wake up

Just as the exercise gym and diet booms impacted on the collective psyche of the designer 80s and holistic 90s, the next decade is set to be dominated by multiplex health and wellness packages – from such obviously daft ideas as yogalates and speed meditation to a growth in health centres, wellness clinics, sabbatical holidays, spa hotels and spiritual or holistic resorts and retreats, as the wellness economy becomes the new economy. Watch out then for a growth in preventative care brands; an upturn in the fortunes of the therapies and technologies sectors; of the alternative going mainstream; of lunchtime cosmetic surgery procedures; of standard wellness contracts between employees and employers; of off-the-shelf doctoring and online diagnosis; the rise and rise of nutraceuticals (foods impregnated with everything from Ritalin to third generation Prozac); of dermal medicines (patches to cure tobacco addiction but also overeating, headaches and hangovers); cosmeceuticals (face creams that pump vitamins, hormones or vaccines into the body); sonic surgery and sonic alignment (sound used to boost serotonin levels, eradicate tumours, soothe stress-friendly personalities).

## ▓ Health really does mean wealth

What we are seeing then isn't just medicine as an economic shift, but a wellness bubble about to burst, and a welcome one at that. By 2010, according to the US Labour Department, healthcare jobs will increase faster than any other except data processing. Biotechnology too is an area that is sure to benefit from this shift. According to the US Food and Drug Administration, as many as 3 million US citizens can benefit from an implantable fibrillator that helps maintain a steady heartbeat, while companies like General Electric say that medical equipment alone now accounts for 9 per cent of its overall profits, with its biotech division valued at $60bn, producing health-related biotechnologies.

## ▓ Life prism improvement packages

The real pay-off, say economists who have started studying this wellness shift, will come from quality-of-life medicines and lifestyle improving initiatives. Currently, lifestyle-related illnesses such as strokes, heart disease, back problems and overeating cost the US and UK as much as 20 per cent of its health spending bill. Yet many of these are preventable by changes in how we eat, exercise, work and relax.

And this is where many future brands need to position themselves. Not as fighters of disease, but as wellness coaches, health and 'wealthare' managers. Brands that are 'wholistic' rather than holistic, ones that offer 360-degree service from cradle to grave.

# Bibliography

Abrams, W., *The Observational Research Handbook*, McGraw-Hill Educational 2000

Axelrod, R., Cohen, M.D., *Harnessing Complexity*, Free Press 1999

Barabási, A-L., *Linked: The New Science of Networks*, Perseus Publishing 2002

Bevan, J., *The Rise and Fall of Marks & Spencer*, Profile Books 2002

Bloom, H., *Global Brain*, John Wiley 2000

Burton-Jones, A., *Knowledge Capitalism*, Oxford University Press 2001

Cairncross, F., *The Company of the Future,* Profile Books 2002

Clare, A., *On Men: Masculinity in Crisis*, Chatto and Windus 2000

Davis, S., Meyer, C., *Blur*, Capstone 1999

Dawkins, R., *The Selfish Gene*, Oxford University Press 1999

Dixon, P., *Futurewise: Six Faces of Global Change*, HarperCollins 2002

Doyle, D., *Tyranny of Numbers*, Flamingo 2001

Economist, The, *Globalisation: Making Sense of an Integrating World*, Profile Books 2001

Faludi, S., *Stiffed: The Betrayal of the American Man*, Harper Perennial 2000

Fetterman, D.M., *Ethnographhy: Step by Step*, 2nd edition, Sage Publications 1998

Florida, R., *The Rise of the Creative Class*, Basic Books 2002

Frank, T., *One Market Under God*, Secker and Warburg 2001

Fukuyama, F., *Our Posthuman Future: Consequences of the Biotechnology Revolution*, Profile Books 2002

Garner, H., *Frames of Mind: the Theory of Multiple Intelligences*, Basic Books 1993

Gladwell, M., *The Tipping Point*, Little, Brown 2000

Godin, Z., *Permission Marketing*, Simon and Schuster 1999

Grant, J., *After Image*, HarperCollins Business 2002

Hammer, M., *The Agenda: What Every Business Must do to Dominate the Decade*, Random House 2001

Hertz, N., *The Silent Take Over*, Heinemann 2001

Homer-Dizon, T., *The Ingenuity Gap*, Vintage 2000

Iyer, P., *The Global Soul*, Bloomsbury 2001

Jacobs, J., *The Death and Life of Great American Cities*, Vintage 1961

Johnson, S., *Emergence: The Connected Lives of Ants, Brains, Cities and Software*, Penguin Press 2001

Klein, N., *No Logo*, Flamingo 2000

Koch, R., *The 80/20 Revolution*, Nicholas Brealey Publishing 2002

Kreitzman, L., *24-Hour Society*, Profile Books 1999

Lawrence, P.R., Nohria, N., *Driven*, Jossey-Bass 2002

Lewis, M., *The Future Just Happened*, Hodder and Stoughton 2001

Micklethwait, J., Wooldridge, A., *A Future Perfect: the Challenge and Hidden Promise of Globalisation*, Random House Business Books 2000

Monbiot, G., *The Captive State*, Pan Books 2001

Moore, G., McKenna, R., *Crossing the Chasm: Marketing and Selling High-Tech Products to Mainstream Customers,* Harper Business 1991

Myerson, J., *IDEO: Masters of Innovation*, teNeues Publishing Company 2001

Ormerod, P., *Butterfly Economics*, Faber and Faber 1999

Price, L.L., Arnould, E.J., Zinkhan, G.M., *Consumers*, McGraw-Hill 2002

Putnam, R., *Bowling Alone*, Simon and Schuster 2000

Rathje, W., Murphy, C., *Rubbish! The Archaeology of Garbage*, University of Arizona Press 2001

Ridley, M., *Genome: the Autobiography of a Species in 23 Chapters*, Fourth Estate 2000

Rifkin, J., *Biotech Century*, Phoenix 1998

Roiphe, K., *Late Night in Paradise: Sex and Morals at the Century's End*, Little, Brown 1997

Scase, R., *Britain in 2010: the New Business Landscape*, Capstone 2000

Schumacher, E.F., *Small is Beautiful: a Study of Economics as if People Mattered*, Vintage 1993

Schwartz, P., *The Art of The Long View – Planning for the Future in an Uncertain World*, John Wiley 2001

Scott, A. J., *Global City Regions: Trends, Theory, Policy*, Oxford University Press 2001

Shiller, R., *Irrational Exuberance*, Princeton University Press, 2000

Underhill, P., *Why We Buy*, Orion Business Books 1999

Wack, P., *The Gentle Art of Reperceiving*, Harvard University Press 1984

Whewell, W., *The Philosophy of the Inductive Sciences*, London 1840

Wilson, E.O., *Consilience*, Abacus 2000

Wilson, E.O., *The Future of Life*, Little, Brown 2002

Wilson, E.O., Holldobler, B., *The Ants*, Harvard University Press 1990

Wolfe, T., *A Man in Full*, Farrar, Straus, Giroux 1998

Wolfe, T., *The Pump House Gang*, Farrar, Straus, Giroux 1968

Zey, M.G., *The Future Factor*, McGraw-Hill 2000

# Index

*Note:* The index does not cover the preliminaries or the bibliography.